THE WORLD, THE WORLD

Norman Lewis was born in London. He has written thirteen novels and eleven non-fiction works. *A Dragon Apparent* and *Golden Earth* are considered classics of travel literature, and *Naples '44* has been described as one of the ten outstanding books about the Second World War. He relaxes by his travels to off-beat parts of the world, which he prefers to be as remote as possible; otherwise he lives with his family in introspective, almost monastic calm in the depths of Essex. The first part of his autobiography, *I Came, I Saw*, is also available in Picador.

by the same author

Fiction

THE DAY OF THE FOX
THE VOLCANOES ABOVE US
THE TENTH YEAR OF THE SHIP
FLIGHT FROM A DARK EQUATOR
THE SICILIAN SPECIALIST
A SUITABLE CASE FOR CORRUPTION
MARCH OF THE LONG SHADOWS

Non Fiction

A DRAGON APPARENT
GOLDEN EARTH
THE CHANGING SKY
THE HONOURED SOCIETY
NAPLES '44
VOICES OF THE OLD SEA
I CAME, I SAW
THE MISSIONARIES
TO RUN ACROSS THE SEA
A GODDESS IN THE STONES
AN EMPIRE OF THE EAST

THE WORLD, THE WORLD

NORMAN LEWIS

PICADOR

First published 1996 by Jonathan Cape

This edition published 1997 by Picador
an imprint of Pan Macmillan Ltd
Pan Macmillan, 20 New Wharf Road, London N1 9RR
Basingstoke and Oxford
Associated companies throughout the world
www.panmacmillan.com

ISBN 0 330 35073 0

5 7 9 8 6 4

A CIP catalogue record for this book is available
from the British Library.

Typeset by Deltatype Ltd, Ellesmere Port, Cheshire
Printed and bound in Great Britain by
Mackays of Chatham plc, Chatham, Kent

THE WORLD, THE WORLD

Chapter One

ALTHOUGH IT WAS years before I realised this had happened, the direction of my life changed in 1937 with the sudden appearance of a breathless young Englishman who dropped into the dining-car seat facing me on an Italian train. I was to learn that he had missed the earlier express he had intended to take, and had only caught this by the skin of his teeth. The seat he now occupied, moreover, had been the only one left vacant. Fortune had committed us inexorably to each other's company on our journey to Rome. Later a shared sense of victimisation drew us even closer together and we exchanged smiles of exasperation when a flustered waiter dumped before us plates of food we had not ordered. By the time the spaghetti came he was telling me about himself. His name was Oliver Myers and he was an archaeologist on his way back from a two-year dig in the Egyptian desert. This explained the deep tan and the slightly faded quality of the blue eyes exposed over long periods to the sun. Now came the coincidence that we should both be re-emerging from the Islamic scene, for I was homeward bound from the Middle East where with two companions I had spent three months exploring the coasts of Southern Arabia.

Studying Myers I was forced to admit that, by comparison with his experiences, mine had been superficial. Apart from his dark skin and pale eyes, I noticed the cramped way four fingers were gathered to hold his fork, as if he had become accustomed to eat with his hand. I had confronted the almost impossible task of learning enough Arabic to get by. Myers spoke it fluently, although it was Arabic of the kind picked up in the course of working with illiterate fellahin. We both tried what we had to offer on each other, but there were vast areas of incomprehension. Myers was somewhat theatrical and the stream of debased Arabic was accompanied by a repertoire of arm-waving and facial contortions, many seeming to reflect the shrewdness, the cunning and the fear of the browbeaten peasantry from whom he had learned them. He seemed proud of the two years he had spent sunk deeply in the primitive world, drawing my attention to a gap where a tooth that had troubled him had recently been knocked out by a hammer. Half a forefinger had gone – crushed under falling masonry. However, even the sharing of interest in a language can provide a little of the social cement with which human relationships are bound together. By the time the cheese was served we were firm friends, and it was a friendship that lasted thirty years, terminating only with Oliver's death.

Coincidentally, we both lived in Bloomsbury, only five minutes from each other, for at that time I stayed in 4, Gordon Street in the house of my Italian in-laws, while he had a flat almost round the corner in Woburn Square. He was back in London for the publication of a tremendous tome of which he was co-author with Sir Robert Mond. It was called *Cemeteries of Armant,* and was just about to be issued by the Egypt Exploration Society.

Gordon Street was a calm Bloomsbury precinct a good mile from the periphery of Soho, and half that distance from the small settlements of foreigners, largely Italian or Greek, scattered like iron-filings round the magnet of Tottenham Court Road. It was largely peopled by those having connections with London University, academics who may have observed with surprise the process by which over a few years a variety of foreigners had crammed themselves into Number Four to produce a singular community. It was probably by pure accident that Ernesto Corvaja had chosen to buy a house in this locality. He and his wife, Maria, and their first child, Ernestina, had arrived some twenty-odd years before this from Sicily via the United States. The Corvajas were from the neighbourhood of Palermo in which people who work in the country return to the town after sunset, and town houses – at least in Ernesto's day – had become little fortresses stuffed with near and distant relations and friends. The original Corvaja family was soon joined in London by Maria's brother, Franco, his wife and son, and as the years passed there were visits by school friends of the children, who often stayed on. By the late thirties my brother-in-law Eugene and two young artists had set up a colony in the principal room. An Eurasian girlfriend of Ernestina who had arrived two years previously was still on the scene, as was Maria Pia, Ernestina's former schoolmistress from Santander in Spain, who showed no signs of wishing to move on. In the meanwhile, Ruth, the Eurasian, had acquired an elderly German lover, whose duelling scars from the Heidelberg days were so numerous and deep that he had some difficulty in varying his expression.

Ernestina and Oliver took to each other immediately, and I was happy that this was the case. Our marriage had been, perhaps, not quite a love match but an arrangement we thought of as a partnership of similar minds. At this time Ernestina appeared to have decided to free herself from the claustrophobia so often accompanying the protection of the Latin extended family. By contrast, I found relief in a refuge from the narrow experience of life in the outer suburbs of London.

The Corvajas, then, were extremely gregarious. They were also fond of animals. They possessed an aggressive and smelly mongrel dog, a large somnolent cat reduced by a diet of pickled mushrooms and tagliatelli con vongoli to a state of chronic incontinence, and a little owl (*Athene noctua vidalii*) imported from Brescia and chained to a perch in the dining room from which it surveyed the scene with imperturbable golden eyes. A kestrel, also imported from Italy, was kept in a separate room, perching usually on the head of a fairish copy of Donatello's *David*. Both these birds were sensibly fed on day-old chicks supplied by a petshop, which they devoured in a lackadaisical fashion, with little evidence of appetite. The basement was the territory of Maria's cockerels reared by her since infancy without access to daylight, on legs sometimes almost doubled over by rickets. Despite this disablement they launched fierce, staggering attacks on all who approached them. 'If burglars break in they will react,' Maria said. 'They are part of our defence.'

It was an environment made to measure for Myers. The house next door but one had something to do with the University Senate, and wandering academics in search of this building regularly rang the doorbell at Number Four in error. This was far from causing Ernesto displeasure. The burden of hospitality lay upon such Sicilians of the old school like a religious obligation. Ernesto ordered the maid to show all such strays into the front room where they would be offered a glass of blackish Sicilian wine before being redirected. This was the Mediterranean ceremony that so enchanted Oliver Myers when he first called to see me. I witnessed his enthusiasm displayed with the usual exaggeration, as he went through the inevitable wine-tasting, lip-smacking farce while Ernesto, troubled by the knowledge that the shipment had travelled badly and tasted like fountain-pen ink, looked on with his huge impassivity, doing his best to offer a smile of welcome but producing no more than a mirthless writhing of the lips.

For Oliver it was an evening of fulfilment. Conversation at the dinner table was in French, Spanish and Italian and he listened happily to the polyglot chatter, coped well enough with the French, and threw in the standard Arabic interjections which were quite obviously in praise of the food and accepted as such. The ill-travelled Sicilian wine had been replaced by Orvieto Classico.

'Very generous, isn't he?' Oliver said to me later. 'What's he do for a living?'

'He's a professional gambler,' I told him.

Oliver, too, was generous to an extraordinary degree, losing no opportunity to thrust gifts upon a friend, or even a casual acquaintance. Sometimes these were inappropriate. On the next occasion of a visit to the Corvajas he presented Ernesto with a carved ivory pipe from Aswan. Ernesto did not smoke.

For my birthday that year Oliver presented me with *Cemeteries of Armant*, his work of prodigious scholarship following two years of labour in the field. The results of this vast undertaking, to which forty-six authorities in various fields had contributed, seemed to have evoked symptoms of disappointment. Myers' preface sets the mood in its opening sentence: 'The cream has been skimmed off Egyptology, and the bulk of the information on the register is of no interest whatever to the ordinary reader.' Later we are told that most of the sites investigated had been 'nearly completely destroyed' by robbers. Nothing of exceptional value to the museums was found in any grave. Among the 'interesting material' the robbers had not bothered to carry off were two beads showing pre-dynastic influence in their glazing. There were several thousand items of lesser interest, but the authors clearly accepted that this was not the stuff to make the reader's pulse beat faster.

The fact was that by this time Egyptology had fallen under the shadow of Tutankhamon, and from the year 1922 that saw the opening up of his tomb and the recovery of the unrepeatably magnficent treasure it contained, Egyptology began to fall into decline. It was in a discussion of this melancholy topic that an unusual aspect of Oliver's personality, of which I had already some inkling, became more clearly defined.

The popular press had moved on from their fulsome coverage of the original treasure hunt and its glittering climax and now began to report on the fact that within months of opening the tomb several members of Lord Carnarvon's expedition had died 'in mysterious circumstances'. Next, Carnarvon himself had succumbed, reportedly of a mosquito bite that turned septic, to be followed by pneumonia. With that, all the talk was of Tutankhamon's curse, said to have originated in a monitory inscription at the entrance to the tomb. It was a story that could have been lifted from the plot of one of Conan Doyle's Sherlock Holmes thrillers, popular at that time, yet when I asked Myers how he felt about the Pharaoh's curse, I was staggered to discover that, in all seriousness, he was keeping an open mind.

Oliver occupied himself at the British Museum and by lecturing at the University. The Armant expedition had furnished a huge number of varieties of mummy, both human and animal. The rarest remained those dating from the Old Kingdom and continued to be much sought after. Consequently Myers found himself on the periphery, as a spectator, of a scandalous affair in which the Museum was said to have been induced to pay a record sum for what was described as a unique Old Kingdom mummy. Myers and his intimates who had worked at Armant and elsewhere believed that this spectacular acquisition was in reality the brother of the Cairo antique dealer by whom the mummy was procured, who had mysteriously disappeared as soon as the order was placed. Eventually ranks were closed, it was agreed that the man so wonderfully encased in ancient wrappers, although the cast of his features could be made out, had died in the distant past, and despite the misgivings of certain experts the mummy remained a centre of attraction at the museum for many years.

The fateful year of 1938 was upon us. It was the year of the peace at all costs at Munich, of disillusionment and the feeling – instinctive rather than intellectual – that this country was under a growing threat of war. Ernestina's brother Eugene had gone off to join in the Spanish Civil War on the Republican side. A subtle change in the national atmosphere hinted at storms to come, and curious behavioural symptoms began to manifest themselves. *The Times* suddenly noticed that the membership of miniature rifle clubs had doubled in a year. I responded to this mood by taking a crash course in German, and was soon able to increase my income by translating sensational and pugnacious articles from the German press for publication in English newspapers.

Those were the days of the last fading flush of autumnal light over literary Bloomsbury, the bohemianism of the Fitzroy Tavern, the lectures on sexual emancipation at the Conway Hall, Bertrand Russell and Dr Joad's pleasurable reshapings of London bourgeois life. Myers and I met often and got to know each other better. He refused to eat anywhere except at Prada's restaurant in the Euston Road, where charming Italian waitresses, all born in London, forced themselves to speak broken Italian to such obvious cosmopolitans as my friend. Despite his flamboyant manner (embarrassing to many Italians) and banter and confident gallantries in the presence of girls such as these, Myers belonged to that category of men like Scott Fitzgerald who are prone to whisper to a friend their doubts over the size of their penis. I suspected that some such lurking fear had promoted his friendship with a showgirl from the Windmill, a practically speechless little Siamese with two-inch fingernails who tottered into view from the wings in support of any of the theatre's frequent oriental settings.

The only occasion, he told me, on which he had felt obliged to break faith with Prada's had been when he invited this lady to dinner. Having learned with delight that she preferred to eat with her fingers, he had scoured London and finally heard of an Indian restaurant in Charlotte Street where it was reputed this could be done. It turned out that by the time of their visit the place had changed hands. A number of the diners wore black ties, and when Myers explained what was proposed, the owner showed hesitation and finally led them doubtfully to a table in an alcove at the back of the restaurant, where nevertheless they remained objects of curiosity.

Emblazoned as his personality was with eccentricity, Myers was able to make himself liked by all who knew him well. He became a frequent and welcome visitor to Gordon Street where Maria had instantly been won over by the hyperbole lavished on her cooking, Eugene listened entranced by stories of armed conflict with Egyptian tomb-robbers, Ernestina teasingly corrected woebegone attempts at Italian, and Ernesto, expressionless as a death-mask, watched as he might have some performing animal.

In the spring Myers was obliged to return to the Middle East, and his contribution to the house's social hubbub was missed. It was to be a year of disruption in the Corvaja household. Ernestina's Eurasian friend and her German lover pulled out, and the uncle who had become an alcoholic was taken to the French Hospital in Shaftesbury Avenue, where as soon as he was left on his own he committed suicide by jumping from the nearest window.

*

Perhaps these upsets fostered Ernestina's sudden desire to go to Cuba. The Corvajas were a family of Spanish origin who had settled in Sicily in the seventeenth century while it still remained part of the Spanish kingdom and its ancestral links remained sufficiently strong for Ernestina to have been sent for part of her education to the Colegio Rodriguez in Santander. In culture and temperament she was incurably Latin.

The latest news from Spain was of the inevitability of Franco's victory, and without waiting for this to happen a Spanish family with whom she had spent short holidays had fled to Cuba. They now wrote begging her insistently to visit them, and this she wished to do. She was at this time having treatment for nervous tension, and her doctor thought it a good idea. 'It's something that's turned into a bit of an obsession,' he said. 'Awful place. We used to call there when I was a ship's doctor. Probably seen the film *Weekend in Havana*, but it isn't like that. Stinking hole. Might get it out of her system once she's seen it.'

This was the advice I followed, and we arrived in Havana in July 1939.

The doctor's picture of Havana was misleading indeed: it abounded with pleasure of the kind that London could not supply. It was an anarchy of colour, for rather than jettison unfinished cans of paint, people splashed what was left on the nearest wall. The city resounded with cheerful noise, of street-corner boys tapping drums, tramcars flashing and showering sparks from overhead contacts, the whine of fruit juice mixers, and the chatter of one or two of the thousand canaries the dictator Batista had recently released. It smelt of electricity and cigar-smoke, and in places of overburdened drains. There was a leisure not to be found elsewhere, with twenty-five men enthroned in a row to have their shoes polished for the third or fourth time in that day. At nine every morning a religious procession formed to study the numbers of the lottery tickets on offer as soon as they were put up on the stand. In Havana it was normal, as we ourselves found, to be stopped in the street by absolute strangers wishing to communicate their thoughts on anything that happened to have caught their attention. The mulatta girls of Havana were seen to flaunt the biggest posteriors and the narrowest waists in the world.

Havana exposed the newcomer to an overpowering vivacity, the street overflowing with beautiful bronze bodies, dressed as if part of the overflow of a carnival taking place round the next corner. A comfortable white minority, although less in evidence, were hyper-active with financial manoeuvrings, for everyone now believed that a world war was certain, and the international news, after a previous slump in the sugar market, induced a happy frame of mind. It was accepted that neutral countries everywhere did well out of wars, and the first battles of the conflict to come were being fought on the stock market. The Havana sugar brokers sat up half the night at the Hotel Naciónál drinking to Chamberlain's failed appeasement at Munich. Already the city was awash with money and with the news of the foreigners buying sugar for stockpiling at record prices. The *Diario de la Marina* published the first photograph of a happy speculator lighting a cigar with a fifty-dollar bill.

We stayed a few days in the small villa of Ernestina's friends the Molas, then moved to a run-down hotel. Havana was bursting at the seams and rooms were hard to find. The situation put an idea into Juan Mola's head. While teaching at Madrid University he had picked up left-wing ideas, and faced in consequence with the possibility of years of exile, he was obliged to look round for some way of earning a living in Cuba. It was clear that accommodation would always be scarce in Havana, and rents in this booming city went up with every week that passed. Only foreigners could now afford to stay in a decently run hotel. Why not, then, Mola said, kill two birds with one stone by opening one. Spacious old colonial-style houses could still be picked up cheaply enough out of town, and in this Niagara of speculative cash in search of investment, there would be little difficulty in buying one of these for conversion.

It was agreed that we might fit very well into this scheme of things. Eighty per cent of the customers for Havana's hotels were Americans, thus fluent English in the reception was essential. Juan and Gloria Mola and Ernestina were full of enthusiasm, I a little less so. Cuba attracted and stimulated me in every way, but I was alarmed at the prospect of burning my boats and settling without a period of trial in a country of which I knew so little. The search for a suitable house for conversion was still in progress when the war broke out, and despite the general feeling in Havana that it might be possible to turn one's back on what was happening on the other side of the world, something in the depth of my being whispered that the course of our lives was at the point of change.

The general view in Britain at this time, which the government made no attempt to play down, was that the country must be prepared for all-out attack both by the Luftwaffe and the submarines of the German Navy, and in response to a bombardment of requests for information and official counsel the embassy in Havana advised all British nationals able to do so to stay where they were until protection could be provided from dangers they might encounter from submarine attacks. Once again, despite the experiences of the First World War, the enduring fallacy had survived that the war would be over by Christmas. Wars, according to ancient inherited memories, started when the harvests were safely gathered in and stopped when the first snow fell. Despite the size, strength and obvious determination of the two sides that now faced each other, more people could still find cause for hope that they might take up their normal lives again in a few months. Nevertheless I found myself temperamentally unable to stay in Havana as less than a spectator of world-shaking events. It was agreed that Ernestina should stay on, as recommended, at least until the spring, while I took the first ship passage I could find, arriving by an American cargo boat in Tilbury on 29 November.

To my delight I found that Oliver Myers was already home from Egypt, and had exciting news for me. The threatened all-out air attacks in London had not happened, and war at that moment was a matter of unlit streets, rationing for those unable to eat in restaurants, and a determination not to carry gas-masks whatever the threat of a surprise gas attack on the capital. Myers' news was that there was an urgent demand for speakers of Arabic. He had presented himself at the War Office where he was told to put what polish he could on his peasant Egyptian dialect, and in the meanwhile hold himself in readiness for some occupation of a special kind. My interview was with the same elderly and bookish lieutenant. He gave me a simple English sentence to translate, and I did what I could. 'Where did you learn your Arabic?' he asked, and I told him that I had picked it up in the Aden bazaar. 'Yes,' he said, with a sort of gentle disdain, 'so I would have thought. And would you be prepared to tackle the considerable task of making it work for North Africa?' I said I would. 'In that case we'd better get you into the School of Oriental Studies,' he said. There might be months before my call-up, he thought, and so there were.

I took the school's course, and to fill in time crammed in a six-month course in Russian, but a year passed slowly before I was called for an interview in a Mayfair office. Although I could now cope with the Algerian alphabet's extra letter and its invention of a future tense (seen as irreligious in other parts of the Islamic world), the interviewer made no attempt to test my Arabic. Instead he studied with satisfaction my Celtic aquilinity of feature and dark eyes, asked me how I was as a swimmer, and I glossed over the fact that I was bad. Had I ever done any amateur theatricals, and would I be happy about dressing up a bit? he wanted to know. I told him about a school play, and that seemed to satisfy him. 'The main thing is a sense of adventure,' he said, to which I nodded in agreement. They were not ready to use me, he said, nor could he say when that was likely to be. In the meanwhile he wanted to enlist me in the Intelligence Corps, but to apply for deferred embodiment, just in case the waiting period was longer than he hoped and I might suffer the misfortune of being called up in the ordinary way. When I asked him what was the Corps' function, he told me that he knew that it existed, but no more than that.

I enrolled in the Intelligence Corps, underwent four months of training with an infantry unit in Northern Ireland, then three months at the Corps depot at Winchester, where they specialised in ceremonial drills invented by Frederick the Great and taught recruits to ride motorcycles downhill after the brakes had been disconnected, with the result that one third of them went to hospital. The call to dress up – I could only suppose as an Arab –

and be deposited from a submarine on the Algerian shore, never came. It was a lucky escape indeed for a poor swimmer. Most certainly I would have drowned, for according to a newspaper report published in the last few years, the three or four volunteers committed to this adventure all died.

The last meeting with Oliver before the tides of war were to sweep us in different directions was, inevitably, at Prada's restaurant. By the purest mischance it was on the night of the first so-called thousand-bomber raid on London. Bombs were falling everywhere on the city and we watched through a tiny peephole in the blackout while a fiery glow enlivened with golden sparks rose over the roof-tops across the road and the fire-engines jangling their bells went racing by. Mr Prada joined us, looking remarkably composed but convinced that his business was about to come to an end. In view of this he offered to sell us any bottle or bottles from his much-acclaimed collection of rare vintages for one pound apiece. We chose a Madeira in a long narrow bottle that he swore was from 1822 and an 1878 Chateau Yquem, drank them slowly and awaited with fatalism the decisions of destiny. When we staggered out it was to discover a new beauty revealed by fire in the normally dismal surroundings of Euston Road. We accepted that years might pass before we saw each other again, and this proved to be so. Oliver was off in a matter of days to some unknown destination in the Middle East, while in the same week I embarked with my Intelligence Corps section on the *Maloca*, bound for the invasion of North Africa.

Service with the Corps, always interesting and supplying occasional excitements, took me to Algeria, Tunisia, Italy, Austria and Iraq. In October 1944 I embarked on the most extraordinary of these experiences: escorting 3,000 unfortunate Russian prisoners back to the frontier of their homeland. Our ship, the *Reina del Pacifico*, stopped at Aden to take on fuel, and received a visit by two sergeants of the port security section, limp with the boredom of such desolate outposts of empire that is temporarily relieved even by the sight of a new face. In the course of an exchange of professional chat mention was made of an eccentric supremo named Myers in charge of the Aden defences. 'Red face, gap teeth, finger missing?' I asked, and was told that that was the man. 'Any chance you could see him and tell him I'm here?' I asked, and the sergeant, clearly astonished by such a request, said he would try. The two went off, and within a matter of minutes a launch roared out from the shore and Oliver stepped aboard.

He hesitated by the taffrail, caught off guard by the inhibitions of the occasion. I had rarely seen a less military figure, certain that this was the only soldier wearing a solar topee and Sam Browne who could still contrive to look a bohemian. 'What on earth?' he said. 'What on earth?' The two Field Security sergeants who had come back with him brought a rope to exclude intrusion, and behind this Asiatic Russians prowled softly, as if over the black, spongey earth of the Siberian forest, and watched us with almond eyes. I explained what I was doing there. 'Supposed to be exceptionally ferocious, aren't they?' he said. 'Must say they don't look it. Do you have much contact with them?'

'Constant,' I said. 'They compose wonderful surrealistic poetry in Tadjik and the battalian commander translates it into Russian, after which I have a go at putting it into English.'

'What a marvellous experience. Tough soldiers and still poets. What do you put it down to?'

'They've managed in some way to retain the imagery of childhood. Their heads are full of fairy stories.'

'Well, I think that's marvellous. But what's likely to happen to them?'

'I think they'll be shot.'

'How unfortunate. I'd have loved to see one of your poetry sessions in action.'

'Well you can. All you have to do is say the word. They'll reel out poetry at the drop of a hat.'

'Unhappily you're leaving in a matter of minutes. Have to get you out of Aden as soon as we can. We've received a garbled signal about a possible attempt by persons travelling on this ship to get ashore. Well, I suppose it makes sense. It's a pity. I won't even have time to tell you about the afreets, the Arabian demons in the Lahej desert. See them any time you like. I'm in the middle of some tremendously exciting experiments.'

'But hasn't it all been explained away as something to do with luminous gas?'

'It's much, much more than that. I only wish we had the time to go into it in a properly detached and scientific way. This is an awful place but being here has at least helped to confirm my attitude, for example, to such things as E.S.P., for which I can only be thankful. I do hope we'll have more time together on your way back.'

There was a blast on the ship's siren, followed by shouts and the rattle of a heavy chain. The sergeants, blank-faced in their pressed shirts and white blanco, closed in, reminding me of sanatorium attendants about to take over a patient back from an outing. Myers was suddenly limp and forlorn against the great, grey slagheaps of the Aden background. Returning my salute it was almost to be foreseen that he should knock his topee slightly askew. '*Ma es salaam*,' he bleated softly as the party turned away.

Infantry soldiers of the accompanying guard rounded up the Tadjiks and took them below.

Senior Lieutenant Golik, the Russian Commander, discussed the prisoners' future and the entertainment the Asiatics were staging that night. There had been a last-minute decision that this particular batch of prisoners should be treated as allies, because there was proof that they had freed themselves from the Germans and actually fought them before surrendering to the British. Therefore at Port Said, in the midst of the voyage, they had been told to get out of their German uniforms, and had been issued British uniforms in replacement. The uniforms were joyfully accepted and even the subsidiary equipment such as zinc water bottles, mess cans, nail- and tooth-brushes and combs, for which a Tadjik would normally have little use, were ingeniously dismantled and turned into musical instruments. Miraculously, almost, the Tadjiks converted such items as gas capes and camouflage netting into colourful and extravagant costumes and slily filched ochre paint used to touch up the ship's bare metal, and with this decorated faces and bodies with fantastic designs. The three Russian officers did not understand the Tadjik theatre and were bored by it all. The Tadjiks impressed them in other ways, notably by their attitude to death. Golik explained: 'In our case life and death are very different things. We see them as entirely separate. With the Tadjiks this is not so. You may be chatting to one and he will say to you "Well, of course we are now talking about the time when I was alive." "So at this moment you think you're dead," I say to him, and he tells me, "Yes, and you're dead, too." The Germans put 100,000 of them in the camp at Salsk and provided food for only 10,000, so they ate each other and put it into their poetry about their adventures in the demon land.'

'Did you eat human flesh, lieutenant?' I interrupted him. 'Only cannibals survived,' he said. There was a Tadjik stretched out on the deck nearby and Golik called him over to show me the hole in his thigh. 'This one had a fever and didn't know what they were doing to him. We had no knives at Salsk but there were men who grew thumb-nails like daggers and they used them to scoop the flesh out. The Tadjiks were the best fighters we had. They were never sure whether or not they were dead, and that made the difference.'

I was down in the hold every night with the Russians, trying to write down the poetry, and watching the Tadjiks act out their dreams. In addition to the British Army issue of kit they had managed to scrounge all kinds of useful litter from the crew and these they turned into antique-looking fiddles, lutes, and rebecks which they played with an ear an inch from the strings to listen to the soft resonance, inaudible to outsiders, of the music of the other world.

Ten days later at Khorranmshahr all this came to an end. The ship tied up under the soft rain and I looked down on the glum prospect of a marshalling yard in which, synchronised as a piece of theatre with the dropping of the anchor, an extraordinary train came puffing into view. This, drawn by three pigmy engines, was composed of an endless succession of miniature cattle trucks of the kind the Russians use to transport pigs. It stopped when level with us and instantly a column of Russian great-coated infantry came into sight, halted, then deployed to form a line between the ship and the train. This was the moment for the prisoners and their British infantry escort to disembark. Two of the 200-odd soldiers of the British infantry escort faced two long ranks of Soviet troops in between which were ushered the returning prisoners. There followed prolonged shouting of orders, the stamping of boots and slapping of rifle-butts as both British and Russians performed ceremonial drill movements appropriate to the occasion. The OC Troops and the Soviet commander then strutted to meet each other, saluted and shook hands, and the documents formalising the handover were exchanged and the thing was at an end. Or almost. As explained later by one of the Soviet interpreters, such was the Soviet commander's distaste for the returning Russians that he refused to speak to them even to give the order to entrain. He asked a representative to talk to me. This man, wearing a commissar's star, was exceedingly overbearing in his manner. 'Comrade Interpreter,' he said. 'Kindly tell these pigs to entrain.'

'Tell them yourself, Comrade Commissar,' I said, and turning, I walked away.

On its return to Port Said a few weeks later, the *Reina del Pacifico* failed to stop at Aden as announced and it was two years before I saw Myers again, immediately after our demobilisation in 1946. We met at Gordon Street, where only the basement rooms were habitable, one of which I shared with a hundred or so old motor tyres. In those days of shortages, Eugene had found there was a brisk demand for these.

About one third of the west side of the street had been demolished with much loss of life by a parachute bomb dropped in the last night of the big air attacks. On the east side, including Number Four, some mysterious phenomenon of this blast had spared the façades of the houses while virtually ripping out many of the interiors. Partition walls crumpled, all windows and most doors were blown out, staircases collapsed. There were freaks of almost impish destruction; a flying missile wrecked a valuable picture in a room otherwise intact, while oil dropped on the tapestry seat of a single chair.

Oliver had been hardly recognisable as a soldier in Aden. Now, in a rumpled jacket and black hat, he had turned into a Bloomsbury regular of old, although Bloomsbury as he had known it had disappeared.

'I've got something for you,' he said, and I found myself holding a small articulated fish, possibly of silver. 'It's a fertility charm, worn during intercourse to ensure pregnancy by the tribal women of Lahej.' His last present to me had been a moose horn, and now I was ready for him with an enormous collection of philosophical works for which I had paid £1 in Charing Cross Road.

I made hazelnut coffee over a primus while Myers untied the parcel.

'Where are the Corvajas these days?'

'They found a cottage in Kent,' I said.

'And those wonderful copies of the Sistine Chapel ceiling he was working on?'

I had almost forgotten. Ernesto was no original painter, but a superb copyist. He had arranged for expensive reproductions on a reduced scale of the Sistine paintings to be sent from Italy, and had spent two or three years using the paintings made from them to enrich the ceilings of his best rooms.

'What happened to them?' Myers asked.

'They fell down. Like everything else they returned to dust,' I said. 'There are a few chunks lying about the place somewhere, if you'd like a souvenir.'

He had finished unwrapping his gift and took out the first volume, turning over the pages with obvious delight. 'I say, this is rather exciting,' he said. 'What do you think of it yourself?'

'It's tosh,' I said.

Myers shook his head sadly. 'Oh well.'

'Still investigating E.S.P.?' I asked him.

'I keep an open mind in these matters as you know,' he said. 'And now we're on the subject, I wonder if you'd object to helping me with an experiment I've always wanted to do?'

'Not necessarily,' I said. 'So long as it's not absurd.' He expected me to talk to him in this way, and gave a good-humoured laugh.

'It would mean a trip down to Stonehenge,' he said.

'I've always wanted to see it.'

'The question is how would we get there? Half the trains don't seem to be running.'

'I managed to get hold of a car last week, so there's no problem.'

The car was a baby Fiat. There was an old airship hangar in a field at Isleworth full of cars that had lost their owners or been repossessed, all selling at £100, whatever the make, model or age. There was a Mercedes SSK that had cost £3,000 but the baby Fiat did fifty to the gallon and 200 miles' worth of black market petrol coupons bought from farmers went with the car. 'Fine day and empty roads,' I said. 'Let's make it tomorrow.'

The night in early April had dusted the fields with frost, and there were still patches of mist, and stiff little clouds in an otherwise clear sky leap-frogged over the hills. We'd come down through Basingstoke and a dozen small towns and the first building of Andover showed over the grass.

'Quiet, isn't it?' Myers said.

'Bound to be,' I said, 'with half the people still away.' The main road was empty apart from a few sad farmcarts. In some places they had started repairs and there were ropes across the road and diversions into lanes. In these, hedges that hadn't been cut back for six years threw down trailers of brambles that clawed at the small bonnet of the Fiat as it poked its way through. England, this April, was an everlasting Sunday morning, lying under a spell of emptiness and silence. Six lost summers in these small towns had done away with colour, leaving faded paintwork and the tatters of advertisements posted on hoardings before September 1939.

In Andover we stopped for late breakfast in a hotel that had been re-opened only a week before. They were still scratching flies' wings out of the wood-work in the dining-room. A girl with her face whitened like a geisha's brought us the rare treat of a boiled egg apiece. Pasty as she was, she still had plenty of flesh on her bones. Londoners these days looked like Romans with high cheek-bones and aquiline noses. Somehow the emptiness and boredom of the years of listening to the distant noises of war had fattened these people. We finished our eggs and the girl was back to offer us two more, which we declined. There was coffee, too, which she warned us was made from toasted nuts, and this, too, we turned down.

'So when are you off to see Ernestina?' Myers asked.

'Monday week,' I told him. 'I'm still on the wait-list for Guatemala City, so I'm living in hope.'

'What made her go there when she took such a liking to Cuba?'

'The cost of living in Cuba went through the ceiling, and only fairly small sums could be sent out from England. She made Guatemalan friends who were going back and they took her with them.'

'Six years is a long time,' Myers said.

'It can be very long,' I said.

Stonehenge was a half-hour further into the morning, a tightly packed megalith cluster throwing down long spears of shadow over the yellow sapless turf. There were pigeons on the stones and many in the sky above, but nothing else in sight that moved.

'Worth the journey?' Myers asked.

'Of course,' I said. 'Rather smaller than I thought.'

'But very impressive.'

'Even after Karnac?' I said.

'Yes,' he said. 'The feeling I have is that it's older. And . . . how can I put it? More universal. This is not a monument for a cat god, but the sun and the universe.'

'Should have been ravens and crows. Not pigeons.'

'Pigeons are doves. Remember that. They're just as symbolical. I wonder if you feel moved by the grandeur of these surroundings in the way I do.'

'There's no way of knowing. Probably,' I said.

'Atmosphere and mood enter very strongly into the kind of experiments that interest me. I've been investigating telepathy in a friend's flat in Highbury, but so far I must admit without positive conclusions.'

'The conditions were wrong,' I suggested.

'Well, yes, they were. Every few minutes a tube rumbled past somewhere beneath us in the bowels of the earth. Intensive concentration was impossible.'

I was studying the monument and thinking about it. Apart from the various cosmic purposes ascribed to it, I seemed to be in the presence of something reflecting the mind of a young child that seeks to challenge nature by unnatural re-arrangements of objects that come to hand, by precarious feats of balancing, as in the case of the colossal lintels here on the standing stones. It was a childish impulse carried to extremes.

We had reached the central feature known as the Middle Archway, a compound of four uprights supporting three massive lintels. 'What I'd like you to do is to place yourself against the end stone with your back to it,' Oliver said. 'I shall then go to the stone at the far end, which I imagine is about twenty yards away. You will transmit thoughts and I will receive. It is now twenty past ten and we'll start in exactly five minutes' time. You could visualise a well-known scene, or select some episode or experience and think about it with every ounce of concentration you can put into it. What is essential is the exclusion for, say, three minutes of all random thoughts. We'll repeat the experiment four or five times then if you can possibly muster up the patience to cope I'd like to go over it a few times with me on the transmitting end.'

He went off and I stood against the stone, still wet from frost in the feeble rays of the sun, and did what I could to enter into the spirit of the thing by starting to concentrate. Shortly he was back, smiling and confident. 'Perfect conditions,' he said. 'Couldn't have been better. Can't help thinking you went out of your way to make things easy for me. Simple stuff. You were thinking of nude women with fair hair.'

'Wrong,' I said. 'I was thinking of an item in yesterday's *Telegraph* about a bear holding up the traffic on a Spanish main road.'

'Oh, hum,' he said, suddenly crestfallen. 'Hold on, though. Wait a minute. Nude – bear – bare. Surely that's a possibility? Or don't you think so?'

'No, I don't.'

'Well, I'm not at all sure. I find it encouraging. Perhaps you're just tired. Anyway, we'll have another go tomorrow.'

Chapter Two

LETTERS FROM ERNESTINA had arrived regularly while I remained in England. They were cheerful and interesting and described life in a Central American republic with such inspired powers of description that friends like Myers urged me to keep them carefully with a view perhaps to eventual publication. I had persuaded her to follow the recommendation issued through the Embassy to remain in Cuba after the outbreak of war, and she accepted that it was prudent and reasonable to put aside any thoughts of return while the blitz continued, especially after bomb damage left the Corvaja home in Gordon Street virtually uninhabitable. Thereafter I was sent overseas and so long as Ernestina could support herself in Cuba, or subsequently Guatemala, there seemed little point in her returning to England. Fewer letters arrived from that time on, and in the period from 1943 to the end of 1944, all news ceased for a period of five months, to be followed by a silence of seven months. This was not an unusual experience, for with changes of sections and theatres of war correspondence was hugely delayed and some letters never delivered. I attempted to break the silence through our Florida section which had some connection in Central America, but their news seemed wary and non-committal: Ernestina had been contacted and was alive and well; no more than that.

Non-military planes flying in any direction continued to be rare for months after the war's end and Britishers stranded anywhere in the Americas were warned to expect long delays before repatriation. Flights in the other direction were less heavily booked and I wrote to say that I expected to be able to come to Guatemala in a matter of weeks. This produced a rapid and enthusiastic response, but somehow I sensed a lack of spontaneity in the writing. It was a long letter that seemed almost too literary, too well-written, too full of nicely turned phrases. I could discover in these sentences no evidence of joy.

The flight to Guatemala was confirmed within a week of the trip to Stonehenge. Ernestina met me at the airport and for a moment I had difficulty in picking her out in the crowd waiting at the barrier. She was smaller than she had always appeared in my memory, the six years had reshaped her face in such a way that she might have been a sister or a cousin, and her stiff, nervous smile probably matched my own. This, I was compelled to admit, was a stranger. Over six years the letters we had written each other had been conventionally informative and cheerful. We had acted as our own censors, but as I well knew the professionals with their scissors left little but banal scraps so that too often not even our literary links had survived.

A standard defence in such emergencies as this is to keep talking. Everything personal was skirted round, and even any description of the fate of the Corvaja family still sitting in the ruins of their house drew little response. So many of us in Europe had settled to a uniformity of crisis. My last experience of life in a foreign land had been Cologne shortly after its near-obliteration in the fire-storm raid when I had watched the flies stream in and out of the holes in the ground. Here in Guatemala City there was an unchallenged normality and stress was unknown. We dined in a restaurant where barefoot Indian girls brought tray after tray of food: ham, tortillas, cheese, dishes of black beans with chillies, joints of grilled guinea pig, meat impaled on little skewers and overflowing baskets of tropical fruit. At one point Ernestina called over the girl who had served her, took a boiled sweet from her handbag, unwrapped it and gave it to her. When she spoke to the girl, who could have been in her twenties, she spoke as if to a young child. 'Of course they are children,' she said, clearly intercepting my thought. 'The hotel doesn't allow tipping so we like to give them sweets instead.'

I commented on the interesting ethnic design woven into the serving girl's garments, all of which I had noticed were different. Immediately Ernestina's expression took on life. It was a welcome distraction, and we were both on safe ground.

'Every girl is obliged to wear real tribal dress,' she said. 'It's a tourist attraction. The huipils you see here belong to a dozen different tribes and a lot of people come here just to study them.' She was clearly well on her way to becoming an expert in such matters. I remembered now of mention made in a letter of part-time work for the National Museum. 'They hope to open a textiles department,' she had written, 'and I'm giving them a hand. Unfortunately it's already late in the day and many of the best designs have been lost.'

The view through the window was of the avenue, like a film set in colours from Eisenstein's *Thunder Over Mexico*. A policeman with an obsidian face stood at a street corner, and an Indian stumbled by on burdened legs. He swore a vermilion kilt and carried the first *cacaxte* I had seen, a wooden cage strapped to his back filled with cans of Coca-Cola. I commented on this and Ernestina said, 'You won't see many delivery vans. They put people out of work. That man keeps a family on thirty centavos a day, which is what he's paid. Five centavos of that goes to the policeman for allowing him to use the avenue, which cuts a mile or so off the walk.'

I said nothing. These were the abuses one expected of a banana republic, but the next small surprise came when the girl arrived to clear away breakfast. I had noticed with concern that the contents of an ashtray from a nearby table had been emptied on a plate of untouched food. 'What happens to all the perfectly edible left-overs?' I asked.

'It goes into a swill-can, and ultimately into the ravine.'

'God,' I said. 'All that food.'

'Sometimes the Indians get at it, but not often, the attitude being if they get free food why should they work?'

The people surrounding us messed with five meals a day, and I was keen to get away from them. I hired a car and we drove a few miles out of town. I wanted to get the feeling and the shape of the country. All the villages were crammed close to the ground which was the colour of burned brick, but, as in Cuba, the people had taken pots of paint of whatever colour they could find and splashed it over the walls. Of human activity there was little to be seen but the servitude of those struggling legs almost doubled under the terrible weight of their *cacaxtes*, the wild freedom of zigzagging drunks, and the teams at street corners hammering sad music from their marimbas. Eight volcanoes with menacing names like Fire and Water encircled the city and these paint-plastered suburbs, and the eight perfect cones floated in the soft light over this scene, with vultures like ash from a bonfire drifting hither and thither in the sky.

The theatricality of the surroundings seemed to do away with evasive talk.

'I believe you enjoy life here,' I said.

'In a way, yes. I used not to and then I changed. At first I laughed at men who wore spurs even if they didn't ride horses. Now I accept it as the normal thing.'

'It's a better life than in England, then?'

'Yes, it is.'

'As you remember England, of course?'

'Naturally.'

'You can't imagine how much better you'd find it now. Do you want to come back?'

'Let's come into the open, Guatemala fashion, and be frank. I'm well occupied here. I do useful work at the Museum, and I have friends. This place is a citadel of privilege of the kind you've never known, but I'm used to it. I fit in. Do I want to spend the rest of my life here? I don't know. The thing is I'm happy enough as things are, and it's clear that you can manage without me. The only problem is money.'

'It's bound to be worse now the army pay remittances are at an end, and with the tightening up on sending cash abroad.'

'Pity,' she said. 'The investment openings here will never be the same again. You can pick up a coffee finca for nothing. For the first time ever we have a liberal government which promises to give land to the Indians. All the finca owners are mad with terror.'

'And what happens if the government takes your finca away and gives it to the Indians?'

'They'd never do that to a foreigner. It's out of the question.'

At that moment it seemed to me at least an interesting experiment, and even, possibly, an exciting one.

Lazlo and Lena Papas, two Hungarian refugees who appeared to be Ernestina's closest friends, had worked hard to enthuse her with the possibilities of this finca project. We called on them in their house which smelt faintly of goulash and looked out over what was commonly called El Mercado de los Zopilotes – the vulture market – in the lower end of the town. The Papas were merchants of hope who had left Budapest in haste some ten years before and lived here ever since by a series of schemes that had never brought prosperity but had somehow kept them afloat. They had taken the house in the market because nobody wanted it, and its windows overlooked Indians dressed in all the colours of the rainbow, selling vegetables, and the *zopilotes* that had been there since the days of the Maya, and were so audacious that they would come flapping down to snatch some edible scrap from the bag carried by a shopper.

Being compelled to live among Indians as he did, Lazlo set out to extract profit from it and advertised himself as an expert on Guatemalan textiles, eventually becoming probably the only non-Indian, I learned, to be able to interpret most of the symbols woven into Indian garments. These often recorded in compact form the wearer's tribal history, his or her age-group, profession, status in society and even sexual potency. This led to a badly paid Museum job. Once in a while Lazlo managed to buy a good example of disappearing textile art and sell it on to the Museum, but these days, he said, such windfalls had become rare indeed. Upper-class ladies had started to collect. When they went to market they took cheap, commercially produced blouses with them and, having spotted a fine *huipil*, would order the market-woman to take it off, and hand her the blouse and possibly five dollars in return. Nowadays Indian women who might have inherited such a *huipil* from a mother or grandmother, wore it inside out when going to market to avoid such compulsory sales.

The Papas knew all about the coffee business. Briefly, and for a pittance, Lazlo had been a government inspector of coffee estates, carrying out coffee control on crops for export, and was offered bribes for good reports and threatened with beatings for those in any way critical of the production. He produced samples of different grades for our admiration or contempt. The best buy for anyone wanting to go into the business was in the Altiplano, he said, where soil and climate contributed to the production of what was generally accepted as the finest coffee in the world. He knew of a small finca going in this choice area that was very cheap indeed, and had everything to recommend it, including relative freedom from earthquakes and proximity to the main Quetzaltenango highway. Labour costs, too, were possibly the lowest anywhere.

'So what's the snag?' Ernestina wanted to know. 'Why are they selling it?'

'There's a widow involved. A woman can't handle a finca on her own. There was some trouble with the Indians when Ubico was here, and he hanged a few. But now the liberals are in that's all cleared up.'

It would take a day or two, Lazlo said, to get in touch with the people in the Altiplano and arrange to have somebody show us round. I was eager to see the north-west of the country. All the Indians of Guatemala seemed extremely poor, and those of the Altiplano, Lazlo assured me, were the poorest of the lot. This in its sad fashion added to their interest for me, for poverty and isolation had helped to conserve their ancient traditions. The *traje,* as the traditional dress was called, was to be seen here in its purest form, according to Ernestina's observations, and many customs and ceremonies that had died out elsewhere with the improvement of communications still took place.

In the meanwhile I made the useful acquaintance of Julian Berridge, the ceramics curator at the Museum, which possessed a huge collection of Mayan artifacts. Most of these were ceramic objects such as drinking vessels and images recovered from lakes Atitlan and Amatitlan into which they had been thrown as sacrifices to the gods. They all demonstrated workmanship of the most exquisite kind. The Museum's collection was the start of my interest in the pre-Colombian culture of Central America, and induced me to embark on a serious study of the subject, finally abandoned some years later after it became clear that its range was so vast that it could never be brought to completion.

It took twelve hours and three changes of bus to reach Santa Maria de la Sagrada Concepción in the Altiplano. The buses were labelled 'third category' and had seven-inch wide seats which were normally used only by Indians who were both small and ready to put up with a minimum of space. Third category buses had a deserved reputation for unreliability, too. In the absence of genuine spare parts during the war years, they had been kept on the road only by miracles of ingenuity performed by village blacksmiths. Lazlo and I were wedged in position among Indians returning to the north, almost all of them in traditional *traje* woven with the symbols that spoke of the history of their tribe. Some of these were brief: 'We came from the mountains, we lived by a lake,' others were venturesome, even challenging, 'Call us the horse people. Four children per horse.' Of the Spanish conquest and near-obliteration nothing remained but the respect for this fecund and powerful animal. First the law then custom prevented an Indian from riding one, yet a kind of close mystical association drew Indians to horses, and successful pregnancies resulted even from the spectacle of horse copulation, so frequently illustrated in woven design.

In these poor Indian villages the people settled uncomplainingly, and without the distractions of hope, to the hard life. The bus stopped at a market to cool down. Porters bent under their *cacaxtes* trotted in to unload their baggage then refilled the vacant space with the stones piled there for this use. It was their belief that muscles should never be left idle. We climbed down to stretch our legs, spreading a local silence among the Indian crowd who followed us with their eyes without turning their heads. Lazlo, who spoke Maya-Quiché, picked up an occasional *sotto voce* comment. The Indian's absence of facial expression, he said, concealed subtle thought processes and much wit.

The long drag up into the Altiplano ended abruptly in a bedraggled cluster of yellow shacks under a mountain scarred all over from the conflagrations of slash-and-burn cultivation. 'Ixtahuacan,' Lazlo said. 'Famous for Mexican smugglers and iguana baked in clay.' The driver put us down, turned back with a desperate squawk on his bulb horn, and went off. A tall, disappointed-looking ladino came out of the cantina accompanied by a child dragging a hawk with a broken wing on a length of string. The man cuffed the child softly away and approached to introduce himself as the agent charged by the widow with the sale of her finca. He walked with the suggestion of a swagger picked up from Western movies and in local style wore four silver rings on the fingers of each hand. He had picked up some English by working in a fish-freezing plant in Belize. The finca was six miles away, he said, and if we were ready he would drive us there. He ducked out of sight into a ruined shed, re-emerging a few moments later at the wheel of a car – once an old Ford saloon, the top of which had been cut away to turn it into an open tourer. Harness bells had been strung round the edge of the body, and from these as soon as we started off came a prolonged festive jingling that was out of place in these surroundings.

We bumped and slithered for an hour through the red dust before stopping outside a square windowless building with an entrance covered by torn sacking. We climbed down from the car and the Ladino pulled aside the sacking for us to pass through. I found myself in a yard of the kind to be seen anywhere in the East or the slums of a Mediterranean city. There, it would have housed odds and ends of machinery or household objects for which it was hoped that, sooner or later, some use could eventually be found: a car axle, an engine block half buried in litter, a ruined tyre, a chicken coop in need of repair. Here, poverty of a different kind possessed nothing surplus to immediate needs and nothing ever to be dumped and forgotten. A search for the purpose of this place recorded fire-wood stacked in a corner, a slab of stone with an iron ring in it, a ram's skull, and steps in a wall that led nowhere.

'Santa Maria de la Sagrada Concepción,' the ladino said, with a touch of pride and a flourish of a beringed hand.

'Where's the village?' I asked.

'This is village,' he said. 'All peoples living in same house.'

'Where are they now?'

'Now they are in the mountains looking for food. If you call them to work and give them food they will be glad.'

'Is this place run with child labour?' I asked Lazlo.

'It comes into it in most fincas. The planters always tell you it's the Indian system. At first the Indians find them light jobs to do round the house. And when they're a little older they're supposed to help collect food in the fields or woods. "Why should we worry?" they say. "It's the way the Indians do things." '

The ladino nodded his agreement. 'Young children very good for coffee picking,' he said. There was a pause between sentences while he organised the wording of what was to come with eyes raised as if for inspiration and the tip of his tongue, as bright as coral, appearing momentarily in the opening of the full, dark lips. 'You may beat them if they don't work fast,' he said, 'and their fathers will be pleased.'

'Don't take any notice of that,' Lazlo said. 'That's meant to impress you. Indian parents no more beat their children than ours do.'

'At what age do they start?' I asked.

'In the finca, normally at eight.'

'How do you feel about that?'

'I'm totally against it. If we manage to get something going my plans are to start some sort of reform in the hope it might spread.'

'Good,' I said. 'It's something we'd better discuss before we get much further.'

The ladino had sensed disapproval of the harsh disciplining of child workers.

'Coffee-picking not hard,' he said. 'They will kiss your hand if you say they may work for you.'

Back in Ixtahuacan we found there was no chance of getting to Guatemala City that day so there was no escaping the cantina's dormitory, which was clean and quiet enough although it had to be shared with two other travellers.

Before returning we discussed the events of the day in the bar over several tequilas which encouraged Lazlo's expression of altruistic views.

'My hope would be to start a movement,' Lazlo said. 'Many planters are reasonable and humane people. The Church might even give us its blessing. The word would get round. This could be the start of a big thing. What do you think?'

'I'm not convinced.'

'You mean you don't see yourself as a coffee planter?'

'Not at this moment.'

'Is it the child-labour thing?'

'That's certainly part of it.'

'The first thing I would do would be to push up the minimum age,' Lazlo said.

'To what?'

'Say, ten.'

'Two years one way or another hardly count. It's still child labour.'

'And cut the working day to eight hours. To some extent we'd be falling in with government policy. There was a reference to labour abuses in the President's inaugural speech.'

'Julian Berridge mentioned it the other day. He said that nothing would be done.'

'You have to remember this is the first liberal president this country has ever had.'

'As soon as he does anything to scare the hard-liners they'll get rid of him. Berridge gives the liberals three years. Let's suppose you manage to start the ball rolling with your one-man land reform, and get yourself known as a liberal supporter, what's going to happen to you when the liberals are no more? The answer is you'll be wiped out.'

'Whatever Berridge thinks I don't feel like giving up,' Lazlo said. He drained his glass and in local style sprinkled salt in his palm and licked it off. 'If necessary I'm ready to take a chance on my own. The time has come when I feel I have to do something with my life.'

At that moment a tall, elderly man advanced on us, stooping a little as he came through the doorway. I was struck by the fact that he was wearing an ill-fitting tropical suit of the kind rarely to be seen in Guatemala where members of the white upper-class – as this man clearly was – are careful about their appearance. He smiled through a ragged moustache in the process of going grey, and held out his hand. 'Edmundo Rios,' he said. 'I'm the owner of this establishment. I've just been told I have English-speaking guests. Happen to have spent several pleasant years at Cambridge. Do either of you know it?'

'I live fifty-odd miles away,' I told him.

'Wonderful,' Rios said. 'I was in Foreign Affairs here until recently but took early retirement after falling out with the late General Ubico. All the better for it. Good climate, splendid mountain walks and pleasant people. I gather you're up here to look over a finca.'

'We've just come back from Santa Maria,' I said.

'Were you favourably impressed?'

'The buildings were in a run-down condition. That was all we saw. If we decide to go any further we'll have to call in an expert to go over the finca itself.'

Rios stroked the bridge of his nose in a local gesture expressing doubt. 'You would do well to do that,' he said. He shook his head. 'This is none of my business but I feel a certain degree of responsibility where foreign visitors are concerned, especially those from England.'

'The price asked is very low,' Lazlo told him.

'It has reason to be,' Rios said. 'They will take less. Were you told any of the history of the place?'

'Nothing. We only know that the owner is a widow. We didn't see her.'

'No mention was made of trouble with the Indians?'

'None at all.'

'The price is very low because there is a dispute with the Indians. They have a claim at Santa Maria. The government doesn't accept it, but the way they see it you're on their land.'

'What form does the trouble take?'

'They come in the night and cut through the roots of the coffee trees. At first you don't realise what's happening. A tree goes here and another goes there. Then you notice all the leaves are falling off. You call in a specialist and he breaks the news. They've cut through the roots, he tells you and holds out his hand for a hundred quetzals.'

'Is there any way round this?' I asked.

'You have to settle it. If you're smart you ask for a meeting with the heads of the families, and they bring one of their priests along, and he burns copal to their god and you drink three or four shots of aguardiente together. You say to them, "I admit this is your land, but I want to pay rent to you to go on using it. You can send all your children along to work for me and I'll pay them thirty centavos and give them five tortillas a day." '

'What happens if you're not smart?'

'If you're not smart you go to the police. The widow at Santa Maria lost her husband that way. The couple bought the finca cheap and the Indians let him go on selling his coffee at good prices because they thought he didn't know the rules of the game. When they cut through the tree roots as a warning this man gave the police commandant ten quetzals and he caught a couple of Indians and broke their legs. After that all was quiet for a few months then the husband disappeared. The story went round that they threw him down the Tajamulco volcano. I don't necessarily believe this story, but that's what they all say.'

Next morning Rios saw us off on the bus.

'So what did you finally decide about the finca?' he asked.

'Nothing at all,' I told him. 'There are one or two points we want to take up in Guatemala City. After some of the things you told us last night I'm a little less keen, perhaps, than I was.'

'This is an interesting part of the country to live in,' Rios said, 'even if the finca's a doubtful proposition. Let me make a suggestion. Why go into the coffee business and stop sleeping at night? I'm moving back into the city in the autumn and this hotel is for sale very cheap. You could buy the hotel and have nothing to worry you. The darned Indians aren't going to throw you down a volcano for running a hotel.'

The next day but one, Thursday, brought with it the beginning of Easter's transfiguration of the city's life. Suddenly the streets fell calm. Forty days of Lent had dutifully passed in a pious lack of activity. People ate less as directed, stayed in bed when they could, and emerged from their houses in the cool of the evening for visits to nearby churches and shrines. The Indians put the last touch to the preparations of the splendid processions with which they would take possession of the streets on Sunday. As one had explained to Lazlo, 'When the Lord is crucified the rains will fall.'

Ernestina had missed the exhausting journey to Santa Maria because she had an infection. We met again at the Papas' house in the vulture market, where the matter of the finca was to be discussed. Lazlo, always the optimist, would have been happy to go ahead, the only problem being the considerable one of raising the cash. He had learned how to live with Indians, he claimed, and I believed that he was right. Lena, as usual, went along with her husband. In reality it was Ernestina who would have been the backbone of this project. Her opinion of primitive societies in general was lower than Lazlo's, but she was a born organiser and if anyone could have got the thing off the ground it was she. But I doubted that she would have stood up to the isolation of Santa Maria. Lazlo was close enough to the Indians hardly to have been affected. For Ernestina the isolation offered its threat in two forms, the first of the place, and the second of the people.

I was the only real, entrenched pessimist. Most of my time since our return had been spent mugging up on the discouraging history of the country, which only confirmed what I had already begun to suspect.

Fourteen families, the book said, were generally believed to rule Guatemala, and perhaps a thousand more shared between them most of what was left of the national wealth. Most of the top autarchs genuinely believed themselves appointees of God. It was a religious tenet and those who opposed it were considered political heretics who deserved extermination. Nobody could explain how, in a country in which all elections were assumed to be fixed, the liberal president had come to power, which to the ruling conservatives made it all the more sinister. Some suggested it was part of a foreign plot. Distantly I could hear the rumble of tumbrils. I could not believe in the possibility of democratic collaboration in coffee growing with emancipated Indians, and this I said.

My flight back to Europe was booked for Easter Monday, and this meeting was followed by a discussion with Ernestina about the future. She remained uncertain about her intentions and wanted time 'to sort herself out'.

Chapter Three

I FOUND MY mother to be suffering from the after-effects of influenza and also the frailty to be expected of her age. Once she had recovered her energy and spirits, it became clear that she felt like a change of scene. It was arranged that she should go to stay with Welsh relatives in Carmarthen.

By chance the move fitted in with my plans. I had gone recently for a medical check-up where the doctor informed me that I was suffering from the peacetime aftermath of the constant and sometimes frenetic activity of the war years, and advised me most emphatically to adopt a more active and demanding life-style. I was to keep moving, revert as far as possible to the health-giving occupations the army had provided, be on the alert – ready to spring into action both by day and night. 'But it's not necessary any longer. I don't need it,' I objected. 'Your body and your brain do,' he said. 'Do you enjoy sport?' he asked and I shook my head. 'How about horse-riding, tennis, squash?' I couldn't work up an enthusiasm, I told him. 'You like the countryside, you tell me. You could go for long hikes.' Knowing myself, I told him, I would never keep it up. A final suggestion was rock-climbing, which had some appeal for me. At least the scenery might be good. He was delighted. 'As it happens it's one of my principal interests,' he said. He usually climbed in the Grampians where the climate imposed a valuable test with the added stimulus of risk. I was no masochist, I told him, and he recommended Pembrokeshire, where he had also climbed, 'and you get your kicks the easy way'.

The area particularly recommended was only thirty miles from Carmarthen, where my mother intended to stay for the rest of the year, so I set out to find a suitable cottage somewhere along the Pembrokeshire coast. I was all in favour of Pembrokeshire, where the people lived on boiled mutton and bacon you had to wash the salt out of before cooking it.

To my amazement, on consulting a Carmarthen house agent I was told that he had nothing of the kind I was looking for on his books. What he could offer was a castle and he read out a few of the overwhelming details. It possessed four turrets, each containing three bedrooms, a banqueting hall flanked by six spacious living-rooms, ample servants quarters below stairs, an exceptionally large kitchen, wine cellars, and the usual offices. It was furnished, he had been informed, but not in a lavish style. The rent was £6 per week. This struck me as low for what was on offer, and he said that the demand for castles was limited, to some extent due to the impossibility of finding staff in these days. Castles could be awkward to live in, he thought, and the people who occasionally took them, sometimes organised themselves so as not to occupy more than a minimum of space. The castle in this case had not been occupied for the past five years.

I pressed for further details and it turned out not to be a castle at all, but St Catherine's Fort in Tenby, situated on top of a rock about thirty yards offshore in the bay. It had been bought as a speculation by a local solicitor who had attempted to change the name by painting Tenby Castle in huge black letters on a fairly small rock surface facing the town. There was no legal way of stopping this piece of impudence, although Tenby Post Office refused to accept letters carrying this address. The solicitor meanwhile ignored letters addressed to St Catherine's Fort.

Going to Tenby to view the property, I found it roughly as described. Among minor additions to the agent's description was the inexplicable presence in the banqueting hall and rooms of the corpses of many small birds, some of which had been so long dead that they had virtually turned to powder. Letting myself in through the fake baronial doors, the first thing that met my eye was a gigantic bearskin rug, the head gazing up at the visitor with penetrating yellow eyes. The flat roof was home to innumerable nesting seabirds among the deep stench of guano deposits accumulated over a half-century.

When I took the place the agent seemed surprised, and it was only at this second meeting, and with my signature already on the document, that other disadvantages of life at the fort came out. I learned that there were no deliveries by any tradesmen, due to the difficulty in hauling goods up the steep and slippery steps cut in the rock. Likewise mail had still to be collected from the post office. He could find me a housekeeper, he said, mentioning that she was a missionary of one of the many obscure religious sects of the area, who would bring with her a daughter who was understudying her. Inconveniences might arise when she asked for days off to preach at chapels, where sermons were not only preached on Sundays but on weekdays. At some time during this conversation he mentioned a general belief that the fort was haunted by more than one ghost, and I told him that I imagined that that could well be the case. There was a special warning, 'Watch out for the tides,' he said. The rock was cut off by the tide for six hours at a time. This meant that you were frequently imprisoned at times when you had hoped to 'go ashore'. It was important to remember that if you failed to beat the tide closing in when you decided to return, the shore visit would be prolonged for six hours longer than intended.

Life at St Catherine's, as I had suspected, turned out to be a game of chance, offering mixtures of mystery, frustration and adventure. There were times when I felt halfway on the road back to early man with none of the tools he had been able to make for himself to tackle the problems of his day. I was unable at first to discover how the gas system operated and caused an explosion. This left me deaf for a few seconds, after which I gave up and fetched an expert who came grudgingly from the town to demonstrate the working of the battery of gas cylinders and their related equipment kept at the bottom of a dark cellar.

On the first night I slept in a bed in one of the town's pubs, and next morning Eiluned Price and her eighteen-year-old daughter Rose of Sharon arrived at the fort. I heard an unidentified sound I first ascribed to the soughing of the wind through the immense keyhole of the baronial doors and went out to find my new housekeeper and her daughter in full flight of the well-known hymn *Let Us With a Cheerful Mind* (praise the Lord for he is kind), sung in this case in Welsh in robust contralto voices. This at an end, Mrs Price explained that the hymn was their standard preliminary to any job they took on. A kind of prophylactic, as she explained beamingly, against the power of evil which was everywhere to be encountered. Both ladies were dressed in brightly flowered dresses worn with short, religious capes in the style of the Salvation Army, but after the initial burst of religiosity the capes came off and the pair got down to work with such vigour that by the end of a hard-slogging day, most of the grime of five years had been expunged. Rose of Sharon, despatched to the town for essential provisions, returned with blood sausage and unleavened bread specially made by one of the bakers for the sect. Mrs Price hoped that it would be the first of many meals she prepared for me. I was relieved to learn that her sect, the Beth Miriams, followed biblical dietetic rules and the Welsh standby, over-salted bacon, was out.

Rock-climbing, the announced reason for my presence in Wales, was not to be avoided, but being a bad performer at sports of all kinds, I was convinced that no good would come of it, and this proved to be the case. Westward of Tenby, the road through Solva to St David's frequently passes close to the edge of the cliffs, offering seascape views unchanged since pre-history. On my first exploratory day I tried an unambitious preliminary climb and found myself in an uncontrollable slide among shale which brought me within yards of a hundred-foot drop. From this dangerous amateurism I took refuge in long and hopefully invigorating walks and bird-watching. This, in an area devoid of the human presence, was extraordinary, with peregrines to be seen at their nesting-sites on cliff ledges, and on one occasion a parliament of ravens, as described in the bird books, with fifty of these excessively rare birds gathered to perform some mysterious social ritual in a farmer's field.

In a way the fort was a good place to work in. Weather in Pembrokeshire was a little worse than in Southern England. The massive stone pile on its rock top seemed to draw on itself the full bluster and rage of storms, and for days on end the town, so close when the sun came out, disappeared behind sheets of rain. Bad weather freed me from the obligation to go ashore and take long, lonely, beneficial walks, and I would settle to work in the central redoubt of the banqueting hall. Here I escaped the worst of the gale's shindy, although the living rooms reverberated and clanked endlessly and the wind whimpered through keyholes and round the edges of loose-fitting panes of glass. On these days of strict confinement, I plunged deeply into the books and documents I had brought back from Guatemala and planned the structure of my book on pre-Colombian culture although with every month that passed its completion date became more problematical and remote. Almost by way of light relief I began my first novel, based on my war-time experiences in Algeria. It was now nearly two years since peace had been declared, and I wanted to write about the war while it was still fresh in my memory.

In the meanwhile the loneliness and sense of isolation lying in wait in such a place was kept at bay by the presence of the two Prices, scrubbing woodwork, polishing windows or over-cooking off-the-ration scrag-end of neck to the accompaniment of resounding and triumphant songs of praise.

'Mr Lewis, bach, please say if we are disturbing you with our singing.'

'You never do that, Mrs Price. I enjoy it.'

'Very kind of you to say that. Pity, but there was only kidney in the butcher's shop today.'

'Then we'll have to make do with it, Mrs Price.'

'With all the fish in the sea funny it is we can't get fresh fish. Are you a fisherman, Mr Lewis, bach?'

'I'm afraid I'm not, but I'll have a go.'

'Tomorrow I'll bring a line and some bait and you shall try.'

'I certainly will.'

She was going then stopped. 'Hymns Ancient and Modern,' she

said. 'We could sing them in English for your benefit. Better it would be if you understood the words.'

'Not at all, Mrs Price. They sound splendid in Welsh. Quite like Latin.'

'Well, that is a compliment indeed. Something we much appreciate. Mr Lewis, bach . . .'

'Yes, Mrs Price.'

'You heard the rumour that the last occupant but one hanged himself from the hook under which you are now sitting?'

'I've heard it, but I've paid it no attention.'

'I am sorry but I have reason to believe it is true.'

'In that case I'll get someone to take the hook down, Mrs Price.'

Next day Mrs Price arrived with a line and a can full of bait and I fished with it in turbulent seas but caught nothing.

'You tried,' Mrs Price said, 'which is the best any of us can do, but Almighty God hasn't given you the knack. I see you here working hard. You can't be good at everything.'

They were to spend the afternoon at a funeral at which Mrs Price would officiate and spent much of the morning practising passionate laments. I listened to Mrs Price's flow of the noble oratory of the funeral service.

'Mr Lewis, bach, do you really believe that your redeemer liveth?'

'It's something many people would like to believe, Mrs Price.'

I missed them, but by way of compensation the sun came out while they were away. The herring gulls resumed their joyful hysteria overhead, and Tenby with its soft, rain-washed colours came layer by layer into focus through the sheaves of mist.

I watched the streets of the town through my binoculars. After the cold rectangles of Carmarthen, the featureless and identical terraced houses and the blunt facades of chapels, Tenby seemed frivolous. This was the capital of an English enclave that had been named Little England Beyond Wales. According to a body of opinion, the English had moved in and taken it over because they saw that it had the makings of the only pleasant seaside resort reasonably accessible to the coalfields and iron foundries of South Wales, where they dominated the scene. When I was in Carmarthen as a child the choice of the summer holiday lay between

Llanstephan, which although exceedingly romantic in appearance was small and somewhat dreary, and Tenby, a real town and a metropolis of pleasure. There was nothing here of the Wales of the stubborn, silent whitewashed villages. To Tenby the English had brought colour and fantasy, with fanciful little buildings that could have been French or even pseudo-oriental stuck into odd corners to drive out the last of the Celtic monotony.

There was no money anywhere else in South-west Wales but the English spenders had brought money here, and walking in the streets you could pick them out not only by their well-cut clothes, but by their size. As the *Western Mail* had noted, the people of English stock who had come to live in Pembrokeshire were taller, on average, by 1½ inches than the Welsh natives of the country. Tenby had dress shops, pubs that admitted ladies to the saloon bars, a single prostitute lurking near the bus station on Saturday nights, and a public urinal with a fine cast-iron screen. It also had an antique shop and in this I was offered a cannon ball which inspired me to take a closer look at the history of St Catherine's Fort, largely to be discovered from old newspaper cuttings. It was clearly a folly of the most expensive kind, built in the fifties of the last century when, improbably enough, the government of the day believed that they had reason to fear a sudden attack by the French and ordered the erection of this and three other such forts at vulnerable points along the Pembrokeshire coast. There could hardly have been any area in the south of the British Isles, even supposing the French had suddenly fallen victims to expansionist madness, where an invasion could have been more pointless. Nevertheless the project was carried out at huge cost, and the forts when complete were advertised as the culmination in defensive military architecture, with a sea-facing curtain wall sixteen feet thick through the embrasures of which twenty-five guns of the largest calibre to that date pointed in the direction of the enemy that never appeared. Shortly after completion a ship attempting to navigate between the rock and the shore carried away the bridge joining St Catherine's to the land. This brought about long confinement of the garrison to the rock, inducing in the end a form of claustrophobia so acute that the fort's batteries bombarded the town. There is no record of the outcome of this mutiny, unique in British history. At the time of my stay cannon balls were still being recovered from the gardens of houses fronting the sea.

A week or so later I went to collect my letters from the post-office, where I was received by a small Welsh lady, with an outburst of melodious astonishment. 'The Fort is it? Quite a collection of them we have, some of them dating back for donkey's years.' The letters were those abandoned by the solicitor. There was one waiting for me from Singapore from a Chinese, Loke Wan Tho. I had met him in unusual circumstances outside a pub in Epping Forest where I had stopped to allow my Alfa Romeo racing car to cool down. The car had won a Le Mans race, and I had had the good fortune to acquire it for an absurdly low price in Italy. It attracted Loke's attention and he pulled up alongside. He was driving a new Mercedes, of which only two had been made, and was accompanied by a beautiful young English girl whose main claim to distinction was her possession, as I later learned, of a hundred or possibly two hundred pairs of shoes. Loke took a fancy to the Alfa and I was dazzled by the Merc, which was the most astonishing car I had ever seen. We each took the other's car for a short spin, and then, as though it was the most ordinary of propositions, Loke suggested a swap. 'You mean here and now? On the spot?' I asked, wondering if this could be some oriental form of joke. 'Certainly,' Loke said. 'You can have my car, and I'll take over yours. Our people can fix up all the legal details.' If it had been possible to put a price on the Mercedes I would have put it at three times that of the somewhat battered Alfa. I had no way of knowing that what was proposed was to a very rich man no more than a trivial whim. For the first time I was encountering great wealth, which was so unfamiliar that it seemed almost incomprehensible. I explained to him that it was not a matter of relative values but that I had half committed myself to a project by which the Alfa was to be converted for racing at Brooklands. The explanation satisfied him. He was at that time an undergraduate at Cambridge and he gave me an address in the town in case I should change my mind.

This I did, for the Alfa proved unsuitable for conversion, and a letter went off to Loke to enquire if he were still interested. Several months passed before a reply came. He had been away touring in Germany and a photograph enclosed with the letter showed the wreck of the admired car. It had been hit by a train at an unguarded crossing and the impact sliced away the rear wheels. Loke had taken me seriously, for the car was now under repair in Frankfurt. There it would naturally be completely repaired and he asked, 'Any particular colour you prefer?'

Years were to pass before we were in contact again, for the Munich crisis was upon us, changing both our worlds. Loke, obliged to drop everything, was called back to Singapore. Escaping the Japanese invasion, he was on the *New Moller* when it was sunk in an air attack, and was rescued from the water with severe burns and temporary loss of sight. Now, for the first time, he was back in England, and was pleasurably astonished to learn that I was rock-climbing in Pembrokeshire, a famous venue for bird-watchers, of which he was one. He said he would like to come to see me, and I invited him down.

For all its zany charm and modest comforts, Tenby was not in fact bird-watching country. This was to be practised at its best some thirty or so miles along the coast, further to the west, and after a quick reconnaissance I found a tiny, semi-derelict cottage in the village of Little Haven which I rented for the period of Loke's proposed stay. The cottage, which would have suited me quite well had I known of its existence in the first place, was primitive indeed, possessing neither electric light, running water nor sanitary arrangements of any kind.

Thirty yards back from the high tide mark lay the frontier of the twentieth century, but down by the shore it was Britain before the Romans waded ashore. Mysteriously, this was one of the Pembrokeshire 'English' villages with an inhabitant even in possession of a double-barrelled name. But whatever the real or assumed family trees Newhaven was a scruffy place, for waste of all kinds that the villagers were too lazy to bury was tipped along the shore in the certain knowledge that apart from tin cans it would be consumed by enormous and confident rats. The contents of latrines were disposed of more discreetly at night, being emptied into the sea at a reasonable distance from the beach when the tide had turned. Some illegal slaughtering went on in times of continuing food shortages and rationing, and small piles of tripes left after sundown on the shore were neatly removed by a pair of foxes tripping delicately over the rocks at dawn.

Loke arrived brimming with enthusiasm and, apart from areas of glistening pink skin round the eyes, little changed in his appearance. The Little Haven scene was one into which he plunged with relish after a brief flicker of surprise at the sight of the house-rat ascending the stepladder to the bedrooms. The fact that the villagers appeared not to notice the presence almost everywhere of the rats seemed to him evidence of a latent Buddhism in the Welsh character. The reverse of the primitive coin displayed summer life by the sea in its most brilliant guise: seals in every cove, a stream with an otter at the back of the hill, and a bluster of wax-white gulls always in the sky. None of the boats from Milford Haven bothered to come here to fish and such, in season, was the largesse of the sea that there were mornings when villagers who could put out of mind what the night tides carried away, brought buckets to the water's edge to scoop up swirling masses of whitebait trapped in the shallows.

In this scene Loke was in his element. At the time of our first meeting, he had been on his way to photograph birds, and now bird photography had become the principal interest in Loke's life. With all the ravens and peregrines, and even the rumour of a Montagu's harrier breeding somewhere in the vicinity, it came as a surprise to find Loke occupied with his first love, the common wren, to be seen hunting its microscopic prey just out of reach of the spume. Ensconced in brambles and bracken he trained his twenty-inch telephoto lens on a one-and-a-half inch bird and there were soft exclamations of triumph when, perhaps once in an hour, he got the shot for which such weighty and sensitive apparatus had been brought huge distances to this spot.

Three island sub-species of troglodytes – the family of wrens – were to be found on St Kilda, the Hebrides and the Shetlands, he informed me, the differences arising largely from the variations in their song performed in the ends of sexual attraction against the never-ending thunder of the surf on such islands. His hope was to identify a fourth variation based on the island of Skomer, which lay only a few miles from Little Haven. This, despite some days of field work in which I assisted, he never did.

Most of the nearby islands showed traces of ancient settlements. On Skomer a sizeable farmhouse, now partially in ruins, had not been occupied for possibly a century, but shortly before our arrival Reuben Codd had taken it in hand and begun a partial restoration, and had recently been joined by his wife and child. Using stones collected from the old ruins, he had patched the holes in the farmhouse walls in such a way that it now stood up to any weather. He kept a cow and a calf, a few sheep, and chickens that were recovering ancestral powers of flight. Where it was evident that crops had been grown in the old days he dug in seaweed to renew the fertility of the soil and planted the basic vegetables. The Codds gave every appearance of enjoying their life-style, and their house was full of laughter. To outsiders such as us this came close to an idyllic existence, and it was clear that this was an experience that had a considerable effect on Loke.

Reuben had made two rooms habitable, and a trickle of visitors who were inevitably interested in bird-life had begun to arrive. The island possessed immense colonies of seabirds, in particular Manx shearwaters, and our presence coincided with the end of a successful experiment carried out in connection with these. R. M. Lockley, the famous ornithologist then living on the neighbouring island of Skokholm, had carried out a study of the shearwaters living and nesting by the tens of thousands in the burrows on the grassy slopes of the cliffs of the island. During the breeding season birds were taken from their holes and released at various distances from home. It was found that a bird released 220 miles from the nesting hole took ten hours to find its way back, and one released in Spain was found in its burrow after two weeks. The Skomer experiment was more ambitious, for a bird was taken by plane to South Africa. This time it took just under 3 weeks to cover the enormous distance. The bird arrived in good shape, with the loss of a few ounces, but clearly anxious to resume its nesting routine. What was even more extraordinary, according to our informants, was that the shearwaters' powerful homing instinct was not exclusively directional, for it had been proved that in preference to a direct flight overland a bird might choose a longer and circuitous oceanic route.

Loke chased after his wrens endlessly with camera and recording gear, but it was the researches carried out here into the mysteries of birds' instincts that captured his imagination. This was life as he wished to be allowed to live it, but he was overshadowed by the melancholy knowledge that within days he would return to Singapore and the compulsions of the world of affairs.

'Surely it's yours to choose what you prefer to do?' I suggested.

'I must admit I would like to spend the rest of my life taking photographs of birds.'

'And can't you?'

'No, but it's impossible to explain why.'

He was a ruler of an empire it gave him little pleasure to possess: an empire of cinemas, rubber, tin and real estate, and he had become one of the rich men of the world. Yet now he admitted that he would return to Singapore with reluctance. His wealth stalked him like a dragon, for custom committed him to the pursuit of riches for which he had little inclination, for, removed from his background, his tastes proved frugal and austere. In the introduction to his book, *A Company of Birds*, published when he was accepted as the best bird photographer in Asia, he lays the blame on destiny: 'I was destined to be a business man,' he writes. Of his ornithology he adds an explanation. 'Every man needs some invisible means of support.' How sad that the empty rituals of a man of affairs should have usurped so much of his life.

Loke went off to Singapore and I back to Tenby in time to assist the Prices in a grand reception of potential converts to Beth Miriam held in the fort's banqueting hall, from which not only the sinister hook in the roof but the bearskin rug with its unsettling eyes had now been removed. There I stayed for two more months, walking, between visits to my mother in Carmarthen, along the gaunt cliff-tops, and living largely on excellent seaweed bread, cockles which abounded in the Tenby sands, and odds and ends of mutton delivered secretly on alternate days. Towards the end of September autumn made its dramatic appearance with Atlantic gales that drew veils of spray across the sky and filled the rooms with the cannonade of huge Atlantic breakers. At their most violent these batterings spread a vibration through the rock that could be felt in the tips of the fingers pressed against an outer wall. There were days, too, when it was impossible to 'go ashore'. In compensation fresh food became unexpectedly available, for small fish, killed or only stunned, were sometimes thrown out of the water and landed on lower ledges where they could be reached.

By the time of this passage through the equinoctial frontier, little had been done to expand the framework of the Guatemalan book. Documents galore, some in old Spanish, remained to be read, and I was beginning to doubt whether these conditions – which I was assured by the locals were no more than a sample of what was to come – would be conducive to literary labours. Mrs Price and Rose Sharon left suddenly to open a mission in Cardiff, earlier than had been intended. Taking me into her confidence, Eiluned told me that she had felt it advisable to cut short the mission in Tenby as Rose Sharon had fallen in love with our butcher, who she regarded as unsuitable as a prospective member of her family, although he offered himself for conversion.

To round off perhaps a rather sad occasion, Mrs Price asked me if I would join them in a verse of that cheerful valedictory hymn beginning 'Now praise we all our Lord', to be sung, she insisted, in Welsh. A little nervously I agreed and, after a couple of run-throughs to try out the words, I added my soft, baritone croaking to their soaring voices. Routine compliments at the end were shown up for what they were by Mrs Price's verdict, 'Well, to be perfectly frank, Mr Lewis, bach, there's no-one will say that as a singer you're not better than a fisherman.'

In the spring of 1948 I returned to London where I sounded out the market for a short first novel. I took advice from a mentor in such matters, a member of Routledge who had published my photographs taken in Southern Arabia. 'It's publishable,' he said bleakly, 'but perhaps not for us.' 'Why not start at the top and go for Jonathan Cape, and then work your way down? You've nothing to lose.'

This I did, and to my utter surprise received a letter from Cape's reader Daniel George asking me to call to discuss modifications which might make the book acceptable for publication. But when I phoned to arrange an appointment, George came on the line with the incredible news that Jonathan Cape had now read the book and would take it as it was. This left me with a feeling almost of having offered myself under false pretences. Cape at this time had reached the summit of its prestige as indisputably the leading literary publisher in Britain. Within a decade of its foundation in 1921, the firm had published such stars of the literary firmament as C. M. Doughty, author of the classic *Arabia Deserta*, H.G. Wells, Sinclair Lewis and T.E. Lawrence - a literary performer who was to make the fortune of the firm. These names were followed by James Joyce, Ernest Hemingway, Robert Graves, and many more of their calibre, so that by the late thirties there were few writers of world-wide prominence who had escaped inclusion in the Cape list.

Summoned to an interview with Daniel George, I was led into his presence at 30 Bedford Square. After glimpses of patrician Georgian interiors, I found him in an oblong cubby-hole, so narrow that it might have been a segment of a corridor. Daniel, hunched at his desk, was hardly visible among a thicket of manuscripts piled to a considerable height on the floor, the window ledges and his desk. In some cases these looked no more promising than the dog-eared, red-taped documentation shoved into odd corners of an old-fashioned lawyer's office. Others had been expensively bound for presentation and I was to learn that both extremes were disapproved of, and lessened the author's chances of success.

Daniel was extremely affable, with a pleasantly sardonic sense of humour that he allowed to come frequently into play. When I commented on the accumulation of hopeful effort over which he presided, he said that he had his method of dealing with it. It was probably at our next meeting that he mentioned this method as being an adaptation of the one invented by his predecessor, the celebrated Edward Garnett. According to an account in the book published by Michael Howard, the firm's junior director, Garnett 'would turn over a few pages and quickly make up his mind whether to read [the book] carefully, and if so put it on one side to be sent down to his flat'.

Garnett had read about ten manuscripts a week. Whether reading them or not, Daniel George had to deal with an immensely larger number. His system was to read the first page, then perhaps two or three pages from the middle of the book, before turning to the end, the whole process occupying perhaps a quarter of an hour. He told me that he was easily put off, as by a single sentence in bad English, pretentious imagery, or ridiculous subject matter. A famous author of that day, venturing upon autobiography, had fatally embarked on page one on an affectionate account of his earliest memory of himself seated on a chamber-pot. Daniel was merciless with literary affectation, and with the repetitive pet phrases with which some authors studded their work. Double negatives were hunted down with ferocity, a special *bête noire* being a sentence that begun with 'It was as if – '. Sometimes persons in high places wishing to try their hand at writing books responded vigorously and with effect to Daniel's criticisms. It was just before our first meeting that he had caused an uproar by attempting to turn down a book of favourite poems by Lord Wavell, then Viceroy of India. Although Daniel George protested that many of the poems had been sketchily remembered and incorrectly quoted, he was officially silenced and the book became a bestseller under the title *Other Men's Flowers*.

Daniel and I went on to see a good deal of each other, and when I felt that it would not be inappropriate to do so, I asked him if the beginning, middle and ending method had been applied in my case, and he confirmed that it had. What had probably saved the day for me was that he had opened the manuscript at a page describing the destruction by artillery fire of an Arab village in Algeria. The gunner in search of some clearly defined object in a background of heat-haze and shapeless mud huts had chosen with huge reluctance to range on a tethered horse. He read on, and I was saved. I asked Daniel what Jonathan Cape liked about the book and he said, 'It's about abroad. He never goes anywhere except New York on business. The only books he really enjoys reading are about travel, and he said yours could have been one. He'd have probably liked it better if you'd have left out the plot.'

Samara was within a few months of publication when I made a second visit to Bedford Square, in early 1949, having been invited to lunch with Jonathan Cape himself. It had been mentioned by Daniel that Irish stew inevitably featured on these occasions, and this was frequently burnt. Such authors as were favoured with an invitation to lunch, knew the place as 'Heartburn House'. Daniel George and the poet William Plomer, who helped out with the reading of manuscripts, were also to be there, and in a brief aside Daniel warned me that Jonathan had just returned from an Easter holiday at Eastbourne with his wife, of which we must expect to be treated to a lengthy description. Both these men stood in awe of their employer who, having started work as an errand boy at Hatchard's bookshop, Piccadilly, had read as many as he could of the books he delivered and through them prepared himself for admission to the world of the famous and the great.

He proved to be tall, imposing and stately, like the most eminent of Strachey's eminent Victorians, cultivating intentionally, it might have been, a slightly outdated appearance. By reputation he was autocratic and blunt, but no-one could have been more courteous on this occasion. He made a brief but kindly reference to my book, after which the conversation moved on as foreseen to the Eastbourne holiday.

'Normally I am an early riser,' Jonathan began, 'never later than seven. On holiday my wife and I set out to spoil ourselves. A real English breakfast in bed. Eight o'clock to the minute. By nine we're out on the front.'

I took a cautious mouthful of the Irish stew. I had been hoping in a diplomatic and round-about fashion to bring the conversation to the subject of Cape's most successful and famous author, Lawrence of Arabia. For years in my youth, long after Lawrence had broken his neck on a Brough Superior motorbike, I constantly ran into people who believed he was still alive. Some even believed that his reported death was no more than a trick by which this huge, if preposterous figure, had been spirited away to re-appear under a different name as a semi-divine defender of the

Empire. Nevertheless, as Daniel had assured me, the Eastbourne holiday monopolised the agenda.

'Routine can be enjoyable,' Jonathan said. 'In the morning two brisk lengths of the Marine Parade, and in the afternoon one. Beneficial both to health and appetite. We're both believers in a square meal at midday, and something light before turning in. Did you say you knew Eastbourne?'

'Vaguely,' I said.

'We stay at Queen's,' Jonathan said. 'The only place to have been awarded an H for merit. Most afternoons we settle to an hour or so of Strauss in the Garden Court, and at five we often pop in at the Southview Café for one of their excellent Welsh rarebits. Something they do very well.'

With that Eastbourne was dismissed. 'And what are your plans for the future?' he asked me.

'I'm hoping to do something about Guatemala,' I told him.

He pretended not to have heard, and I repeated what I'd said.

Jonathan smiled austerely, and shook his head. 'Always write a book about Nelson,' he said. 'Never write a book about South America.'

Back in the office I tackled Daniel George.

'Do what he says,' Daniel said. 'Write a book about Nelson. He'll probably publish it. Jonathan has the market at his finger tips. If he says South America won't sell, it won't.'

'What about Peter Fleming's *Brazilian Adventure*?'

'The adventure sold, not Brazil. It could have happened anywhere. Most of the people who bought the book didn't know where Brazil was. In any case, from what you say your Guatemalan book is going to keep you busy for five or six years. What are you going to live on?'

I packed the Guatemalan material away for another time, and made a start on another novel, *Within the Labyrinth*, describing the Machiavellian Italian scene at the end of the war.

A year later, having submitted the typescript of this book, another lunch at Heartburn House took place, incredibly enough just after Jonathan Cape had returned from holiday. Since my first lunch at Bedford Square I had made a quick excursion to Eastbourne to study its topography and could now speak of the place in a more intelligent fashion. Together in spirit we walked the Marine Promenade twice in the morning and once in the afternoon, listened briefly to Strauss in the Garden Court and were self-indulgent with the Welsh rarebit in the Southview Café. Jonathan responded to my encouragement.

'So what's to come next?' he asked. 'Not Guatemala, I hope.'

'Not if you're against it.'

'How much work have you put into it so far?'

'I've travelled round the country and talked to a lot of people. The Indians go in for the most amazing ceremonies. Few people have seen them. There's a village where a man volunteers to be crucified at Easter. In another place they're supposed to sacrifice a child to the god Mundo every ten years by throwing it down a volcano. I should also add I've read a good deal, my hope being rather to put the thing on a scientific basis. I should have to go back again, of course.'

Jonathan raised his hand to his mouth, then yawned enormously. 'Put it on ice,' he said.

William Plomer said something about there being a market for a child's book on Indians, and Jonathan turned hastily to the subject of travel. 'We've done well with it in the past. But why not go somewhere people will want to read about? Say Indo-China, for example. Nothing's been written about the place for years. There's certainly a book in that.'

The outcome was an offer by Jonathan to back a book on Indo-China and finance travel in the country for a journey taking up to three months. A logistics problem now arose. In the matter of travel, tickets could be bought to any place in the world, but since the war the amount of cash that a traveller could take out of the country was limited to £100. Using his influence, Jonathan was able to increase the sum for this particular journey to £200, but it was difficult to see how this could cover the cost of internal travel and subsistence in a country so vast. In hope of helping the situation I bought a gold watch with the intention of selling this if funds ran out. Jonathan also gave me an introduction to Peter Fleming at *The Times*, who provided a commissioning letter without which travel would have been impossible in a country ravaged by war.

Oliver Myers was back in the Middle East, although archaeological digs were now a thing of the past. In the four years since our last meeting, at Stonehenge, he had entered the Diplomatic Service, but we continued to keep in contact by letter. Having discovered that the Air France plane from Paris to Saigon stopped at Beirut, it was my hope to be able to break my journey there and see something of him again.

When in London I liked to stay, as before, with the Corvajas, with whom I remained on affectionate terms, although there was something unreal in the tacit and never-questioned assumption that Ernestina would eventually reappear. It was to this address that I arranged for the proofs of *Within the Labyrinth* to be sent so that I could correct them before leaving.

The proofs, however failed to arrive, so I rang up the publisher and was told that by mistake they had been sent to 4 Gordon Square. This was about a hundred yards away so I walked across to collect them, only to discover that a second Norman Lewis lived at this address, and that he, too, was a Cape author who had recently completed a hugely successful updated version of Roget's Thesaurus. Unfortunately, I was told, the second N.L. had left the country only two days before, and was presumed to have taken my proofs with him. Three days later I stepped down from the Air France plane at Beirut, where Oliver awaited me. 'We're having a little party for you at the embassy,' he said, and minutes later I suffered a surprise from which I have never wholly recovered, for the first introduction was to the man with whom I shared names, who had also stopped off at Beirut on his way to some Eastern destination. It was a circumstance that further encouraged Oliver's fascination with the paranormal, and inspired him to begin a work to be entitled *The Mechanisms of Coincidence*, although the book was never finished.

Chapter Four

THE INDO-CHINESE JOURNEY – or rather journeys – had been planned with some misgivings, because in 1950 this vast country remained terra incognita. In London there was no-one to whom I could go for information on what I was to expect, and all the French Embassy could do was to send me to Paris. Here the information service provided a guide who took me to the splendid Musée de L'Homme, which dealt in great depth with the culture and history of the many subject races in the process at that time of extricating themselves from the embrace of the French colonial empire. Whatever knowledge there was to be uncovered in this field, it was here. There was one drawback: it was a decade out of date. A curtain had fallen with the Japanese conquest of 1940, and when they pulled out another historical pause was to follow before the French were once more in the saddle of power. With that the nationalist rebellion began, and with it the start of a fresh colonial war.

By the time I arrived in Saigon no-one had much idea of what was happening. The situation was 'fluid'. The French were in control again of the principal towns, but it was anyone's guess as to what was going on outside their defence posts and stockades. I had the good fortune to be introduced to a young Vietnamese girl, Chu Ti, who had fought in the rebel forces, been wounded in action against the French Foreign Legion and smuggled into Saigon to convalesce. Through her I obtained a better understanding of the political and military situation, as well as a more intimate picture of the life and the ancient culture of the Vietnamese people themselves.

The French expeditionary force was weak in terms of men and matériel but it was led by young officers who volunteered for overseas service out of a sense of adventure. These were inclined to view the whole thing, rather as I did, as a kind of camping holiday on a magnificent scale plus a few moments of excitement which hardly added up to a war. Not the slightest objection was raised to including me in forays into the countryside, and in the military convoys by which communications were maintained between the towns. So far, this was an old-fashioned, easy-going kind of campaign with little resemblance to what was to follow with the arrival of Richard Nixon on the scene and the promise of bombing the country back into the Stone Age.

Where I was concerned, very little danger was involved. Convoys were shot up, but not when I was on them. All these expeditions took place through landscapes of unimaginable beauty, through ranges of unscaled mountains and forests full of splendid animals. The enemy, who in a loose and sporadic fashion held nine-tenths of the country, came and went in the night and was rarely seen. As a result we became blasé, and although it was strictly forbidden to slip away from a convoy and travel on one's own, I was twice with officers who did this, dashing through enemy villages in mid afternoon under the correct assumption that the Viet-Minh would be taking a nap at this hour.

These were experiences that no-one would ever repeat, for what was about to happen would strip Indo-China of every aspect of the beauty that then entranced its beholders. A police lieutenant gave me a lift to Ban Méthuot, a small town hardly any distance north of Saigon yet separated from the capital by a thousand square miles of unexplored territory, and marked on the latest map issued by the Information Office *Région Inconnue*. How truly extraordinary it was that in our modern world, a French resident of 'The Paris of the East' could get into his car and at the end of less than an hour's drive find his further passage barred by a forest containing no-one knew what.

The Japanese invaders were the first to penetrate this great arboreal wilderness, through which, ten years before, they had cut a track wide enough to take a single car. In this interval seedling trees, some ten feet tall, had sprung up, spacing themselves with mathematical regularity, the problem now being to avoid them or to hack them down. Over the millennia the jungle had established its patterns and its order. Seen first at a distance, the tall, slender trees with their quite smooth trunks appeared as a plantation, seeming even to have provided themselves with some device eliminating the presence of weeds. They shot up to the roof of the jungle where they put out a parasol of branches trailing ropes of immaculate orchids. At the apex of the parasol it was normal for an enormous hornbill to perch. Hawks, all of the same breed, swayed on the tops of the bamboos growing at the edge of the forest. Once in a while a boar came trotting down the track, kicking up deep purple butterflies as it went. Everything in the jungle had submitted to a discipline. It was our good fortune here to see the world as it would have been tens of thousands of years ago, and our contact with it was all the closer and more intimate after a car-crash forced us to walk a number of miles before reaching an army outpost, where we picked up a lift to our destination.

Our experience of the vanishing tribes inhabiting this region was even more memorable than that of the unspoiled rain forest. Besides buffalo-worshippers there were twenty or thirty versions of the supposedly Malayo-Polynesian people known as the Mois in the mountains and forest of central Vietnam, and Dr Juin, the expert on the subject with whom I spent several days, believed that they had been there almost as long as the trees themselves. There were a number of unusual features in their culture, one being that they succeeded in fitting the population of a substantial village, comfortably and hygienically, into a single long-house, which might be up to 150 yards in length. Juin, who had studied the Mois for thirty years and written a number of learned books on their life-style, claimed that they possessed an unequalled racial memory, recorded in sagas, a study of which he said threw a unique light on man's existence in pre-historic times. Although such information must have been fascinating, I was more impressed by Juin's investigations relating to our day, and above all by his contention that although, as in most primitive societies, crimes as we understand them were few, in this case not only did the Mois not commit crimes but conceptions of right and wrong seemed quite incomprehensible to them. In their place – and incidentally governing conduct by the most rigid standards – were the notions of what was expedient and what was inexpedient. The Mois, he said, were concerned with policy rather than justice. Piety had no place in their ritual observations. Contrition was meaningless, and there was no moral condemnation in Moi folklore of those who committed anti-social acts. Who knows how many of them survived Nixon and the saturation bombing of the forests in which they had believed themselves to be safely hidden.

Laos, the little kingdom tucked away in the north, was the goal and *ultima Thule* of all the escapists of *France-Asie*, and colonial service Frenchmen, office-bound in Paris, volunteered for overseas duties and pulled all the strings to get themselves posted there. It was supremely famous for the charm and the compliance of its womenfolk, and young civil servants who came out as bachelors frequently found themselves happily married within days of their arrival. The unflinching polygamy of the royal family had filled the streets of the capital, Luana Prabang, with princesses, all of them accorded a variety of honours, of which the principal was the right to carry a parasol of five tiers. A Frenchman in the postal service, newly arrived, had married one of these, and a Captain Dupont with whom I travelled through the country and who also possessed a Laotian wife described the circumstances of this wedding. 'At six o'clock on the day of his arrival', Dupont said, 'the postal employee expressed the wish to get married. My wife went out to look for a suitable girl, and was back with one by six-thirty. At seven the *bonzes* came and performed a marriage ceremony which took half an hour. At seven-thirty we opened a bottle of champagne and drank the health of the bride and bridegroom, and by eight they were already in bed.' The man in the *Postes et Telegraphes* took his wife's rank very seriously, Dupont said, and he had had the army engineers fix up a bulky contraption to hold her parasol when they went out in his jeep which, with the parasol in position, could not exceed ten miles per hour.

Such were the adventures and transformations within reach of those whose good fortune it had been to know, or even settle in, Indo-China before war in the Western style had taken it in its grip. Yet, despite the changes, I, too, was the spectator of an infinitely variable pageant, amazed that so many people anywhere could be so happy, and at the subtlety and refinement of their many pleasures.

*

Cape did better out of *A Dragon Apparent*, the book about Indo-China, than expected, and although enthusiasm in my presence was kept under control, Michael Howard's history of the firm which appeared some years later spoke of it as the 'highlight of Cape's spring season' in 1951 and of 'tens of thousands of books' being sold 'to an eager public'. It was at a time when publishing was going through a bad patch, and Jonathan, obviously eager to repeat the success, subjected me to a stream of propaganda – to which I eventually succumbed – on the necessity of subjecting Burma to the same treatment. And so, pocketing – as before – my £200 travelling expenses, I took the plane to Rangoon.

Travelling in Burma proved to be a much more arduous affair than in Vietnam, where even after the years of the Japanese occupation and the war with the French, much of the ordinary routine of life had survived. Burma by comparison had remained isolated and mysterious.

U Thant, the great Burmese statesman who eventually became the head of the United Nations, was chief of the Ministry of Information in Rangoon, but with the best possible will in the world there was little information he could provide. I showed him my letter from the Burmese Embassy in London, and he told me that this was the first request he had received for permission to travel in the country, and was not quite sure of the official procedure to be followed. Thereafter I was passed from office to office, handled always with exquisite courtesy, encouraged in my hope and commiserated with upon my many frustrations. Finally,

I went to the English Consul who told me that as far as he knew he was the only Englishman to travel up-country since the war, and he made a wry face at the memory of the experience. He believed that this was a case when only a certain exceedingly powerful general could say yes or no.

U Thant gave me his name and the general agreed to see me. He was even more engaging than the many charming people through whose hands I had already passed; an Anglo-Burmese who was remarkably English both in appearance and manner, whom I suspected of having been revamped at Sandhurst where he would have been an outstanding student. In the short time I had been in Burma I had come to see it as a simple country, peopled by men and women with a taste for the simple things of life. Whatever this powerful, two-star general had picked up in England was simple, too; the plain watch, the silver ring, the single campaign ribbon, the grey-greenish kerchief that was not silk. When I was shown in he was in the midst of translating a British military manual into Burmese, and I was directed to a seat with a genial flip of the hand. 'Hang on, dear boy. Be with you in a sec,' he said. Then he explained the difficulty he was in. The British manual was far from being the latest and many of the terms had changed. 'Happen to know anything about this kind of thing? I'm absolutely flummoxed,' he said. He passed over the manual with passages underlined on the open page. It was an occasion when the endless hours of basic army training spent on the parade ground at Winchester bore modest fruit, and seated at the desk at his side I sorted out some of the difficulties. 'Wizard,' he said, when at last it was plain sailing. 'Damn lucky you happened on the scene. Oh yes – you wanted to see me about something, didn't you?'

'I came here to write about the country, and was hoping I could travel round a bit.'

'And aren't whoever they are doing the necessary?'

'They say they can't. I've been in Rangoon for a week and got nowhere. Now they tell me you're the only one who can say yes.'

He laughed. 'Well, I suppose I'd better do something about it.' He rang a bell and an N.C.O. came in.

'Where would you like to go?'

'Anywhere I can,' I said.

'This man will write out a pass for you and I'll sign it,' he said. 'Damn interesting trip, I imagine. Won't find it too comfortable, but have a great time. Come and see me when you get back.'

In the war in Vietnam, and consequently in travelling through that country, a certain degree of order had developed by the time of my arrival. Stability and routine of a kind had taken shape. It was possible, for example, to travel by jeep without undue peril between Saigon and Pnom Penh, the capital of Cambodia, to put up there in an excellent hotel, and eat an acceptable hybrid form of Frenchified oriental food. Similarly, by travelling in a military convoy, Vientiane, the principal town of Laos, could be reached, and there, too, comfortable lodgings found. Fighting went on in many areas, but conveniently for a visitor like myself, this was usually called off at sundown, and on more than one occasion I travelled at night through zones accepted as in Viet-Minh control, without ever being troubled by warlike incidents.

Burma was different. In Vietnam the established authority was challenged by a united opposition with a single ideology. In Burma the government was opposed by two separate bands of communists, two versions of a heterogeneous organisation called the PVO (People's Voluntary Organisation) in which many bandits had enrolled, 10,000 or so Seventh Day Adventist Karens, and a small army of mutinous military police. National Security was therefore perfunctory. In Indo-China the social life of a small town remained remarkably untroubled. The Chinese always ran a gambling saloon. It was quite normal for friends to finish a convivial evening in a *fumerie* where they might smoke two or three pipes of opium together. The town could well also possess a cinema – even a little theatre staging oriental ballets of great charm and interest. Burma had nothing to offer of this kind. There were no hotels outside Rangoon, no restaurants, no places of entertainment. In Mandalay, the old capital, I slept in the projection room over the cinema, my slumber occasionally disturbed by the sounds of fighting at the end of the main street a mile away.

Travelling itself provided occasional hazards, and in all I

covered by one or another means of transport nearly two thousand miles of the country. The lorry, for example, preceding mine up the Lashio road in the northern Shan States, was held up, sacked and burnt. This had taken place several hours before we passed through the area, nevertheless we felt it reasonable to congratulate ourselves on a lucky escape. Such was the atmosphere of intimidation in the small town of Mu-Sé, where I found myself a few days later, that the police there decided to take me into protective custody. The language problem made it hard for me to understand what was happening but a heavily armed policeman followed me wherever I went and took me back at night to sleep in the police station. Compassion came into this. My exceedingly tough-looking policeman was sorry for my predicament, and tried continually to force food upon me, some of which, including a mess of mashed-up lizards, I found alarming. A merchant with a few words of English explained what this was about. 'You very weak man. He say you must eat,' he told me. I got out of this by explaining through the merchant that I was engaged in a religious fast. This was accepted unquestioningly by my solicitous captor, but as I could not eat I must drink more, he said, compelling me at frequent intervals thereafter to drink camomile tea, glasses of it being repeatedly thrust into my hands accompanied by remarkably sweet smiles.

Even on the river trip down the Irrawaddy that followed, still regarded by some of my Burmese fellow travellers as a 'pleasure-making excursion', the sounds of conflict were not far away, once forcing me to take refuge from ineffective rifle-fire behind a stockade of bales of malodorous fish. Such inconveniences were minor indeed compared to my journey in the 6.15 am train from Mandalay to Rangoon, celebrated in Burma as the only train which never arrived at its destination. By the time I took my seat in a remodelled cattle-truck and our odyssey began, forty-five bridges had been blown up in this section of line – five in a single night. During my own journey the train was put out of action by simultaneous explosions set off both in front of it, and in its rear. At Yamethin, where we were taken to spend an uncomfortable night, White Flag Communists were besieging the outskirts of the town. Tatkon, next stop, was threatened by a bandit, famous throughout the country as a reincarnation of a cow, subsisting largely on grass.

Apart from the matter of security, the more I saw of Burma the greater even its physical difference from its neighbour Indo-China appeared to be. Indo-China remained quilted by millions of trees. This affected every aspect of life there. The lush, green estuarial lowlands were veined with a network of small rivers. Everywhere there were sparkling lakes with their lively population of birds. Indo-China drew the stranger on continually to new pastoral delights revealed behind forest screens, to views of mountains the mapmakers had overlooked, to ravines and cascades advertised suddenly by the thunder of concealed water, to vast deserted caves with old Buddha images left in corners and recesses by people who had long-since vanished from the earth.

The Burmese scene everywhere could be taken in at a glance: a burnished plain without atmosphere or mystery or surprise: everlasting sunshine in a cloudless sky, temple bells tinkling in a hot wind and with it the grunting of crows in search of carrion. The religious philosophy of the country proclaimed the refinement of humanity through successive reincarnations into a kind of celestial non-existence, and the belief had grown that the building of pagodas was part of the means by which the desired conclusion could be brought to pass. Thus over the centuries, pagodas went up by the million, and all the trees went into the making of bricks. For the outsider the means had become detached from the end, and he was hard put to understand what the building of religious edifices had to do with the evolution of the soul. Unlike the Vietnamese, the Burmese have never freed their religion from the magical procedures of the past, and one of the results is an apparent indifference to social betterment. In 1952 there were forty-two thousand registered lepers in Burma. Nothing was done for them, probably because at the bottom of the Burmese mind the conviction still lay that in this cruel state they were righting an adverse balance of merit accumulated in previous existences.

A British takeover of the country in the last century did nothing to help. A belief in the superiority of their own culture enabled the Vietnamese to remain relatively aloof from their French masters. The Burmese snuggled up to the English and aped their ways, sometimes with considerable success, as in the case of the general who made my travels possible. There were many more like him in the middle class. Under a misapprehension regarding my marital status, a leading citizen of Mandalay suggested that I might consider marrying his exceedingly beautiful sister, but only on condition that I became a Baptist. Christian nonconformism was as fashionable at that time as were Christian names: my friend's name was Henry and his sister's Isobel.

Apart from a reluctance to meddle with the workings of destiny, as in the case of the lepers, I came to see the Burmese as possibly the most generous people on earth, and indeed liberality ranks first among the 'ten shining enlightenments' of their beliefs. Constantly I was the beneficiary of their open-handedness. In the beginning it may have been a matter of shrewd investment in the incarnation stakes, but by now I was convinced it had become a national habit. As my friend with the beautiful sister had assured me, 'If you are hungry you may go up to the first man you meet and tell him that you have not eaten, and he will give you food.' It was inevitable that he should add the rider, 'Thus he will be acquiring virtue,' but I brushed the excuse aside. Who, unless he has visited Burma, can ever have had a taxi-driver smilingly return a tip? Once in my case this renunciation was followed by the gift of an edible bird's nest – a sought-after product of the particular area.

In the matter of hospitality there was the case of Tin Maung with whom I travelled by lorry to Lashio, close to the Chinese frontier. There was an aroma about him of mysterious power, and, piecing together biographical snippets, I suspected him of having been involved with a Shan separatist movement backed by the Japanese. In Lashio there was nowhere to stay, so he took me to his family house in which his old father, his mother and two younger brothers lived in two rooms. Like most of the Burmese I met, Tin Maung was imperturbable. He had been away from home for a year, and when the lorry delivered us at his garden gate, the first news he was given after the calm ritual of his reception, was that the third brother had been killed by bandits. This was delivered by his father, U Thein Zan, while the two surviving brothers took up a kowtowing position, and the old mother, covering her face, retired into the doorway of the house. Tin Maung listened in silence, nodded twice than took off one of the four silver rings he wore on his right hand and placed it on the left. A minute passed slowly and no-one spoke. Tin Maung then asked, 'Have you put up a tablet for him in the shrine?' U Thein Zan said, 'You are now of age. We were waiting for you.' We then went into the house together.

They all slept in the same bed, which would be required now to accommodate five persons – six if I were to be included, as they insisted. Tin Maung, a man of the world, would have none of this and, managing to borrow a camp bed from a neighbour, installed me in the second room. It was a solution the dear old mother completely failed to understand and she complained at length at the family's affront to good manners, and the decadence of the times. Even more impressive in the sphere of Buddhist tolerance was the example of U Thein Zan, who was a lay preacher at all the Lashio pagodas. The drinking of alcohol came close to a deadly sin in such an environment, but the old man trudged down to the nearest stall-owner's house and came back with a pint of country spirits. 'For your friend, who has now become my son,' he said to Tin Maung, handing it over. 'He is a foreigner so he may drink. I know that you will drink too, but I still do not despair of your salvation.'

Tin Maung thought I should see something of the Shan country while I stayed in their house, and paid daily visits to the market in search of a lorry leaving for Nam Hkam. He first offered as a typical local curiosity a pious old man who had willed his body to the vultures. We drank tea with him and we were then introduced to his legatees. Having been a wood carver, he had fitted up perches for them carved with legendary figures in his garden, where he said they could conveniently keep an eye on him while waiting for their inheritance to come through.

Our next trip was a sentimental visit to the spot where, having captured and condemned him to death, the Chinese tried unsuccessfully to hang Tin Maung from a tree. The executioners were so weak from starvation and sickness that although they could haul him off his feet they could not keep him in the air, and he eventually tore the rope out of their hands and escaped.

I spent a week with these people and grew much attached to them, and when I left them it was with regret.

*

I returned in early 1952 to depressing news. To cross the Burmese frontier was to pass behind a curtain excluding all news of the outside world. In Rangoon a letter had been waiting for a month to inform me that, although I had left her in fairly good health and in good hands, my mother had suddenly died. In other directions, too, the news was not good. Ernesto Corvaja, taxed probably with the problem of coping with life in his ruined house, had suffered a fatal heart attack. Eugene had married a wife for whom Maria did not care and the couple had moved away, leaving her alone.

Although the journeys in Indo-China had little physical ill-effect, Burma had taken its toll, for I was compelled sometimes to eat what a western stomach hardly recognised as food, and a routine attack of malaria left its debilitating effect. On my return to Rangoon I found I had lost a stone in weight and, taking a room in the Strand Hotel, I went to bed for a week before tackling the journey home. Medical advice back in England called for a process of recuperation. For this I decided to look for an unspoiled village on the Spanish coast where I could establish a summer headquarters, to which I would return to write books after my winter travels, as well as to fish, swim and settle in tranquillity in the mild, Mediterranean sun.

Having shaken off the malaria, I took a train to the South of France, followed by a succession of local buses through Catalonia down what is now known as the Costa Brava, and over roads left unrepaired for nearly a decade. The Riviera-style development of the Mediterranean coasts of France and Italy had not taken place here. The beaches were empty and the holiday crowds were still to arrive. Tiny fishing villages remained roughly as they had been for centuries in full possession of the charm of the past.

In the semi-medieval town of Figueras I discussed with a hotel owner the project I had in mind. At Figueras main roads came to an end and those that took over, leading down to the sea, hardly improved on cart tracks as they wound their precipitous way through the hills. The owner, a student of local history and customs, was excited by my plan to pick the least accessible of the coastal villages and live in it for a year or two. A wonderful experience, he thought, and one he would dearly have loved to share with me. All five villages in the vicinity maintained minimal contact not only with the outside world, but also with each other, and all their customs were different. In his father's day, he said, most of the people who were born, lived and died in the five villages by the sea had never set foot outside them, and there were still quite a few who took little interest in anything beyond the view from their narrow windows over the sea. He could see one possible obstacle to my proposed investigation into the life of the Spanish past, which was the villagers' notorious mistrust, if not dislike, of strangers. He feared that even if I could find somewhere to live I could expect to be kept at arm's length. All these people were Catalan speakers, too, and they resented being spoken to in Spanish. Did I feel like tackling the language? Not quite yet, at least, I told him.

With the Burma book under way I left England in early spring heading for Farol, described by my hotel-owner friend as the most isolated, self-sufficient and custom-bound of the five villages. I drove a hired car down the excruciating road to the coast, round twenty or thirty hairpin bends, and within a half mile of my objective was obliged to leave it at a bridge that had collapsed.

Farol was what a gifted child with paintbox and chalks and the fresh vision of childhood would make of such a fishing village; a gap in the cliffs with a line-up of almost windowless houses, coloured washing on flat roofs, a scattering of black goats, a church tower with a stork's nest, yellow boats pulled up on the beach, and pairs of women in bright frocks mending nets. Far from suggesting any hostility to the outside world, there was a subdued gaiety in this scene. I found a bar tended by a brown-faced, lively girl who might even have been happy at the sight of a new face, and, Catalan or not, chatted pleasantly enough in Spanish. I risked asking her if there was anywhere to stay, and she told me there was a *fonda,* making clear by her expression that she didn't think much of the place. I went there and stayed for a few days. It was kept by two silent brothers and I was the first guest for a month. They kept sixteen cats under the room in which I slept, and after exposure to the odours that seeped through the floor, I went back to Lola in the bar, explained my plight and she promised to do what she could to find a room in one of the village houses.

My friend in Figueras had been wholly wrong about the attitudes of the people of Farol, for I was handled from the beginning with polished courtesy. By this time I was on easy speaking terms with the fishermen who frequented the bar; they astounded me by their habit of breaking into bland verse after a glass or two of coarse wine. Although no comment was made on the subject I believe that they were mystified by the purpose of my visit, and by my ability to live – as they saw it – without work.

Life, through the shortages inherited from the war, was hard although evidently satisfying. Rationing was severe, and applied even to the basic diet of bread and olive oil. There was no meat, and the normally edible parts of a chicken were reserved for the young, the old, and the sick, the head, innards and feet going into Sunday stews. All marketable fish went to Figueras but certain kinds that lived off seaweed, for which there was no commercial demand, were eaten by the villagers, as were the heads and the tails of the larger fish.

Apart from a part-time schoolmaster, the shopkeeper, a priest and the Civil Guard, the whole of this community was engaged directly or indirectly in fishing, and most of the menfolk in strenuous and often dangerous activities at sea. My hope was to come closer to these people, persuading them to exchange the courtesies owing to a guest for the relaxed rough and tumble of a relationship between friends. The approach to this end, I thought, might be through making myself in some way useful, and an opportunity arose when I noticed how difficult for them the normal transactions of daily life could be through an inability to cope with arithmetic. Since nobody could add up or multiply, shopping for a number of small purchases became a complex and time-consuming process. I therefore made visits to the village shop in the busy morning hours and was available to tot up sums. Following this, one of the senior fishermen asked me to check the agreed figures paid by the wholesaler of their fish, and I was able to put an end to certain irregularities, to the general satisfaction. It was possibly by sheer chance that within days of this success Lola announced that she had found a room for me in a village house. From this time on I felt entitled to consider myself an honorary villager, and retained this status during the summer months I spent in Farol over the next two years.

To be absorbed in the life of an old-style Spanish fishing village called for unquestioning respect for a catalogue of engrained customs and superstitions. Chief of these were certain prohibitions, including the wearing of leather shoes or any other article made of leather in a boat. The superstitions could sometimes seem absurd. In Farol, for example, great stress was laid by line-fishermen on the type of hook they employed, which in design resembled exactly those found in graves excavated at the ancient Roman colony of Ampurias. The only difference between the Roman hook and the modern one was that in the first case the hook was fastened to the line by tying it round a neck in the haft, whereas in the latter an eye-hole replaced the neck, and the line was tied through this. About the time of my arrival supplies of the Roman-style hooks had run out. Only the modern kind were to be had, and the fishermen were quick to attribute to this a decline in their catches. It was of much relief to them when I made the fairly short trip across the French frontier and loaded up with the old-style hook, still to be found in France.

With the distribution of the hooks all the tests of acceptability had been passed. The inhibitions of respect had been put aside and I could be lightly mocked, for example, for an excessive esteem for punctuality, seen in southern countries as a nervous disorder to which the British are susceptible. Especially after a heavy day with the nets followed by a *porón* of scarifying wine, the fishermen used grand language, sometimes pillaging lines from such bards as Luis de Gongora, which in translation carried once in a while an even Shakespearian twist. When the great moment came for the invitation to join the crew of a fishing boat, a small ceremony was to be expected. All those concerned downed a glass of *palo*, the sickly local equivalent of champagne, and there was some boasting about the size of past catches and those to come. My neighbour Francisco then took my arm and we made for the boats. With a sweeping gesture of dismissal he threw down a challenge to a notably stiffening breeze, 'Let us confront the sea together.'

What was on offer was an apprenticeship in the long and tedious processes of preparing a boat for a night's fishing, to be followed at dawn by anticlimax, or at most the small and erratic triumphs of the catch. Nevertheless I could think of no honour and no prospect that had ever delighted me more.

The days spent in Farol were among the best in my life, and it seemed to me that I had stumbled upon a little community that in its geographical isolation had arrived at one of the most pleasant forms of development. Its enclosure in an opening in low cliffs had helped to exclude the village from the violent incursions of the past, and dense cork-oak forests in the rear added to this protection. A fast-running river under the collapsed bridge on the village outskirts contained many trout in which the villagers showed not the slightest interest. The sea in the vicinity was of extreme clarity, and with a face-mask in use large and uncommon fish were to be seen, while an old cannon that must have fallen from a ship lay thirty yards or so from the beach in twenty feet of water and remarkably free from marine encrustation.

Life in Farol was both strenuous and calm. Imperturbably the fishermen rowed their boats in light or heavy seas. Hardly any could swim and on average one a year was drowned (apart from the occasional man alone in his boat carried away by a storm to be seen no more). There was a single policeman and a purely nominal alcalde, but otherwise Farol was free of state control. A charming physician known as Doctor Seduction looked in from time to time with a supply of 'lung syrup' for coughs and strong disinfectant for suppurating wounds. The village maintained its aged poor in a state of dignity, spending more on their funerals than on the cost of their upkeep for a year. Once a year, at the height of the tunny fishing season, a clairvoyant known as the *curandero* arrived from the Pyrenees to settle inheritance disputes and provide wives with birth-control devices made from sponges. His main service was to direct the activities of the fishing fleet which, as he explained to me in a most agreeable fashion, he did by the use of astral charts and 'intimations'. He was always successful, and suddenly and briefly the village was awash with money, to be squandered with all possible speed in readiness for a return to the spartan living and the drives of necessity to be accepted as normal in the life of this village.

I filled notebooks with jottings about the life of a community, seen at first as so deceptively simple but which under the skin was complicated and subtle. Years later I went back to the contents of the Farol notebooks and published an account of the happy adventures of those days. The title was taken from something like a statement of faith made by an old fisherman when news filtered through that a great part of the village of Farol was about to be developed. I asked this man how these changes and others that had already taken place were likely to affect his future. To this he replied, 'How can anyone say? One thing is certain, we have always been here, and whatever happens, we shall remain, listening to the Voices of the Old Sea.'

While still unaware of these unfortunate encroachments, I had begun to form a vision of arranging my life so as to be able to spend every summer in Farol. I had my eye on a splendid shack which had once been occupied by an aristocratic hermit and now mouldered peacefully within feet of the high tide, and I spoke about this to Don Federigo, the part-time schoolmaster who spouted Lope de Vega at every opportunity, although he was weak on simple arithmetic.

'You're too late, he said. 'It's to be pulled down.'

'But why?'

'They're clearing up the village before the development.'

'I don't understand. There's nothing to be developed here,' I said. 'Only the sea.'

'That's just the point. There's big money in the sea. I've had a sneak view of the plans for the urbanisation they've just passed.

A Barcelona firm has bought half the village. They're building a resort with forty villas and a golf course, five hotels, possibly a go-kart track, and a marine promenade with eucalyptus trees.'

'So the shack has to go?'

'They're putting a car park there.'

'How long will it be before this happens?' I asked.

'They start work in the autumn. It's to be finished in about two years.'

'What's to happen to the fishermen?' I asked.

'There won't be any,' Don Federigo said. 'The trawlers from Barcelona will fish here next year. They use radar. Our fishermen will be rehoused. They'll make ten times the money taking foreigners on boat trips.'

'You know my problem,' I said. 'I need peace and quiet to work. Anywhere else you can recommend if the worst comes to the worst?'

'Not along this coast,' he said. 'Everything is out. What you have to do is look for a place where there's no electricity and the water from the river plus frogs is brought round in a tank on a cart. I'm thinking about Ibiza. I was offered a job there once, but I changed my mind when I saw the place. At this moment it's just what you're looking for, but you'll have to hurry. They're building an airport, and as soon as that's opened it will go the same way as this. Anyway, why not give it a try? They're like Africans. Some of the women up in the mountains still wear veils. The plane will soon put a stop to all that.'

'When you say they start work here in the autumn, what exactly will they be doing?' I asked.

'Logically they'd be making up the road and rebuilding the bridge which has to come first.'

'And after that?'

'After that it's winter. They'll go to bed and stay there like we all do. We stay in bed more or less until March. After that we get up and go on with whatever we were doing.'

'So I've got the rest of the year?'

'Leaving out the road and the bridge itself, yes. You're safe until then.'

'Ibiza sounds a possibility,' I said. 'The chances are I'll be on a trip somewhere in the winter. What I'd like to do is give you a call as soon as I get back and if things still sound as bad as you say I'll probably take your advice. You'll be hearing from me in March.'

Chapter Five

JONATHAN CAPE HAD high expectations for *Golden Earth*, as the Burma book had been called, and now reached the conclusion that yet another book about South-east Asia would not be one too many. From the point of view of the peace of the world, the situation there was now worse than it had been two years before, for it was generally believed that with the probable collapse of the French, the United States would step in. In North Vietnam, where previously the French had been opposed by scattered guerrilla forces, regular armies were now appearing in the field, and were prepared to stand and fight. Only the towns and the largest villages were fairly secure. The rest of Indo-China had slipped away into no-man's-land. Any new book would have to be about Hanoi and the North, where it was predicted that the decisive battles of the war were about to begin.

Having been bulldozed into the decision to return again to South-east Asia, it was at least some measure of compensation to discover that on this journey I could at least kill two or more birds with one stone. The Borneo Company, one of the spearheads of Western penetration of the Far East, had been casting round for someone to write a commissioned history of the firm. They now heard of me through Oliver Myers, and the firm's manager in Thailand, Angus Buchanan, had invited me to their headquarters near Chiengmai in Thailand for a discussion over a possible alternative to the book on North Vietnam. This also provided an opportunity to call on Loke Wan Tho in Singapore, with whom I had recently exchanged letters on the subject of an expedition he was planning to Nepal.

Having settled on North Vietnam I phoned Buchanan to say I would be coming, flew to Bangkok and thereafter took the train to Chiengmai, where Buchanan had promised to meet me at the station on his elephant, assuring me that this was part of the company's traditional hospitality offered to visitors. At Chiengmai, however, Buchanan awaited me in a Volkswagen. What happened to the elephant? I asked, to which he replied that it was suffering from ingrowing toenails.

The Company's headquarters were a cross on an enormous scale between a pagoda and a cattle shed, full of the scent of ancient ledgers and exhausted spices although in one corner of a vast room at the time of our arrival the fragrance of kippers for breakfast lingered on. It turned out that the object of my visit had been lost to sight, for by now discussions over the proposed book were going on with Compton McKenzie, although later I was to learn that the fee he had suggested was considered too high. It would have made a fascinating book, for in this same room the contract had been signed for the supply of the celebrated Anna as a children's nanny to Mongkut, King of Siam. It would have been only one of hundreds of arrangements of comparable importance to have been negotiated under the sincere gaze of the Company's Victorian principals whose portraits decorated these walls.

This, as was to have been expected, was a treasure house of outmoded English custom, and of course speech. Elderly staff members clung to the public school slang of the twenties. Low-level employees, who happened to be seen as pretentious, were referred to as they had been in *Punch* before the First World War as 'bumpers', a term applied to those who only rode horses on Margate Sands. Prostitutes were 'polls', and to be caught out with one could be 'deuced awkward'. This picture of men living at the far ends of the earth who had ceased to bother with home leave was complicated in the manner of some of Somerset Maugham's characters by a tendency to go native. It was normal for people who might have spent a third of their lives in Chiengmai to break into the flow of public school English with sharp little interjections of Thai, spoken through the nose. The most senior company servant had taken to wearing a convenient and sensible vest-like garment, excellently adapted to the climate, with black silk Shan trousers down to the knee. For the last ten years most of his spare time had gone into writing a book about the four Idyllic Occupations, which were reading, farming, fishing and the gathering of firewood. The story was that he still kept a Thai mistress who was a 'serene highness' and was entitled to be shaded by three ceremonial umbrellas wherever she went, although now she was old and rarely to be seen.

Representatives of foreign firms such as the Bombay Burma and the Borneo companies were invited and even expected to attend local festivities, which most of them thoroughly enjoyed, and here, if they had any feeling for such things, there were traditional entertainments to be watched that had hardly changed in a thousand years, and which in their poetry and magnificence would have been hard to match anywhere else on earth.

Meadows, one of the Company's old timers, gave me a lift over to the Wat Arun – the tallest building in the area – where a festival was taking place. The first sign of military sponsorship was a large placard bearing a notice in Thai, and beneath it an English translation.

ALL HAT WEARING. BRASSIERES ALSO TO WEAR.
ALL TO DANCE.
PARTNERS TO TOUCH. NOT WALK BEHIND.
LADIES HAIR CURL IN PERMANENT WAY.
LOW CASTE NO UMBRELLA-ING.

Meadows explained that among the new rules laid down in search of power and prestige was the requirement that hats be worn within the precincts of all pagodas. Sensibly, as they were never worn at other times, these were on hire, displayed on tables in long lines outside the Wat's walls, and beside each lady's hat had been placed an orchid, and a safety pin with which to secure it if desired. Behind the lines of hats were tumblers containing mekhong, a locally made whisky drunk hot, with adjacent primuses to deal with drinks that had cooled down. The monks had drawn the line at whisky drinking within the perimeter of the Wat itself, so to be on the safe side many of the males helped themselves to the equivalent of a half pint of Johnny Walker, becoming instantly drunk, and sometimes bursting into loud laughter.

A notice over the richly carved lintel of the entrance to the temple enclosure said: 'All doors are open. Courtesy and affability conciliate.' Through the entrance two wonderfully kept cows ambled past, chewing on the flowers they had snatched in passing from the hands of sauntering guests. To one side of the gate several members of the festival committee came forward to receive us and to present Major Chai Wut, Chief of Police, who happened also to be a registered astrologer. Meadows told me later that the Major had recently had several gold teeth put in 'to make his face wider and happier'. He said he had taken rather a liking to the man. He was at his most pleasant when drunk, as he frequently was, and was well-known for the number of semi-destitute hangers-on whose rice he provided, largely from the proceeds of minor corrupt practices. Meadows complimented him on the new American pistol he was wearing and the Major showed himself delighted. 'We are surrounded by evil men, Mr Meadows,' he said. 'It behoves us to antidote our precautions.'

In the matter of protocol first priority was a visit to the Wat itself, and we climbed the wide marble staircase leading to a L-shaped hall. The floor of this was packed with prostrate figures, and turning the corner of the L the huge figure of an enthroned Buddha came into view. Meadows nodded respectfully in its direction as if to a foreigner of distinction who might or might not feel inclined to return his salutation. Through the deep and throbbing drone of prayer came a muffled babel of sounds from outside the building: the shrieking voices of actresses, the tangled rhythms of several orchestras, and the crackle of .22 rifles on miniature ranges. Now and then we heard a thumping explosion. Meadows explained that this sound would be produced by the most up-to-date of the many attractions – the hand-grenade a midget soldier by a gold-dipped fob-watch, engraved with a stylisation of a bursting bomb.

The front two rows of onlookers seated behind a protective barrier were occupied by the vacant-faced young novice monks who were the town's leading citizens. Behind them, in order of importance, came the big opium smugglers, army and police officers, a few exquisite princesses descended from Mongolian war-lords and condemned to a vacuous liberty through the decline in harems, then the richest shopkeepers and the elegant and dignified prostitutes from the town's leading brothel – each one carrying a plastic shoulder-bag proclaiming a progressive outlook. It was an occasion when the Siamese genius for good humour was shown to best advantage. Each contestant picking up his grenade received shouts of encouragement. When a tank was knocked out a cheer went up. A bad throw provoked groans of disappointment. The management seemed anxious that people should win their prizes and failure caused them to click their teeth in dismay. Sympathetic-looking nurses were dodging about in the background of this and other gatherings in the vicinity, on the look-out for dead-drunks who were tenderly gathered up and carried away for treatment.

Meadows thought that I should go first. An army N.C.O. stepped up and placed three grenades on the bench at my side. In so far as a Thai could look anxious, this man did so. He mumbled something with lowered eyes, and Meadows translated. 'He is concerned for your success and begs you not to fail.' The N.C.O. handed me a white glove and I noticed that the palm of it was blackened by smoke. Meadows saw me staring at it and said, 'There is a five-second delay. Probably better to give it three seconds. Be on the safe side, eh?' At that moment an ambulance siren started up and the ambulance dashed off. I was looking down at the grenades and noticed they were smaller than in the old days, although the Italian 'Red Devil', which was the smallest of them all, could blow your forearm off and with it half your head, if you held it too long.

I picked up a grenade, which fitted snugly into the palm although it was heavier than I expected, and the thought flashed through my mind whether this one could have slipped through with the full charge intact. In the old days of grenade-throwing, either in practice or with serious intentions, the thrower sometimes fumbled and dropped the thing. The N.C.O., perpetually smiling, watched me closely and nodded encouragement. 'Five seconds,' he reminded me. 'But better three.' I noticed at this moment something about the music I found a little unnerving. Several orchestras were going at full pitch and predominantly the instruments employed were xylophones and gongs, but it was the sudden outburst of frantic squealing of rams' horns that I would have preferred not to be obliged to listen to at that particular moment. I gripped the grenade, struck the pin projecting from its bottom on the bench, counted three fast to be on the safe side, and threw it at a midget battle tank that had come jerking into sight on the conveyor. The throw was too high. The grenade struck the iron background sheet before falling to the ground, and there was a two-second delay before it exploded with a belch of smoke and shower of sparks, accidentally almost derailing the personnel-carrier following the tank. 'I have an idea that was a full charge,' I called to Meadows, but he had moved two or three paces to the rear and there was no reply. My second grenade was wide of the mark and did not explode. The third just missed a self-propelled gun and exploded with a thunderous crack the moment it struck the ground. I turned round to Meadows. 'Your go,' I said, but he laughed and shook his head. 'I've changed my mind,' he said.

Fifty yards away they were dancing the Ram Wong on a raised circular stage under the supervision of a police lieutenant whose job it was to enforce the new cultural laws. These obliged couples to take each other in their arms in Western style, which they did so long as the policeman was able to keep his eye on them. He was obliged, however, to look after two other cultural side shows so that as soon as he left the Ram Wong the dancers, including several Europeans, changed back immediately into the traditional dance in which the man followed the girl, both partners jigging and waving their arms rhythmically to the music.

We turned away in the direction of the striptease, but halted by a notice at the entrance to the tent. ***TEASING TO STOP ONE HALF HOUR FOR NECESSITIES OF BODILY RELIEF. TO RESUME SO PLEASE TO RETURN WITH OUR THANKS.***

Just as we reached the gate we were stopped by the sound of running feet from behind. It was the N.C.O., clutching a package which he thrust into my hands. 'Please to open,' he said, and I tore away the wrapping, and found myself holding one of the grenade-throwing bedside lamps. There was a note with it. *For dashed good effort. To accept with compliment.* 'To compensate one grenade not explode,' the N.C.O. said, baring his teeth with pleasure.

We examined the lamp closely. It was beautifully made, the surface incised with posturing figures from the Ramayana. How extraordinary, I thought, that you could only find a really excellent example of the ancient art applied to a shell case. 'I find this', I said to Meadows, 'highly symbolical of the times and the place.'

*

Next day I left for Bankok and Singapore. Meadows drove me to the station in Chiengmai, where it was announced in an almost congratulatory way that the train would be no more than two hours late in leaving. Thus I was given an opportunity of seeing something of the old part of the most delectable of oriental towns in the early morning hours before the bustle of the day began.

Chiengmai, capital of the North, remained beneath a thin veneer of development Thailand's most pleasing city. It was sedate enough at this hour to be explored on hired bikes, with everything worth seeing compressed into the old town within the medieval walls. Part of Chiengmai recalled scenes from old movies, of China before Mao, and a glance at the map confirmed that the remotest provinces of China were not far away. Men and women wearing hats like enormous lampshades hobbled past under the weight of a pole balanced on the shoulders with heavy burdens at each end. Time-defaced human and animal figures, ribald and threatening or merely grotesque, lay abandoned among the rubbish in odd corners. The department stores, open by seven, had special offers of spirit-houses to suit all pockets, from clearance lines in plastic to deluxe versions in richly-grained teak. They were put up everywhere to give shelter to the ancestral spirits of the family, and to such vagrant ones as might be tempted to take up residence, just as a bird may take over a nesting box.

The roofs of old Chiengmai, curling at the eaves, lay upon the city like autumn leaves, and from these arose the spires of many temples, spreading the faintest of haloes into the misted sky. There could have been no more poetic scene than the line-up soon after dawn of the archers with their crossbows, members of a clan enjoying the privilege of shooting at the stationary outlines of fish in the intensely green waters. All these men in their ancient garb presented roughly identical features to the rising sun as they muttered a prayer at the instant of releasing an arrow.

There was only time for one of the many pagodas, the Wat Phra Singh, enshrining the Buddha which, deposited momentarily on this spot while being taken to the king, refused to move further. The pagoda also possesses one of the largest collections of grandfather clocks in the world. We arrived when a stream of male citizens over fifty, who are allowed to sleep there once a week in order to benefit from the holy emanations, were taking their departure. With that the long-drawn-out whistle of the train was heard, and we said goodbye. 'I cannot possibly tell you how much I wish I were coming along,' Meadows said.

'Why do you say that?'

'I've been here too long,' he said. 'In the end you feel a change coming over you but by that time it's too late. Before I know what's happening I'll be wearing Shan trousers. It's time to go, the question is can I pull myself out?'

It was a sweltering afternoon in Singapore when I arrived. Attracted by its reputation for embalmed Englishery, I took a cab to the celebrated Raffles Hotel, and was allocated a room with chintz curtains, a telephone dressed up unconvincingly as a cat, a Gideon Bible, and bedroom slippers for both sexes which seemed only to emphasise the loneliness of the long-distance traveller. A call to Loke's number rang only once before the receiver was picked up and a remote and passionless female voice held me at bay. I sensed well-controlled impatience at the other end of the line as a cautious questioning began. Having described myself as a personal friend of Mr Loke and outlined the purpose of my visit to Singapore, I was told that Wan Tho was out of town at that moment, but she hoped to be in touch with him that evening, in which case she was sure I would hear from him. From this I could only suspect that I had been fed into a system in which calls by the hundred for the great man were filtered and sifted, before a batch of possibles were delivered to a secretary for a final verdict as to who was acceptable and who could be forgotten about.

An hour or two passed. I wandered down to the bar and got into conversation with a man who was in office-building construction and Loke's name came up. Loke, he said, with a laugh of satisfaction, had recently dabbled unhappily in steel futures, and now found himself with several thousand tons of steel girders on his hands. He had had to find somewhere to store these, temporarily, but it was no longer possible to find a square yard of unutilised land in Singapore. The only solution was to stack them in his magnificent garden, largely until then devoted to – and I knew this was coming – Malaysia's foremost orchid collection. The ambience of Singapore, he assured me, was uniquely entrepreneurial.

Having eaten little since dawn, I was now beginning to feel the pangs of hunger. What was the food like here? I asked my friend. He raised his eyes to heaven, and said they prided themselves on traditional English cooking, including steak and kidney pie, with a curry evening meal on Saturdays, which was strongly to be avoided. It was quite pleasant in the garden, and most people ate there in the evenings, although long-sleeved shirts and anti-malarial cream were a must.

I had to leave Singapore the following morning and I had given up hope of Loke, so I went down and occupied the only vacant table in the garden, which may have been turned down by other diners due to its positioning at the edge of a pool, in which large goldfish with sullen expressions and immensely bulging eyes circled endlessly in hypnotic fashion in an anti-clockwise direction. The waiter came with the menu, suggesting before I could speak ragout of beef with herb dumplings, which struck me as unsuitable in a climate in which even the sky seemed to sweat. The alternative to this was savoury meat loaf, to which I had just committed myself when everyone seated in the vicinity was suddenly distracted from whatever they were doing as five white Cadillacs, moving so silently that only the scrunch of their tyres on the gravel could be heard, crept up the drive to form a line outside the hotel's entrance. It reminded me of the funeral cortège of an American gangster, minus the flowers, and I was never more surprised than at that moment when I saw two figures crossing the lawn in my direction, one being someone from the hotel, and the other Loke.

He was full of cheerful apologies, including one for the cars. 'Kind of thing I hate,' he said, 'but I have to put up with. Marvellous you chose to turn up now. We're on our way to my sister's birthday party, dear boy. Black tie, white Cadillac. There's no getting out of it. Hop in.' Five years had passed since the days of our bird-watching in Pembrokeshire, but birds and photography played as great a part in his life as ever, he said. He had a wonderful story to tell: he was now a bosom friend of Malcolm Macdonald, the British High Commissioner for Asia, who also knew something about birds. Loke had found him a house in Kuala Lumpur, in the garden of which an extremely rare eagle was about to build its nest. Loke persuaded Macdonald that the chick-rearing operation ought to be kept under observation, and within days of the Commissioner agreeing to this, he found a thirty-foot tower erected next to the tree with the nest, at the top of which Loke spent most of his spare time for a month.

We were bound for an open-air restaurant a mile or so out of town, the central feature of which proved to be a rotunda set in a garden of flowering trees among which bird cages were artfully concealed, some furnished with real songsters, others with vociferous mechanical bulbuls, used to stimulate birds in the neighbourhood into natural song. About two hundred Chinese guests were seated at long tables forming a hollow square. Within the rotunda a pianist in tails seated at a grand piano worked his way with some panache through a repertoire of Sankey and Moody hymns.

Loke explained that most of the guests were Christadelphians, members of an American fundamentalist sect that attempts to inculcate severe morality in its adherents, including – despite the example of the marriage at Cana – an absolute ban upon alcohol.

For this reason all believers present were invited to wash down the exquisite food placed before them with Dr Pepper, 7-up, or other such blameless refreshments. 'Don't despair, old boy,' Loke said. 'We'll do something about it in your case. You're unsaved, so you don't count.' More white Cadillacs were arriving, and he said of the colour, 'I imagine it's part of our way of showing our faith.' He slipped away and his sister dropped into the empty chair. She was exceedingly pretty, with features veering in the direction of European models, as I had often noticed in the case of upper-crust Chinese beauties. She was carrying a bowl of great delicacy which I later found out was Ming. She picked up the gilt-edged card at the side of my plate, giggled and read the text, 'Let us continue in the breaking of bread, and prayer.' With that the glass was filled from the splendid bowl. 'Malt,' she said. 'I hope you approve ... well, I guess only God sees this. Cheers.' She went, and Loke was back. 'I checked with one of the elders, and I was right. He said the colour emphasises the concept of purity.'

It was a lively affair. The guests exchanged jokes, pulled funny faces, demonstrated conjuring tricks and punned in English – probably in Chinese, too. They were easily amused. A feature of the banquet, which ran to some thirty dishes, was a partridge served to each guest in which a simulated and edible bird's nest had been inserted. Someone stood up and said, 'Normally the bird is to be found in the nest. Now we are eating a nest that was discovered in the bird.' Everyone clapped.

The real and mechanical bulbuls warbled in their cages, the pianist charged for the third time into *Through the Night of Doubt and Sorrow*, played as if it were a wedding march, and a Chinese lady wearing a kind of surplice arose to upbraid us all in a brief sermon in English, which appeared to fall on deaf ears. Now, with the disposal of the last of the simulated birds' nests, the signal had gone out for 'the hour of contagious joy' to begin. Red noses and false moustaches were distributed and a pentatonic twittering arose from the guests as they indulged at this stage in horseplay of a decorous kind.

At the end of the night the scent of the frangipani strengthened, Sankey and Moody had been put away, and I was reminded of the past's indelible grandeur by the strumming of an ancient zither someone had smuggled into this most modern of scenes. With the first flush of dawn Loke drove me to the airport. On the way we talked about his forthcoming expedition to the Himalayas, where for two whole months he proposed to wash his hands of his business concerns, sever communications with Singapore and do nothing more than hunt down, photograph and skin rare birds. The invitation to me to join the party was renewed. Had I ever thought about taking up taxidermy? he wanted to know, and I told him that I hoped to do so when I had the time. 'You're bound to spoil a few birds at first,' he said, 'but you'll soon get the hang of the thing.'

With that, we parted in hope, continuing a regular correspondence but never to meet again. There was to be no expedition, for a year or two later Loke was killed in a plane crash in Taiwan.

*

On the occasion of my first visit to Indo-China in 1950, my flight from Paris to Saigon by DC4 had taken, including a night's stopover, an excruciating four days, but by the greatest of good fortune had provided an opportunity to get to know a senior French policeman, Vincent Lagrange. Shortly after our arrival he had invited me to dinner at his house in the rue Catinat. Here he lived in resplendent surroundings with a Vietnamese mistress of outstanding beauty, Nam Chuan. A curious situation had arisen, for the fourth member of the party was Chu Ti, a bosom friend of Nam Chuan who lived in a cottage in the garden. Nam Chuan and Chu Ti had been born in the same village, but the two girls were poles apart. Lagrange's girlfriend was worldly, a typical French official's mistress, swathed in silk and tinkling softly with concealed jewelry as she moved about the room. Chu Ti was beautiful, but her attractions were of a different kind, including the freshness and simplicity of a village girl in country cottons, and the clogs worn by country people in their muddy fields. In my discussions with the girls, I was astonished to find that, despite Lagrange's position as an upholder of French Dominion, no secret was made of the fact that Chu Ti had been fighting in the jungle with the rebel Viet-Minh, and had been wounded in a skirmish before being smuggled into Saigon to convalesce.

Although Lagrange never made reference to this episode he must have been aware of it, and it was only to be concluded that he was firmly under Nam Chuan's thumb. Later in our relationship he had admitted to a near-certainty that Nam Chuan had something going with his house-boy who took over whenever his employer was on tour. Lagrange was philosophical (*'Ah, qu'est ce que vous voulez? Elle est jeune et jolie et je suis vieux'*). Whatever their domestic complications, I saw a good deal of the Lagrange household. Vincent seemed happy to have me accompany him on official trips, and I took Chu Ti to the movies, which she adored, although with a strong preference for gangster films. How extraordinary it was that this little jungle fighter who had seen prisoners' throats cut and men frizzled by flame-throwers in battle should squirm in her cinema seat not only from the pain of unhealed wounds but at the adventures of Edward G. Robinson acting the part of Al Capone.

Before making this second trip to Saigon, I had written to Lagrange but received no reply. Having settled in at the Hotel Continental, my first concern was to get in touch with him. There was no reply when I telephoned so I took a cyclo to his house where I was met by a concièrge who was new to me. She told me that Lagrange was on three months' leave in France, and that Nam Chuan, who for her was Madame Lagrange, was staying with relations for the great spring festival, the Tet. Chu Ti she had never heard of. I wrote out a note for Nam Chuan which she promised to have delivered, and next morning they phoned up from the reception at the hotel to say that someone was waiting for me. It was Chu Ti, who in the first moments seemed almost unrecognisably changed, although in a matter of moments I realised that the transformation was due to nothing more than the town-clothes she was wearing. I remembered that a reporter on *Le Figaro* had mentioned that because the Viet-Minh were now in most of the villages, a warning had gone out to country girls to leave their pyjamas and coolee hats behind when they came into Saigon to avoid being suspected of spying or worse. I stammered my pleasure and surprise, and we touched hands. Meetings of the kind are not publicly effusive in South-east Asia. I could see that she was daunted by the surroundings. 'Can we go somewhere else?' she said. We took one of the pedecabs waiting at the door, and told him to take us to the Jardins Botaniques.

These, too, had changed, having benefited from the cash-flow of war, although losing none of their charm. For the Tet, the municipality had splashed out, filling the gardens with a purchase of tame silver and golden pheasants, birds that could be seen in the wild on the outskirts of the city, but were here for this occasion in recognition of the good luck with which they were supposedly charged. It was a merit-acquiring exercise to feed these magnificent birds with specially dyed grain on sale for the purpose, and everyone who could afford a piastre's worth for distribution made a purchase.

Luck was seen or stored in the least likely of ways. Spoilt, yapping little dogs of a kind once bred for the old imperial family were brought here for the Tet. For a miniscule fee one could be taken on a lead to urinate against a small post carved with the signs of longevity and peace, in this way discharging luck like a strong electric current. Soft drinks were to be had in the six symbolic colours, but possessing no flavour of any kind: included in the purchase was a horoscope cast on the spot. The pursuit of good fortune seemed often to be linked with absurdities to which even the most sensitive members of the community were prey. Chu Ti, for example, for whose discrimination and intelligence I had the highest respect, was clearly happy to scatter festive grain in the path of a pheasant, and showed signs of disappointment when the birds pecked at her offering in a disinterested fashion.

We sat under a tree to which a little banner had been fastened thanking it for flowering at such an appropriate time, and I asked her about the two years that had passed since our last meeting. 'The future is beginning to smile,' she said. 'By next year the war will be over. We shall be liberated.'

'Do you still go to the jungle?'

'When they need me. I help with the wounded, but there's less fighting.'

'And your own wounds?'

'They've healed. The bullet is still there, but it gives no trouble.'

'I'm glad. And what is the news of Nam Chuan?'

'The news is good. She has been honoured by one of the leaders.'

'The Viets? You don't mean the Viets?'

'No, the Cao-Dai.'

At that moment I remembered Lagrange had told me that both girls had become followers of the strange new religion, based on Buddhism, the teachings of Confucius and Christianity, that was sweeping through South Vietnam and had even been successful in recruiting membership among the largely communist Viet-Minh. Their saints included Victor Hugo and Joan of Arc, Lagrange said. Also St John the Baptist and the Jade Emperor. They had a Pope, archbishops and bishops galore. They held spiritualist seances and went to Mass. Everybody was an official with a title of some sort or another, so there was something in it for all. 'Vegetarians, aren't they?' I had asked, to which Lagrange replied, 'It's not all jam. You live on soya and vegetables. After forty you're not allowed to go to bed with your wife.'

'I forgot you were Cao-Dai,' I said to Chu Ti. 'Last time I was here the French took me to see the cathedral of Tay Ninh.'

'Did you like it?' she asked.

'Well, I don't know,' I said. 'Have you ever heard of Walt Disney?'

'No.'

'He's a man who went in for fantastic things. He could have designed the Cathedral. It's very fantastic. It has a statue showing Jesus Christ borne on the shoulders of Lao-Tse, who is carrying Buddha and Confucius. They've been made to look like Japanese acrobats just about to go into their act.'

Chu Ti's expression made me suspect that she saw nothing incongruous in this. I wondered sadly what was to become of the unapproachable style and taste of these gifted people under assault by the vulgarity of the West, of which Cao-Daism offered a foretaste.

'Nam Chuan is now a member of the Charity Corps. She has been elevated to the rank of fidèle-ardente.'

'And has all this altered her life in any way?'

'Her life is changed. She releases captive birds. She eats rice. Three nights a week now she sleeps in the garden.'

'What does Lagrange think about this?'

'Monsieur Lagrange is not happy.'

'That I can well imagine,' I said.

Next day I had an appointment with my old friend Monsieur de la Fournière, director of the Office of Information and Propaganda, who, as architect and organiser of my earlier journeys into the country, had even been able to persuade his contacts among the military to allow me to travel on their convoys.

He was a man full of enthusiasm. Recognising me as I came through the door, he bounded from his chair and rushed to grab my hand. There was the usual banter about the English winter climate. 'So you couldn't put up with the fogs,' he said. 'I must say I'm delighted to see you, and you couldn't have come at a better time. As you'll see for yourself the war's been won, and it's practically over.' He was a man whose optimism was so blind and persistent as to rank almost with the mildest of mental disorders. He hustled me to a wall map and threw out his arm to show the bold black arrows representing the French Forces in the field hurling back the weak and scattered Viet-Minh, clearly now at the point of annihilation. 'Quite a change since you were last with us, eh?'

I congratulated him warmly, but for me this map had not changed. I waited for him to say, 'We have them on the run,' and he did.

'I can't tell you how much I resent being chained to this desk,' Fournière said, 'at such a time, when you writing fellows go round having all the fun. How about your taking over here for a week or two and I'll do your job? Well maybe it's less exciting than I think. Still, you had a few nice trips. I remember that Dalat run when they got the Chef de Convoie.'

'I missed that one,' I told him.

'Yes, of course you did. You missed all the bad ones. They should have taken you along as a mascot. Still, we've put the bad times behind us now . . . So what can I do for you? Would you like to go somewhere? I suspect that's what you've come to see me about.'

'If at all possible I'd like to go to the North.'

'You mean Laos, say Luang Prabang? But didn't I send you there before?'

'It was Hanoi I had in mind,' I told him, and I saw his eyebrows go up. 'But why? Why Hanoi?' he said. 'Where does the interest lie?'

'For a writer it's interesting because not much gets written about it.'

'Yes,' he said, 'I suppose that's true, but I have to be frank with you. This is an awkward time.'

'The last thing I want to do is be an embarrassment.'

'There is no question of that. I must explain that until now all our energies have been concentrated in the South. A policy, I may add, that's been crowned with success. Hanoi has been left to wither on the vine. One thing at a time. Now perhaps there are signs we are turning our attention to the North.'

He followed my eyes as I turned again to the map. Up in the north there were no bold, black arrows, and rivers spread from Hanoi like the legs of a spider across an empty landscape to the sea. Scattered to the south of the town were small zones cross-hatched in red. 'There is no established resistance,' Fournière said. 'What you see are areas of temporary intrusion. Is this really interesting to you? Do you still want to go?'

'If possible, yes.'

'There are no convoys. You cannot get through by road.'

'And by air?'

'One plane a week. It is usually monopolised by the army. There is a plane in two days' time.'

'Any hope?' I asked.

'I will do my best for you, as I have always done. An even chance, I suspect. Come and tell me all about it when you get back,' he said.

*

Next day was the first of the Tet, involving the many foreigners in Saigon in a crisis of the kind I'd been through before. It could be summed up in the fact that all the Vietnamese who looked after their bodily and spiritual needs had deserted them. Although the hotel had done its best with all manner of inducements to enlist a temporary staff, the innumerable maids, the bell-boys, the floor-cleaners, the waiters, the kitchen staff and the cooks had simply packed up and gone home. There, dressed for the most part in plain white garments, they would spend much of the day on their knees, burning incense before the shrines set up for the spirits of their ancestors, and praying for a year that would be at the very least an improvement on the last.

The hotel had given little advance notice of this dislocation, but late on the previous night, as panic struck, little agonised notices had been pushed under bedroom doors warning that only tea and biscuits would be available for breakfast, and that beds might not be made the next day, and supplying the addresses of restaurants likely to be open, although these were mostly in Cholon, two miles away, to which, in the probable absence of pedicabs, guests would be required to walk.

I was awakened by the room-boys running up and down the corridors beating small gongs. This was followed by silence. I got up, dressed, went down to the dining-room to swallow two cups of tea, and then went out into the street. This, normally one of the busiest on earth, was now not only transformed but unrecognisable in its emptiness, in which the clatter of sandals of the hotel's head porter and his wife hastening homeward was audible fifty yards away.

I had arranged a meeting in the morning with Chu Ti, the victim of a common predicament in Saigon at this time, having been orphaned by the war and left with no home to which to return. She had been born in a village near Vinh Long, believed to have been an early stronghold of the Viet-Minh, and one morning while out digging clams the village had been attacked by a single plane which had dropped a single bomb on its centre. The legend was that the French had been trying out a bomb fitted with liquid air possessing many times the destructive power of conventional high explosives. Rushing back at the sound of the fearful blast, Chu Ti found that little was left of the village but heaps of rubble, one of them entombing her parents. It was a loss that had left the first day of the Tet with little meaning for her. Nevertheless the emerging new religion of the Cao-Dai had adapted itself to such situations with sympathy and protection. After a spiritualist seance with Victor Hugo whose opinion the Pope Ho-Phap always consulted, followers like the bereft Chu Ti were told that they might pray for their ancestors in the temples of any religion.

I found Chu Ti in the garden of the house in the Rue Catinat. 'So how have you decided to spend the day?' I asked.

'First of all I shall burn incense in the Cantonese Pagoda,' she said.

'And am I allowed to come with you?'

'I was hoping you would.'

Remembering Lagrange's description of this celebrated place of worship I was delighted by her choice. We walked the two miles to Cholon and found the pagoda in a mean street with seriously ill people left by its doors to die in peace. 'They're nervous about women,' Chu Ti said. 'But if you buy enough incense they'll let me stay.' The pagoda was dark and full of the cold reek of antiquity. All the shapes it contained were seen through smoke, which had a strange, heady smell, and people were standing in rows in the misted depths of the building, swaying with their eyes closed. Whispering, Chu Ti explained they were seeing visions. I listened to the bass grumble of monks in prayer somewhere out of sight. A sound came and went like the rattling of shaken bones, but underlying all these was the incessant purr of some great gong, like the breath of a sleeping tiger. 'You'll find it very strange,' Chu Ti said. 'If you want to we can leave.' A monk had followed us from the door and we greeted each other, hands clasped together. He smiled continuously showing black-enamelled teeth in the surface of which tiny patterns had been cut to reveal the white bone beneath. The monk lit two spirals for us, then stood back holding the long tongs with which he would snuff out the burning end of the spiral when the amount paid for had been used. Another monk was there to hold out a plate with our horoscopes: illegible splashes of ink on fragments of crumpled silk. Of these practices Lagrange, a willing target of superstition beneath the sceptical façade, had said, 'It's only an amusing old con but so well done you almost fall for it. There's no charge for the horoscopes, and they're always favourable, which is rather pleasant. As for the visions, my guess is they sneak some drug into the incense. I managed to have one once, but it was the usual highly idealised female, and even then only lasted a few seconds.'

Chu Ti's eyes were tightly closed, and she was swaying with the rest. 'Any visions?' I whispered. 'I'm trying hard,' she whispered back, 'but nothing so far.'

Having satisfied the ancestors, Chu Ti wanted to go down to the river, where we found that despite the restraints of the first day of Tet this part of the town was coming to life again. It was said that nearly half the population of Saigon had transformed themselves into boat people, thus forming over a century or so an aquatic society, equally complex if certainly more mobile than the old. Standing on a small hillock, we looked down on many hundreds of sampans, moored in disciplined rows, occupied usually by large families who could only move along their boat like trained soldiers on manoeuvres. Further out the bigger boats began; the nearest of the junks belonging to the aristocracy of the river were anchored in deep water a hundred yards away. The owners kept chickens, ducks and piglets, had pot plants, and washed themselves comfortably on deck instead of jumping into the river. There was a bluish tinge in the light here that was more restful than the brazen yellowness of the town, and the air was several degrees cooler. For this reason it was the custom of many of those who could spare the time to take an hour or so off work in the heat of the day and go down to recuperate near or among the boats. It was both restful and instructive for people who had lost all notion of how to relax to study the lives of the boat people who could. Through openings in the sampans' sides you could watch every conceivable incident of the domestic routine, most of them conducted with exceptional calm.

People were sprawled about under the canopies of the sampans, playing cards, dicing, chatting, being visited by doctors who did little more than study the whites of their eyes. A fishing rod poked over the side of every boat, but I never saw anyone catch a fish. Round about midday members of a society of pig-admirers came ashore and exercised their pigs on leads. Chu Ti took me to a waterside café where people dropped in for a snack of semi-hatched eggs with small apertures cut in their sides tc allow choice in the degree of incubation, but I refused to experiment.

Chu Ti was not here for the river-front scene but because most of the town's Cao-Dai supporters had gathered down by the river for an extraordinary event that was to take place. Opposition from the established religions had been successful in preventing the Cao-Daists from setting up a pagoda in Saigon itself, so now they proposed to bring a large and splendidly equipped junk round from their headquarters at Tra Vinh, and establish it as a floating pagoda in the river. The news was that the junk had sailed from Mytho on the previous day and was due to arrive at any time. For Chu Ti there was no doubt that this would happen. She fished in her bag and pulled out the horoscopes. As in the case of such transactions the world over, the future as presented was comforting but vague. Chu Ti was to experience a marked change for the better. It seemed likely that I had been summed up as a visitor who would not be staying long, and the horoscope assured me that the journey upon which I was about to embark would be successful.

In the late afternoon the Cao-Dai junk nosed its way through a jostling encirclement of sampans. Even at a distance it stood out in the extreme maritime diversity of its surroundings, for it had been painted white with a somewhat ghostly effect. As it came closer to the shore, unusual features were discerned: the masts, for example, were sheathed in gilt decoration, imitating the foliage of parasitic plants, into which – I noted through my binoculars – plaster monkeys were scrambling. A profusely ornamented background had been erected on the deck, in front of which assembled, as if for a group photograph, the visiting delegation of Cao-Dai notables. They had been assembled in rows, with the most important on a stand at the back. The top row included legislators, inspectors, bishops and an archbishop. At the top of this flattened human pyramid the tiny, wizened figure of a cardinal, swaddled in silks and sprouting wings, was enthroned under a large portrait of Victor Hugo. The great writer, now principal saint charged with transmitting the ordinances of Heaven in verse form, had been orientalised by the artist with the addition of a few straggling white hairs at the corners of his mouth, and his subject seemed faintly amused.

I made the mistake of laughing. Two of our immediate Vietnamese neighbours in the crowd looked up, plainly shocked. 'Why do you laugh?' Chu Ti said. 'Is this funny?'

Snatching at an excuse, I said, 'A little boy was making faces.'

'Ah,' she said, nodding. I had had a lucky escape.

By this time I knew her well enough to realise that, despite a show of imperturbability, she was intensely excited. 'It's the horoscope,' she said a moment later. 'Now you will see.'

A small scarlet barge had been lowered into the water from the junk and was being rowed in our direction, and the old-fashioned winged hat worn by the man standing in its bows indicated the distinction of its wearer. Another bishop, I almost said, but checked myself in time. The barge wound its way through the sampans, and the boat people gathered on their decks to wave their flags. 'The messenger is coming,' said Chu Ti, with the almost unnatural calm held in reserve by any Vietnamese rejecting unseemly excitement. She made for the water's edge and I followed her through the thickening crowd. The boat bumped into the bank and the man in the winged hat scooped up his toga and jumped nimbly ashore. Chu Ti went to meet him, they both bowed and the man unrolled a paper and began to read. Several other young men and women had come running and placed themselves at Chu Ti's side. The man in the winged hat was reading from a list. He would read out what seemed to be a name, followed by an interrogatory grunt, and someone in the rapidly forming crowd would grunt back. Mysterious things were happening on the junk, from which came the shrilling of the boatswain's whistle and the popping of small fire-crackers. A party of rich Vietnamese in Western tropical clothes had just climbed aboard and were making deep obeisances to the cardinal, who had come down from his position under Victor Hugo's portrait and now sat on a golden throne.

Chu Ti came back from the gathering at the waterside. It was good form not to show curiosity, so I waited for her explanation of what had been going on. The Cao-Dai had issued an information leaflet describing itself as the 'Universal Religion of the Age of Improved Transport', proving that there was no absurdity of which it was incapable. It was hard not to laugh at the pompous old men who had taken everything that could be used from Confucius and Lao Tze and fitted it into the new faith. Chu Ti said, 'They have come to their decision.'

'About what?'

'The promotions,' she said. 'There are five new fidèles, and two fidèles ardentes. I am one of the two. They have given me a grade one.'

I took her hand. 'That's wonderful news. You must be relieved.'

'What is relieved?' The word was outside her vocabulary. Something from the no-man's-land of the emotions with no equivalent in the firm definition of Vietnamese speech.

'You must be very pleased,' I said. Grade one, I thought. So even the ghost of the old examination system lingered on.

'Tomorrow I have to make the three prostrations,' she said. 'Then I receive my toga. Will you come?'

I shook my head. 'Tomorrow I'm going to Hanoi,' I said, in effect detaching myself from her future. Then suddenly I found I was embarrassed. Surely I could have said that better? I asked myself. I knew by now that ceremony lurked everywhere, smoothing out human relationships among these people. Blunt announcements of all kinds were ruled out, and correct forms followed. The prostrations would almost certainly be the supreme moment to date in Chu Ti's life and her invitation had been an honour. I wanted to explain in self-defence that as an outsider I had been given no models to go on. Doing my best to save the situation I said, 'I am disappointed not to be with you, but the Information Office has booked a flight for me. I shall be back in two or three weeks' time. I hope you will still be here.' Nothing in her expression revealed her thoughts. Very often, as now, the faint beginnings of a smile might have recalled a pleasant memory. 'There is no way I can tell,' she said. 'From now on I must listen to the orders of my superior in the Cao-Dai. Let us say, perhaps I will be here.'

At this point at least I knew what was expected of me, for I had already been warned that Vietnamese who have rejected the influence of the West do not say goodbye. We each turned and walked away, and the speechlessness at this conclusion of our meeting was part of a ceremony correctly performed.

*

De la Fournière came to the hotel to see me off. To emphasise that this was a social occasion he was dressed informally in sporting attire which included a tropical version of knickerbockers. 'I can't tell you how much I envy you,' he said. 'They're real people up there. You'll find it quite a surprise.'

The check-in formalities were conducted on the pavement, before boarding the bus. The police were there to inspect passes and there was a perfunctory frisking for weapons. At this point accompanying friends were turned back. The armoured car that would lead the way to the airport rumbled into position, but there was a further wait for news of conditions on the road.

'You'll enjoy Hanoi,' de la Fournière said. 'A nice, old-fashioned town. The hotel is a disaster but I'm glad to say we were able to get you into the Camp de la Presse. Cheerful atmosphere, besides which you'll be with people in your own line of business. All the home comforts and a wonderful directrice with a bunch of keys dangling from her belt. And, by the way, the chef is from Perigord. Do you enjoy frogs?' Someone blew a whistle and I was clasped in a Gallic embrace. 'Well, I'm afraid I have to leave you in peace. Have a good time. I'll look forward to hearing all about it.'

We boarded the plane. There was a further delay while airport staff scrambled all over it searching for hidden explosives; then we took off. Few such experiences in this life turn out as expected. Despite De la Fournière's forecast, we were carrying no soldiers. The handful of passengers included several Vietnamese government officials, immersed in their paperwork, and the Emperor Bao Dai's ex-mistress who had risen to fame as Miss Saigon two years before. Now, according to the Vietnamese stewardess, she was popping up north for a brief visit to a French general she had got to know. She was exceedingly outgoing, flashed smiles in all directions, and fell almost instantly into a close-knit conversation with a French passenger who moved into the next seat. Hardly had we sat down when the captain came back with the chief steward carrying champagne and squares of toast spread with caviar. After a pause for him to settle his distinguished passenger's nerves, he moved on to me and there was an opportunity to talk about Hanoi. All he could think to say about it was that it was a good place to pick up antiques. There was a market for Buddha images, stashed away over the centuries by the thousand in local caves. You could pick them up for nothing from the local peasants. He had brought back a crateful on his last trip, flogged the best of them and given the rest away to his friends for Christmas.

'Any drawbacks at all?' I asked, and he said that he couldn't think of any but the diabolical weather. 'Think to bring a raincoat?' he asked. I said I hadn't, and he said, 'Pity. You'll need one and they can't be had for love nor money.'

I looked down through the window at the most brilliant bird's-eye-view I'd ever seen. A huge swamp, shining green lamp-light up at us, turned away with mechanical smoothness, and was invaded by a purple segment of sea. A chessboard of fields drifted into sight with a minute ivory pagoda like a chess-piece waiting to be moved.

'Where are we?' I asked.

'We just passed Qui Nhon,' the captain said. 'That's the lake. An hour and a half to go.'

'Do you have any troops down there?'

'No, it's all Viet-held territory.'

'Is there a forecast for Hanoi?'

'Yes,' he said. 'It's raining, and that's the way it's going to be.'

His prediction was correct. It was raining in Hanoi and exceedingly cold. Bao Dai's girlfriend was whisked away out of sight in an American car while the rest of us waited in the minibus for confirmation that the road into town was safe. This kind of rain, which would go on for a couple of months, was called here *le crachin;* it was something between mist and drizzle which formed and dissolved shapes with a curious animation. Awaiting permission to leave, I noticed the way the *crachin* had filtered the colours from this landscape, leaving nothing but greys and a depressed bluish green. There were paddies nearby in which the peasants were transplanting rice-seedlings. They wore over-size conical hats and their enormously long, tapering thighs protruded from straw cloaks of the kind illustrated in Japanese woodcuts. The owner of each paddy was seated in a raised chair under a huge, black umbrella. I tried to photograph this scene, and stood for some minutes inhaling the soft feathers of rain and trying to clear the lens before giving it up. At one moment the hammering of distant machine-gun fire was to be heard. I drew the driver's attention to it. He said, 'It's nothing. It happens all the time. You get used to it.'

The two soldiers who were to escort us now emerged from the airport building, climbed aboard, and we took off and were shortly on the outskirts of Hanoi, appearing largely as an assortment of palm-thatched shacks among boulders and pines. Closer to the centre the fussy, over-elaborate houses of the rich began to appear with pillars decorated with auspicious lettering and flattened dragons on the rooftops. Next came the commercial centre plastered with advertisements for cough-mixture and Coca-Cola. There was a last stop for checking of passes, then I was dropped off at the Camp de la Presse. This was a back-street mansion in French, end-of-century style, bulky and a little severe, with an unnecessarily wide flight of steps up to an entrance imposingly guarded by a pair of gryphons, both seriously vandalised.

A Monsieur Jouin, head of the local information service, awaited me under a portrait of General Jean de Lattre de Tassigny who had recently announced that France would be in Vietnam for a thousand years. He had been at the London embassy, spoke English excellently and took a pride, as I was to learn, in a habit of understatement he claimed to have picked up from the English. Welcoming me to Hanoi he described it as a nice little provincial capital where you could put your feet up and relax, although I could not help noticing the workmen engaged in fitting wire-mesh screens to the windows to keep out the bombs.

Jouin hoped I'd join him for lunch and, remembering the chef from Perigord, I willingly accepted. There was a strong smell of cooking about the place, of a kind I could not associate with French cuisine. This was soon explained when Jouin asked me if I had any likes or dislikes in the matter of food. 'I ask', he said, 'because buffalo tends to feature on the menu up here. It's an exotic experience for people straight out from Paris, but as it's the only meat it can get monotonous. We're lucky in having a cook who's full of ideas.'

'I hear he's from Perigord.'

Jouin spread his hands in sorrow. 'Ah, that one has left us. This man's Chinese but he was quite a find. The last chap left his cookbook behind and he's working his way through it. Today it's tripes à la mode de Caen, except that buffalo will stand in for cow. If you're feeling adventurous the alternative is duck's feet cured in fragrant pine-smoke with sour sauce. Well, anyway, see you in a half hour.'

Jean-Paul Baudouin was present at the lunch. He was a journalist on the staff of *Le Monde*, a man in his fifties, doyen of the French press corps in Indo-China, whose fame had reached my ears, although we had never met. At this moment Baudouin struck me as not entirely happy with his lot. Having allowed himself to be served sparingly with the main course, he carefully pushed the buffalo tripe aside with his fork and took a cautious mouthful of the riz Tonkinois, which from his expression failed also to awaken enthusiasm. Ill-advisedly, Jouin now began a fulsome account of his journalistic achievements and consequent fame both in Hanoi and Paris, to which Baudouin listened gloomily, eyes averted. Until now our conversations had been conducted in English, but as soon as Jouin came to the end of his speech Baudouin dismissed it with a flip of his hand, adding in French, 'Ne dites pas des bêtises'. He then turned to me. 'I've been sent here at great cost to my newspaper', he said, 'and inconvenience to myself. But what am I doing? The answer is, nothing whatever. This is the Siberia of Indo-China to which unsatisfactory war correspondents, or those raising their voices against the absurd policies of our government, can expect to be banished.'

Jouin seemed to enjoy the outburst. 'Pay no attention to him,' he said to me. 'He's upset because we refuse to allow him to get himself killed by taking part in an operation. Isn't that so, Baudouin?' The correspondent of *Le Monde*, who had lifted his glass, sniffed it and put it down again. 'Where does this wine come from?' he asked.

'The forces' usual suppliers in Saigon. Why?'

'Tell them to go somewhere else,' Baudouin said.

'Well, as it happens, I've good news for you,' Jouin told him. 'After all these unfortunate delays, permission has come through for a little excursion tomorrow. The army will be taking you both to Can Son.'

'And what does Can Son have to offer?'

'An outstanding achievement. Something that's been kept under wraps until now. You two gentlemen are going to be the first to have the honour of being taken up there. We've built a new-style voluntary co-operation village where our friends among the tribal peoples will live in peace and security. The name it's been given is Vietnamese for Harmonious Presence. It's all part of General de Lattre's "Operation Turning the Tide".'

'You are victims of your own propaganda,' Baudouin said. 'As for the tide turning, what you don't understand is that it's already done that, but you can't see it.'

A Captain Doustin picked us up in a command car next morning at dawn and we drove through streets where the Tet lamps of the night were still burning feebly behind window panes blurred with rain. 'My problem', said Doustin, 'was that after three months of the jungle all that interested me was to find a quiet place. You're up against people who never let up. You can't imagine the luxury of sleeping in a bed with a mattress once more.'

'Let's hope you don't find this too quiet,' Baudouin said. 'It's been too quiet for me. I need a battle with plenty of blood for the customers, V.M. atrocities and a story about one of our heroic generals.' He switched on a light to study a map. 'Any idea where we're going?'

'No more than that it's up in the mountains. There should be a guide waiting for us at Thai Nguyen. Four hours, more or less, from here. Great scenery, they say. Harmonious Presence is quite a name for a village. I can quite understand you've seen enough of harmonious presences, but it might amuse the readers.'

'And what do we do when we get there?' Baudouin asked.

'Sorry to spring this one on you, but there's a little ceremony to perform. A loyalty and medals, as they say in the trade. The Chef de Canton reads out an address, we pin medals on the notables, they sacrifice a cockerel or two, then we eat.'

'Oh God,' Baudouin said.

'Sorry, the General absolutely insists we eat whatever they offer us. It could be absolutely anything from a length of snake's gut to a bat, but whatever it is, down it goes. These people are important to us and we can't risk offending them.'

'I offend the bastards all the time and shall continue to do so,' Baudouin said.

We bumped along over the rutted track leading to Thai Nguyen and the mountains and the dawn opened a pallid fan behind the *crachin*, and played tricks with snatches of landscape seen through the rain. Clear vignettes came and went in the watery opacity, peasants in their straw capes, yoked buffaloes, the ruin of a pagoda, a weeping tree. 'Why aren't they observing the Tet here?' Doustin wanted to know, and Baudouin told him, 'They're tribals. They don't come into it.'

We came over a low hill and Thai Nguyen grew suddenly out of the earth like a grey mass of toadstools, and when we went down into the town the people, men, women and children, were out in the streets gambling under umbrellas of all sizes and shapes on the third day of the Tet. The guide had not shown up at the checkpoint, and as the rain had slackened off we found our way down to the market place to drink tea, and in doing so discovered a most extraordinary collection of painted clay figurines specially made for the Tet, and displayed on a large number of stalls. These depicted in charming and vivacious forms every aspect of village life in Vietnam. A man scraped the mud off a buffalo, boys flew kites, families picnicked, watched acrobats or went for rides in boats, a doctor looked into a woman's eyes, an old man led a duck on a lead, a little girl held up a bird, lovers admired a flowering tree. These scenes, so lovingly recreated, were the enjoyments of an ancient civilisation that has hardly been bettered. We collected as many as we could carry, exchanged greetings with a group of smiling patriarchs who had staged a chrysanthemum show, then went back to the checkpoint, where there was still no sign of the guide, so we set off again.

Twenty miles north of Thai Nguyen the calcaires began – a sudden visual impact that took me by surprise. We are accustomed to a gradual approach to mountains through foothills, a cooling in the climate, and vegetation of a less restrained kind. Here it was a confrontation without warning. Starting from a base well below Thai Nguyen, the Vietnamese had pushed their light orderly tessellation of fields for fifty miles up a wide valley, then abruptly the advance came to an end against a great blue-grey limestone wall topped by pinnacles like gnarled old fingers scratching at the sky. With this every aspect of the plains was instantly cancelled. Gone were the buffalo and the peasants groping in mud under their big coolie hats. Mountain people lived hard, frugal lives among these peaks that continued for a thousand square miles across southern China as far as Kunming. One of the Chinese emperors, carried here some centuries back in search of exotic adventures, fell in love with the exaggerated landscape and ordered court painters to get more crags and mist into their work. This they did, inventing a classical style which has become so familiar. Here, an hour by slow road from Thai Nguyen, where a two-thousand-foot cliff with great trees growing from the cracks in the sheer face appeared to bar the way, we were seeing China (as this had once been) as the emperor had seen it.

It was slow going from now on along the track avoiding colossal limestone obstacles, and the Vietnamese who persisted in pushing on with their buffaloes to the north did so by circuitous routes and by eventually isolating themselves from the main body of their countrymen behind the towering ramparts of the calcaires. The mountains themselves had always been in the possession of Thai and Mon tribes, both closely related to the Siamese. At the Camp de la Presse I had spent an interesting hour with two cartographers from Paris who presented me with a magnificent ethnological map they had made of the area. It showed Thais and Mons dotted through the mountains, and most numerous at Can Son. Here we were to see the recent Vietnamese immigrants installed under the army's surveillance in their voluntary co-operation village of Harmonious Presence.

It was approaching midday by the time we were through the last of the calcaires, with a view over a wide plateau and the swamp to be converted by the Vietnamese settlers into paddy-fields. All these pockets of humanity scattered through the mountains had always managed to get along with each other well enough in the past. One of the cartographers told me, 'Somehow or other we managed to shake things up so things aren't so good as they were.' The first evidence that all was not well was the appearance suddenly by the roadside of a buffalo lying in a pool of fresh blood.

Round the bend the Harmonious Presence came into view built on high ground over the swamp. A fenced enclosure of densely packed roofs and narrow lanes was allied at a lower level with an assembly ground for markets and the occasional ceremony of the kind we had come to take part in. It was here that the notables of the village should have awaited us, flying kites painted with messages of welcome. Not a villager was to be seen, instead several French soldiers came through the fence and scrambled down the slope.

Doustin pulled up. We got down from the car and went to meet them. More soldiers appeared from the wings of this scene; parachutists who carried themselves with a certain weariness, slouching almost under the weight of their equipment. Without a word being exchanged between us I knew that something was wrong. A sergeant-chef detached himself from the rest, and there was something in his posture and that of his parachutists and also in their silence that reminded me of the strange sequel of calm, the aftermath of near-sleep, I had known to follow violent events. The sergeant-chef and Doustin drew aside, they talked together without emphasis, shrugged shoulders, shook heads. Doustin came back. 'There was an infiltration and an attack,' he said, in a resigned and lifeless fashion. 'It was quite a battle.'

Baudouin gestured to the sergeant-chef. 'What happened to all the people? The villagers?' he asked. 'Where are they?'

I could see that the sergeant-chef resented the bitter, ironical manner, and he chose his words as if addressing an officer. 'They've been conducted to safety,' he said. 'The Viets have sustained heavy casualties.' He led the way to a shallow moat separating the assembly ground from the village itself. This was still dry, and lying at the bottom we saw a long row of bodies, some showing dreadful injuries. They exhibited a good deal of physical similarity of the kind often imposed by violent death. Most of the victims lay on their backs, eyes open and lips drawn back in a contorted half-smile through gritted teeth. One man had lost the top of his skull, and his brains lay nearby in an intact membranous sac, varnished smoothly with blood.

'Why are they not in uniform?' Baudouin asked.

'With respect, half of them never are,' the sergeant-chef said. 'Prisoners tell us there aren't uniforms to go round.'

Baudouin bent down and with some effort rolled a dead man over on his back. 'The hands are tied,' he said.

'We carried out executions as ordered.'

'With hand-grenades. You threw grenades at them?'

'We completed the orders given. I refer to Major Leblanc who was in command of the operation.'

Baudouin turned to me. 'As an unprejudiced observer,' he said, 'I am asking your opinion. Are you ready to swallow any of this? Do you believe these stories of infiltrations? Why have all the people of this village been suddenly spirited away? Who are these people with their hands tied before they are killed?'

'Could it have been the Viet-Minh's punishment of collaborators?' I suggested.

'Then what were the paras doing here?' He rounded on Doustin. 'I demand to see the commanding officer.'

Doustin shook his head. 'I suspect you will be unable to do so.'

'At any rate I can count on your backing?'

'To a limited extent,' Doustin told him. 'I was sent here to conduct a ceremony which turned out to be impossible. I shall report the facts as you and I saw them, but I am absolutely debarred from comment. Nor could I allow myself to be involved in an on-the-spot investigation. This would be seen as a breach of discipline.'

'Of course,' Baudouin said. 'I understand you cannot compromise yourself.' He turned his head away. 'In that case may we return?'

Doustin went ahead to the car and climbed in without looking back. Baudouin and I followed. 'These things are always fixed up for their New Year,' he said. 'The hope is to hit them while they're playing cards. Sometimes it still works, but not so often these days. They're learning fast.' He sighed. 'Well so much for the third day of the Tet with one more to go. Let's see what tomorrow brings forth.'

*

There had been some talk on the previous day of a visit to the 'front', and when Captain Doustin picked me up at the Camp de la Presse he was wearing a Colt automatic, as was the driver who came along on this occasion. The front was thirty kilometres along the road to Hoa Binh on which we should be travelling, and the order was that all troops would be armed. Exactly as promised, at the thirty-kilometre milestone war awaited us. Suddenly faces were harder, and all the military personnel in sight were moving in a brisker and more resolute fashion. Orders were given in resounding tones. Foreign Legionnaires in white kepis and bearded like fierce Santa Clauses advertised the proximity of real combat, and somewhere far away bombs were thumping down with the sound of prize potatoes being emptied out of a sack on to a solid floor. 'Sadly the requested extension for Monsieur Baudouin's permit did not come through in time,' Doustin said, although there was little evidence of sorrow in his voice. 'He would have much enjoyed a visit to Hoa Binh, although they are saying now that the chances of getting through are no better than fifty-fifty.'

We were shunted off the road by the security guards and directed to take our place in a line of tanks and lorries waiting to move off. As soon as the security officer turned his back Doustin told his driver to pull out of line and go up to the head of the queue, and I noticed that in this environment he had become a little piratical. Waiting until the half-track in front had a lead of a hundred yards, we started after it. This method of moving vehicles singly through a danger zone had replaced the convoy system I had experienced on several occasions. Before reaching Hoa Binh there were a hundred natural death traps. Whenever the Viet-Minh felt like doing so they could pick off an isolated car, but the new arrangement had put an end to the regular massacres that took place when a solid jam of vehicles, immobilised, say, by the blowing of a couple of bridges, was annihilated at the pleasure of the attackers. 'Until now we have been unable to get at them, and success has gone to their heads,' Doustin said. 'Now they want to fight a big battle. We've enticed thirty thousand of them out of the holes in the mountains, and we're waiting for them at Hoa Binh. We can look forward to an exciting day.'

We were in calcaire country again. On all sides these massive limestone ruins soared from the matted jungle, their surfaces seamed and pitted like carious teeth. Whole armies could have played hide-and-seek about their bases, protected from the air in innumerable caverns and from ground attack by impenetrable pallisades of tree-trunks. Heavy artillery had been manhandled into position here. Fisherman naked from the waist down dangled nets hardly larger than handkerchiefs in the streams beneath, and watching them I saw the water's surface twitch and shiver with the explosions of the heavy guns in the casemates above. Doustin reached for his camera but changed his mind when we passed an abandoned car floundering on flat tyres, and puckered with bullet holes. 'They're in the woods all round,' he said, glancing over his shoulders as we accelerated away. A more compelling opportunity for photography encouraged risks a few moments later when we ran into the aftermath of an ambuscade in which two men had been wounded – one disastrously with the loss of a leg and his genitals. Doustin leaped down to record this atrocity. Rain and plum blossom blew in our faces and the *crachin* hung like webbing from a tapestry of branches woven overhead into a grey and dripping sky. Doustin composed his picture: the restless bodies, a middle-distance with a roofless pagoda under the jagged mountain background – a click of the shutter, then back into the car and we moved on. This brutal scene alone, with the ambulance men tussling with their gear, and the gulping rhythm of groans, had detached itself from the ordinariness of battles. Peasants passed, threading their way through the jumble of stalled military vehicles going about their business with a terrific indifference, willing themselves, perhaps, to be no part of these happenings, with not so much as a side glance at a drama having less reality probably for them than an episode from a sub-plot of the Ramayana. Two woodcutters stopped for a moment to shift the positions of their immense loads. At the end of the valley a white flake broke from a cliff struck by a shell and fell, trailing a comet's tail of chalk, into the woods. What were they firing at? Doustin wondered aloud, and a tank gunner popped his head out of a turret to explain that the howitzers were targeting the mouths of caves, and this was a radar error. Below us in the shallows of the Black River nothing had distracted the fishermen's gaze into shallow pools, and never for a moment had they ceased to wave their arms as rhythmically as dancers as they guided the tiny fish into the nets.

A mile or two ahead the last of the great limestone peaks closed in on the road to form a minature Khyber, and as we joined the queue through this we found that the tanks, half-tracks and armoured cars were squeezing cautiously and at a terribly slow pace, overlooked (as was feared) by the advance guards of a tenacious and resourceful enemy. In a mood of gloomy prognostication, Doustin recalled methods adopted in past situations of the kind, when a column had been encouraged to dissipate its strength by allowing half the vehicles through such a bottleneck before the middle sections and both ends were attacked. In the long wait to enter the pass Doustin explained the task faced by this force. For the first time the Viet-Minh had succeeded in putting a real army in the field, which, advancing down the Black River Valley at great speed, threatened to cut off Dien Bien Phu and Hoa Binh, both garrisoned with insufficient French troops. We were now ten miles from Hoa Binh, from which the news was far from good. Up to this point, Doustin said, the Viets had been content to take over villages. Now, such was their confidence and strength, they were ready to attack towns.

There was time to be used up in the delays and confusions of such operations and Doustin was suddenly eager to talk. He had been in this war since the beginning, holding down a comfortable staff job at Army HQ, Saigon, until after a year at a desk, he had suddenly been overtaken by a craving for action. 'They put me in command of a strong-point overlooking the Ho-Chi-Minh trail,' he said. 'Can you imagine what it was like sitting in such a post for a year, two years, even three years, without ever seeing the enemy, waiting to be attacked. Then one night your first action happens, and for many of us it was the last. I don't mind confessing, I still get the eerie sensation that I had in those days. In the end it may have become noticeable, and they switched me to what I'm doing now.'

'Is it cowardice?' he asked. 'I hope not. It is the feeling I get at this moment that we are at grips with something ant-like rather than human. These unemotional people driven on by some blind instinct. I feel that my intelligence and my endurance are not enough. Take, for instance, those fellows they send up to dig holes close to the wire, before an attack. You'd expect them to show some human reaction when our supporting guns start dropping shells among them, but they don't. They go on digging until they're killed, and then some other kind of specialist fellows come crawling up and drag the bits and pieces away. Some time later that night you know the shock-troops are going to come up and get into those holes and then you're for it. Losses simply don't bother them. All they're concerned about is not leaving anything behind. They actually tie a piece of cord to every machine gun, so that as soon as the chap who is using it gets knocked out it can be hauled back to safety.'

I nodded. 'I had a brief close-up view of them last time I was here,' I told him. 'When a man reaches his fortieth birthday his friends club together to buy him a coffin,' I said. 'They have a great party. It's a different attitude to death.'

An hour or so passed before they waved us into the column, and we began the long, slow, suspect grind through the sinister labyrinth which finally opened on to a distant view of the military installations, the earth-works and the lined-up cannonry of Ao-Trac, the principal defence-post of the southern valleys, and the supremely important Route Coloniale No. 6 to the west. A huge effort was being made to strengthen the defences on this side of the small town, and engaged on this were several hundred

Vietnamese civilian suspects, kept hard at it by a number of gigantic Senegalese soldiers who rushed among them screaming abuse and lashing out with their switches.

At this point there was a halt while a scout car was sent ahead to report back on the situation, and during this pause I noticed the onset of what might have been a malarial attack of the kind I suffered at irregular intervals when exposed – as I was at this moment – to excessive cold. In Saigon it had been hot and I had mistakenly assumed that Hanoi would be at least warm, too. Instead it was both cold and wet. Fortunately I was prepared. At the Camp de la Presse, Monsieur Jouin had eyed my tropical cotton doubtfully, and said, 'You should be better protected. I have just the thing for you,' and he went away and came back with an amazing overcoat discarded by a foreign visitor who had left the country. It was a coat of the kind with a velvet collar worn until a few years previously by men of affairs. Dismissing the pretended enthusiasm with which I took up the offer, Jouin went on to say, 'The weather here can take you by surprise. It may come in handy.' He stuffed the coat into a brilliantly patterned ethnic bag made by a tribe called the Kala Nyangs, and handed it to me. The moment had come, I now decided, when I could no longer put off covering my shivering limbs with this garment, and I was wearing it gratefully an hour later when we arrived in Ao-Trac. Here we followed the road signs to the sand-bagged dug-out where Doustin was informed that the senior officers of this redoubt of the French colonial possessions were at that moment gathered for lunch, and that we were expected to join them.

The officers' mess was in a dug-out with enormous guns pointing at the sky all round, and each time one of these fired, earth slid down like loose snow from the sloping roof. Within, we sipped Pernod while waiting to be seated, chatting in lowered voices out of respect for the presence of the commanding officer. Around us bottles were ranged with almost mathematical exactitude on the shelves, among photographs of French film actresses on display in unsuitable plush frames. The colonel was exuberant and euphoric, holding forth confidently on the prospect of rapid victory. We clinked glasses. 'I do apologise for the coat,' I said, 'I'm suffering from the shivers.'

'Of course you are,' he said. 'Think nothing of it. Happens to the best of us here all the time.'

He made frequent jokes which the junior officers listened to obediently, ready with their guffaws.

'I echo', the colonel said, bursting with optimism, 'General de Lattre's words, namely that we are here to stay for ever. To these I add my support – in the humility befitting my lesser rank – if God wills it, plus a single stipulation: that they continue to send us a sufficiency of shells and a half litre of wine per man a day.' He laughed suddenly: a full-blooded man acting to perfection his part of happy acclimatisation to the proximity of death. The junior officers added their guffaws, and an immaculate Senegalese mess-boy went round to replenish glasses.

Seated at table we enjoyed an excellent wine with the fish and a '47 Patriarche to accompany the beef. 'We try to look after ourselves here,' the colonel said, 'with particular emphasis on rations.' He turned to me. 'The men get the same food as the officers. Might as well be as comfortable as we can?' The diabolical crash of 155 howitzers drowned the rest of his words, set the burgundy glasses chiming thinly and a bottle fell from a shelf. Shells plunged with harsh sighs into the sky and exploded six seconds later in staccato thunder. The colonel's easy smile was unchanged. 'By the way,' he said to me. 'I'm afraid Hoa Binh's out unless you feel like being parachuted in, which could probably be arranged, although I'm afraid you'd have to leave your coat behind. The Viets are shelling the Black River ferry now. Sank the ferry boat yesterday with the second round at 2,000 metres which is something of an achievement. They use those recoilless mountain guns they make up themselves. Very easy to manhandle. Means they can keep shifting them all the time, and all we can do is plaster the whole area and hope for the best.'

Suddenly a dull, grumbling undertone of heavy machine-gun fire filled in the silences between the cannonading, and crashing echoes chased each other across the valley below. 'It's unusual for the tanks to be in action this time of the day,' the colonel said. He pushed his chair and got up. 'I'm afraid I must leave you. Hope you'll be staying the night. You'll find it a bit primitive – and, of course, noisy. We've hardly settled in yet, but I've great plans for the future. Come back and see me in a year's time, and I promise you you won't recognise the place.'

The colonel left us with dignity and no evidence of haste, but as soon as he had gone there was a scramble for the steps to follow him, in which Doustin joined. I was last, suddenly caught up in the huge loss of energy of the second wave of the malaria attack. Reaching the open, I made for a gap in the buildings. There were shouts and twenty yards away a howitzer fired and the concussion was like a heavy blow in my ears. Yellow fields sloped down to the Son Boi River over which the *crachin* raised and lowered its veils, and I walked towards it until two tanks came into view, moving along the bank like badly adjusted clockwork toys in a series of jerks. Droplets of water blown into my face carried with them the staccato of machine guns, and something I took to be a mortar bomb thumped powerfully between the tanks and myself, opening a ragged fan of blue smoke. In a matter of minutes my ridiculous city overcoat was soaked through and my teeth chattered uncontrollably.

But where were the enemy the French must eventually fight it out with? I was beginning to understand that the battles of the past were no more. The word 'battle' once conjured up Lady Butler's defiant guards in their squares at Waterloo, the orderly advance of cohorts and legions, the bugle-call for the charge, 'standing fast' and 'face to the foe'. Now all was improvisation and chaos, with an invisible enemy in limestone labyrinths, in a pine forest as black as night, or simply wrapped up in mist. There was a rumour that the fishermen I could still see down by the Son Boi hid their guns on the river bank while they scooped up their small fish, and it now occurred to me that I was well within range of them.

I turned back and began to walk uphill towards the Colonel's dug-out and met Doustin who was out looking for me.

'We're leaving immediately,' he said. 'The road is under fire. Here, put on this tin hat.'

Back in the Camp de la Presse in Hanoi I went to bed and stayed there for four days, getting up on the fifth to attend a press conference called by the general. The point of his lengthy harangue came after forty minutes, but the assembled correspondents, knowing what to expect, could take only a mild, connoisseur's interest in the peroration. 'People put it to me this way,' said the general, his fine, brooding eyes fixed reproachfully on his audience. ' "Having achieved your purpose in forcing the enemy to give battle – having destroyed in that battle his two best equipped divisions – why do you retain so many men in a position where from lack of opposition they can no longer be effectively employed?" In deference to this logic, which is unanswerable,' said the general, 'I have decided to displace the centre of gravity of our forces, which will henceforward be concentrated in the delta, and Hoa Binh, which is now without value to us, has been evacuated.'

On this occasion I saw Baudouin for the last time. 'I've eaten my last duck's foot for a year. Off to Paris tomorrow.'

'But you expect to be coming back again?'

'There's no way out of it. I'll have to be in at the end.'

'And you put that at a year hence?'

'More or less,' he said. 'They'll take Dien-Bien-Phu, then the Americans will come in. At least we will be out.'

Chapter Six

In March 1954, with North Vietnam behind me, I telephoned Don Federigo in Farol to receive the expected reply. 'It has happened,' he said. 'They didn't even knock off for the winter, such is the power of money. Your shack was the first thing to go. Come and see us when you can.'

The ship that carried me some weeks later from Barcelona to Ibiza had also brought the executioner to deal with a youth sentenced for robbery and murder, who would be garrotted in the old style reinstated by the dictator, on open ground in use on normal occasions as a football field. The executioner had occupied the only first-class cabin, remaining invisible to the other passengers until the moment of disembarkation, announced by a blast on the ship's siren spreading a thousand shrieking echoes through the ancient town. He stood for a moment at the head of the gangway, a small man in a dark Norfolk jacket, with immaculate grey hair under an alpine hat. Then he climbed down slowly, looking straight ahead, followed by two young men with the faces of devotees in a religious procession who were to assist him in the most theatrical of public performances. A horse-faced old Renault had been sent to collect them, into which they clambered and were driven away, and the scramble of the ordinary passengers to disembark began.

People who came to meet the ship had been constrained by new enactments under the heading Public Order to form orderly lines on the quay while they waited, in the manner of soldiers on parade. It was a system that had never really worked, and now with the appearance of disembarking passengers at the top of the gangway intense and clamorous confusion broke out among the crowd below. There was a rush rather to capture than merely to welcome those arriving. An hysterical outcry went up. People were being pulled out of each other's embraces, and there were tugs of war for the right to help with the baggage. Part of the ritual of arrival was the food forced into the mouths of the newcomers, the bread – stale at that time of the morning – and the slices of mountain ham. In the background the terrible old taxis, one or two even powered by wood-burning stoves, hooted desperately to attract fares. A policeman who was there to keep the situation under control had given up and was now trying to head off two gypsies who had arrived with a performing bear.

A friend of mine had written to the painter Antonio Ribas on my behalf, and he was there to meet me. He was often referred to as the Goya of Ibiza and enjoyed immense local prestige, easily selling everything he painted. Nevertheless, he gave most of his money away and lived in extreme simplicity in a house of many empty rooms in which it was usual to find that homeless gypsies had taken shelter.

He was a small, cheerful, lively man in his fifties, with a face easily creased by mirth, and wearing a flat and floppy beret of the type that had become extinct elsewhere in Spain between the two wars. He was clearly overbrimming with the desire to be of use. 'Your friend tells me that you work alone and are looking for a quiet place,' he said. 'The question is how quiet? I can show you a house where you would not see another face from one week to the next. This is an island where we offer solitude in all its degrees. In the circumstances I'm taking you to see an empty farmhouse which provides peace in moderation. If you wish to take this, a woman can come in every day to tidy up and there is water in the well to last to the end of the year. If this is too noisy for you, or even too quiet, there are many other places we can look at.'

We took a taxi out to the farm, which was situated about five miles from Ibiza town. It was decided that I would spend the day exploring the vicinity and that we would meet again that evening.

The farm had a double door like that of a fortress, a single window, but most notably a roof composed of pine-trunks layered with earth that might have been six feet thick – a typical feature of local architecture where plundering incursions from North Africa had been commonplace down the centuries. The house was in a stony field in which nothing but the occasional almond tree grew. There was something a little gimcrack and skeletal about these trees, in the branches of which in each case a single motionless crow perched on watch for lizards, although I never saw one take its prey. All the shapes in this landscape were different; even the air itself carried a dry, spiced scent. Screwing up my eyes to peer into this flinty wilderness, I tried to reconcile any part of these surroundings with my memories of Farol. Ribas was right. This was Africa. This was a different world.

In a way it would be a good place to write in, because there were no distractions apart from those you made for yourself. At intervals of an hour or two a farm cart would pass with the squeal of an axle and the crackle of the wheels over the flints. Towards sundown, cream-coloured coursers came sprinting into sight, running over the stones at speed in pursuit of flying beetles, with desolate cries of hark! hark!, before disappearing into a purple mist. I had understood that these birds only thrived in desert surroundings, but they had evidently decided that Ibiza was the next best thing.

Night fell, and Ribas was back to pick me up.

'Did you like it?' he asked.

'I did. There were bats hanging from the rafters, but as it happens I'm fond of animals.'

'I've been thinking,' he said. 'Solitude is all very well if stimulation exists. Now I remember that your friend said you would have liked to be near the sea, but where would you have stayed?'

'In a fisherman's house, I was hoping. As I did in Farol.'

'In Farol the twentieth century has arrived. Here they are still afraid of foreigners. If you were staying a year or two you might get an old couple to adopt you. The priest would splash holy water over you and turn you into one of us.'

'The schoolmaster in Farol thought there were villages here where the women still wore the veil.'

'They did when I was a child,' Ribas said, 'but I haven't seen one for years. They still call on Allah if anything surprises them.'

It was a dark night, brilliant with stars, and the flints in the path crunched under the rope-soled alpargatas I had taken the precaution to bring. The high-pitched barking of watch-dogs came distantly, and closer to us the nightjars rang their small bells. An oasis of light was provided by San Felipe, where there was a white church with lamps all over its façade. A flight of steps descended to the small square, and on these many motionless black cats had seated themselves. The square was enclosed by about thirty small white houses, none possessing windows. It was the scene of a local version of the *paseo*, with files of youths and girls of marriageable age encircling the square in opposite directions, with the girls walking on the inside.

Ribas led the way to a bar where, under an oil lamp suspended on massive chains, I found myself in an interior from Zurbarán. The Spanish painters have always revelled in the drama of still-life. This place might have been furnished for our admiration by a master of the seventeenth century with its assemblage of great-bellied pitchers, fire-scarred pots and cauldrons, a cleaver hanging on the wall and the sinister black amputations of mountain ham suspended from the beams. Above all there was the proprietor himself, half-ferocious, half-foolish, his brawny arms thrust through the sleeves of a leather jerkin, despite the softness of the night. He shuffled towards us to slide the plates of beans down the table and splash the wine into the thick glasses. Outside in the square the youth of San Felipe continued to circle. The boys were now shining torches in the faces of the girls, and there were outbursts of laughter. The priest had come out of the church and stood looking down from the top of the steps. Ribas said, 'He's a member of the Fascist Falange. He carries a pistol under that cassock.' Ribas had already mentioned that he had been brought up in a Catholic orphanage, and was no lover of the church.

'How long do you expect to be staying with us?' Ribas asked.

'Five years, perhaps more if all goes well. I'd spend the summers here and travel in winter. This is a trial run.'

The man who owned the bar stood close to us, and there was a touch of insanity in his grin. When I glanced in his direction he held up invitingly the flagon of bluish, local wine. 'Think about it carefully,' Ribas said. 'If you stayed in this village, for example, this would await you every night after your work. This man's beans and his wine and the *paseo*, in which you cannot join. Soon the priest will put the lights out and they will all go home, and only you and the cats will remain. Tomorrow we will go to look at a place I know near the sea.'

The Casa Ses Estaques Ribas found for me was some ten miles from the town of Ibiza up the eastern shore of the island. The name means House of the Mooring Posts, for part of its garden was included in the port of Santa Eulalia, but it was generally known as the House of the Turkish Princess after an oriental notability who had occupied it until six months before my arrival. This woman had lived in a state of feud with the local fishermen who used a flight of steps leading down to the water to dry their nets, and strung up their catch to be sun-dried on posts in her garden. In retaliation she had frequently bombarded them with empty gin bottles hurled from the flat roof, and in certain lights the garden still glistened, as if with a variety of gems, with the fragments of these embedded in a carpet of pine needles.

Ses Estaques had ten rooms in none of which it was possible to live with any comfort, for they were crammed with the ruins of superfluous furniture brought there by the Princess although never put to use. These included chandeliers, although electricity had not reached this part of the island, and illumination was by oil lamps like those of the Foolish Virgins in children's illustrated bibles. The principal salon was choked with lengths of piping and there were cracked wash-basins and a demolished bath, but the only water to reach Ses Estaques was the few gravelled inches that accumulated nightly in the bottom of a well, or a supplement, complete with a frog or two, from the water-delivery tank carried on a cart. The only intact object in this limitless confusion was a huge gilt mirror. This possessed the amazing knack of shifting the human expression from elation to gloom, in an arbitrary and inexplicable way according to the angle of view.

In these surroundings I camped with enthusiasm but slowly diminishing hope in my attempts to duplicate with my new neighbours the easy familiarities of the fishermen of Farol. Although Santa Eulalia was in some ways more primitive than Farol, arithmetic was unaccountably better, so I could be of no help in totting up purchases, and I was soon to discover, as warned, that the temperament of the people of Ibiza was poles apart from the mainland of Spain. The resources of the sea here, too, were of a different kind. The forms of fishing of which I had gained some slight knowledge were little practised in this community, and the great seasonal windfalls of tunny and sardines upon which dearth or prosperity turned, did not exist. Here fishing was on a small scale and largely carried out by individuals. This was the cardinal fact that highlighted the difference in the lifestyles in the two communities. In Farol the arrival of the tunny or sardines was the prelude to spontaneous fiestas far outdoing the celebrations of Christmas and Easter. Suddenly there was surplus cash to be mopped up and the fishermen dashed off to Figueras to buy new dresses and cheap jewelry for their wives, and new outfits of all kinds for their children, although spending nothing on themselves. These were the occasions both of marriages and conceptions, although the latter were rare, and few couples produced more than a single child. In Ibiza there was no excuse for such joyous irresponsibilities, and, apart from impetuous killings and emotional funerals, life was conducted on a relatively even plane.

The attitude towards women had hardly changed in Ibiza since the long presence on the island of the Moors. In Farol smartly dressed women sat on the beach in the cool of the mornings and evenings mending the nets. In Santa Eulalia they were not allowed to do so. The fashionable girls of Farol wore dresses copied from those of the French tourists they had seen. By contrast the country women of Ibiza had hardly arrived at the

Middle Ages, and bundled in their black clothing, wore up to fourteen underskirts. Some of them carried lace handkerchiefs with which they flicked casually at their face as if to dislodge a passing male's gaze. They were supposed, as I later learned, to dose their men with aphrodisiacs made from the innards of crawling animals. According to local gossip, in which I was soon included, the peasant women (although not the fisherfolk, who were more honourable in such matters) disposed of unwanted husbands by poisoning or other methods. A local beauty who ran a bar a few miles away was said to have got rid of hers by throwing a stick of dynamite down the well in which the man was at work.

*

Ribas called on me. I tunnelled into one of the rooms, dragged partially dismembered chairs into the garden and we sat at the top of the marble staircase which led down to the water. The three lowest steps were draped with nets, and boats were tied up to the pilasters at the bottom, one of which still carried a disfigured head in the Greek style. Two fishermen who paid not the slightest attention to us were baiting their hooks. A boat painted in the old illegal yellow (a colour associated with superstitious practices) flopped at anchor on the wavelets, and an enormous cat contemplated the water from its bows.

'Is this more to your liking?' he asked.

'I have to admit it.'

'This is a good place for work. Output depends on barometric pressure. Here it is always high. In the town I take a week to finish a picture. Here I may take as little as two days. Only Formentera is better.'

'Interesting,' I said. 'I seem to be turning out more than usual, too.'

'Why do you come to places like this?'

'It used to be doctor's orders. I had to lead an active life. Now it's a habit.'

'Are you making any progress with the fishermen?'

'A little. I put up a notice in the garden saying "This place is yours to do what you like with", but so far no result.'

'I think they took it for sarcasm,' he said. 'They are conservative. Next week they'll say *bon dia,* and after that who knows?'

'One of their kids made an evil eye sign at me yesterday.'

'It's to be expected. This is an interesting place. They're all members of a clan. If a girl wants to marry some nice-looking outsider she's taken a fancy to, he has to put his case to the heads of the families. Intelligence, strength and good looks don't come into it. The only thing he has to do is solve the riddle they set. If he fails and still insists, they'll stone him.'

He was in a hurry to go. There was only one bus back to Ibiza town that day and there were no taxis to be had.

'By the way,' he said, 'the prisoner who was going to be garrotted has been given a last-minute reprieve.' He thought over this, shaking his head. 'Here only the innocent suffer,' he said.

Two days later Pepa Boix came to work for me. She was a small, grey, shapeless, furiously energetic woman in her fifties, who was under supervision by the police. This was due to imprudent curiosity shown at the beginning of the Civil War when within days of the outbreak of hostilities Nationalist planes swept down to bomb civilian promenaders on the town's sea-front one Sunday afternoon. By way of reprisal, several supporters of the fascist cause were taken to the castle to be executed by being shot through the eyes by firing squad. Spectators were allowed in to watch the spectacle, among them Pepa. All those who accepted this macabre invitation had been subjected to police harassment ever since.

Her husband had been killed in the war and now she worked in a kind of grim and fatalistic way to support a daughter and an old father who had never quite recovered from a terrible beating by fishermen who accused him of stealing fish from their pots. To add to her miseries a large area of woodland between Ses Estaques and her own village was haunted by what was accepted at all levels of society as a Carthaginian ghost, forcing her to take local advice as to sightings before making detours of a mile or two on her way to or from work.

The existence of Carthaginian tombs locally was well-known, and Carthaginian ghosts were relatively frequent in the area, regularly appearing to scare the wits out of villagers in this coastal strip. It was normal for them to take shape silently among the trees, human in form, taller than average and smiling in a way that those who came face to face with one found exceptionally terrifying. Pep Salvador, owner of the local shop, and probably the first man in Ibiza to wear gold-framed mirror spectacles, was the authority on this subject. When digging lower than usual in his cabbage patch, Salvador had discovered a tomb and taken the trouble of measuring the skeleton it contained, finding it to be the equivalent of 6 feet 3½ inches in length. He then carefully replaced the earth and replanted it with his seedling potatoes. I did not presume to ask what became of the grave-furniture such burials could be expected to include. It was an episode and a subject that would have entranced Oliver Myers, who was by this time lecturing in Nigeria. I wrote to urge him to come to Ibiza, but for one reason or another the visit had to be put off and never took place.

Ribas showed no surprise at my mention of the ghosts. 'There are a number in the town in the neighbourhood of the Carthaginian necropolis,' he said, 'but what with the traffic and the building that goes on these days they tend to be overlooked.' We sat on our ruined chairs watching the sea. Thirty yards away a flying fish glittered briefly in space before splashing back. In the distance the unearthly sound of a conch shell being blown announced the landing of a new catch. An old woman, sepulchral in black, waved her arms and shrilled high-pitched, birdlike sounds calling her chickens to be fed.

Now that the Carthaginians had come up, Ribas thought we should lose no time in making a trip to Cala San Vicente, to the cave-shrine Es Cuyerám which had been rediscovered then ransacked by a German a matter of weeks before my arrival. 'They were peddling statuettes of the goddess in the streets of Ibiza town for two hundred pesetas a time,' Ribas said. 'Eighteen times the price of a bottle of beer. We ought to see the place before more damage is done. We could make an early start and get there in the day.'

We set out on our walk next morning soon after dawn with three hours' easy going along the coast before the turn-off inland to San Carlos. The easy part was very beautiful and enlightening, too; in the presence of Ribas, I was almost able to borrow the vision of a painter, and I saw the most alluring of all seas as never before. I realised that, in some settings, it could be even wine-red, as in antiquity. Inland the landscape was faded and sun-sapped, with bleak, windowless houses, the wind ripping at scarecrows nailed to crosses, the scorched remnants of crops, and then hunting dogs with pink eyes and snouts dragging at the heavy logs that frustrated them in their attacks on chickens and cats.

'Here', said Ribas, 'the sickness from which all people suffer is boredom. There is nothing in their heads. They bring up a single child, then they settle to await death. In uneventful lives they will go to any extreme to create an incident. The husband murders a stranger. The wife seduces the priest.' He shook his head. 'Fourteen black petticoats hide the most sensual of all bodies.'

San Carlos, capital of the region, was at this time in a state of feud with its neighbours, including Santa Eulalia. It was the home-town of the vendetta, and in consequence a regular supplier, as Pepa Boix had assured me, of sacrificial victims for the garrotte on the football field of Ibiza town. San Carlos was a tidy place: clean streets, white cubic houses with closely barred windows, and a patch of municipal garden in which the heads of sunflowers slowly gyrated. Ribas pointed out a tall building with a flat roof in its centre from which in the last month a young man on the run had sniped at and wounded three guardias before making his escape.

This being a Sunday, the youth and beauty of the town were parading in the square, the young men in freshly laundered cottons and the girls in country-style outfits covering them from their throats to their toes. I was steered into the village bar, which had a picture of Christ at one end and a picture of Franco at the other. It was bisected by a long counter on which were ranged about thirty tumblers filled with a milky fluid. One at a time in orderly fashion, spruce young men of the kind we had seen in the square passed down the counter, took up a glass in the left hand and emptied it quickly and in silence. In each case the shirt sleeve of the right arm had been rolled up, and the arm extended across the bar. This was taken in the grasp of a young woman behind the counter with a hypodermic syringe who administered an injection, waved the man on and gestured to the next in line to come forward. No-one spoke.

Ribas, who had been contentedly sketching this scene, was now at my elbow with his explanation. Male strength was achieved and preserved in this manner, he said. 'In this way they protect their virility and sense of aggression.'

'And what's in the syringes?' I asked.

'Ah, that now. Nothing more than vitamins.'

The girl who had plunged the needle with apparent indifference into a couple of dozen arms had dismissed the last of her customers, and now pointed the syringe invitingly in our direction and smiled tolerantly when we shook our heads.

She had the face of a celebrant or a goddess on an Attic vase that some might have considered too strong to be beautiful. Ribas said, 'She had fourteen suitors before she married, which is the limit they allow. After that she would have been put out of the village.' For all that, the marriage had turned out badly and the husband had disappeared, or as they said in San Carlos, leaving you to form your own conclusions, he had 'gone to Algeria'.

Cala San Vicente had to be approached at low tide along a strip of shingle, slithering over seaweed and splashing through rock-pools. According to Ribas, this village had been chosen as possibly the most isolated in Europe, and so Raoul Villain had been spirited here after his assassination of the French Socialist leader Jean Jaurès who opposed France's entry into the 1914 war. In San Vicente he had built himself an ugly house like a vast slab of concrete with fleurs de lis painted all over the grim facade. The oldest villager was half led and half carried into our presence, and supposing that all foreigners were French, produced a few words in that language for my benefit. By the time he had arrived to commence his exile, the old man said, Villain had come to believe that he was a reincarnation of Joan of Arc and had been sufficiently persuasive to convince many of the villagers that this was the case. The fishermen, therefore, including himself, brought their catches to Villain to be blessed, and he accepted with great dignity the small fish set aside as his reward. It was in this guise that he confronted the anarchists who landed here in the first days of the Spanish war, and was shot down on the beach.

We climbed a mile or so up the steep hillside to reach the cave-shrine through a narrow opening in the rock. It had undoubtedly been chosen as residence of the Goddess Tanit because by great good fortune the entrance offered a view of the great sea-girt rock of Tagomago, where the Carthaginians had also left indications of their presence. The German had hacked away a section of a wall and removed the treasure concealed behind, but a few square yards remained intact, suggesting that the robber had been disturbed at his work. Detritus left by him was strewn all over the floor. It is said that children were sacrificed here to Tanit. Raking through the primordial rubbish I found a tiny black sliver of bone that the museum of Ibiza thought might have been part of a child's finger, although this was never confirmed.

In Farol it was not permissible for a fisherman to carry a priest on his boat, and there was a strict veto on carrying or wearing any article of leather, in particular shoes, as opposed to rope-soled alpargatas. Prohibitions in the port of Santa Eulalia were more comprehensive and I quickly noted that a fisherman seemed embarrassed when an outsider touched his nets. Despite an otherwise cordial relationship with my neighbours, an uneasiness remained.

It was a disappointing situation relieved in some measure a month or two later by the arrival on the scene of Juan Ripoll, a native of San Carlos. Juan was a smallholder, like a substantial proportion of the males of San Carlos, but also an incorrigible gambler and eventually lost not only his house and his land, but his wife. No pressure had been put on him to leave the village, but such was his loss of face that he did so, establishing himself in a vacant shack a mile down the shore, and scraping some sort of a living by doing odd jobs for local farmers. In his late thirties, Juan was good-looking in a piratical sort of way and of cheerful disposition. We were soon on friendly terms and he got on well with Ribas who turned up at Ses Estaques almost every second day to take advantage of the sudden high barometric pressure which kept him busy at his painting.

Ribas was of peasant origin and therefore had a predisposition to be fascinated with the sea, and to know very little about it. At times when pressure was high in Ibiza town and low on the eastern shore, he told me it was his custom to spend the day walking up and down the sea front, encouraged by the sight or sound of the waves and ready for inspiration to strike. Ripoll managed to come by a small boat and occasionally the three of us went for short and dangerous trips. None of us knew how to sail, and the fishermen drying their nets in the garden would shake their heads when we set out and cheer us like successful bullfighters when we returned.

One of the many splendid things about this island was its resistance to change. People and events stayed in the same happy groove. Spontaneous activity quietly settled to routine. Life adapted itself to peaceful and reassuring objects and procedures, and nerves quickened to the pleasures of familiar things: the surge almost of hysteria that greeted the arrival and departure of the ship, the solemn blastings on the conch shells that signalled the fishing boats' return, the honk of the taxis' horns supplicating for fares, and at midday when the villages were suddenly full of the odour of frying in crude oil, the clatter of the big-wheeled carts over the cobbles, and the millennial Arabian cries of hih! hih! with which the mules were urged up the steep streets.

For a whole season Ribas chased after his atmospheric pressure, managing to spend half his time admiring the sea and painting the heedless fishermen at Estaques. Whenever we had time on our hands, Ripoll carried us on risky expeditions on his boat. In the end one of our neighbours who had injured himself and could no longer work on the nets took pity on us and agreed to come on a trip round the island. One minor snag arose. The fishermen here were members of a patriarchal society, and the permission of the senior male of several families had to be sought. This was obtained and a date settled upon when a letter from Lazlo Papas in Guatemala arrived that brought about a change in my plans.

No news from you for a long time. I wonder if you've been getting my letters. A friend is posting this from Miami, but make no mention of it when you reply. We're swallowing a heavy dose of censorship right now. Did you get my letter telling you that against all good advice I took a chance on the finca? This turned out a disaster because within weeks of fixing up the paperwork there was a revolution and, just as you said, it turned out I backed the wrong horse. President Jacobo Arbenz Guzmán and all his reforms went, a local gun-slinger called Armas took over, and a lot of people, mostly Indians, got shot. I was pulled in on a charge of being a crypto-communist and the finca went. I gave the kids who worked for me an extra fifteen centavos a day and I put up the bottom age to ten, and that put paid to it. So I'm not only broke but under police surveillance. At the moment I'm in Huehuetenango where even if they're starving they go on playing the guitar.

If you're still working on your book about this part of the world I believe you should drop everything and come over as fast as you can, because it's what's happening here now, and perhaps a little less history (sorry!) that should be in the book. I don't have a fixed address but if you decide to come all you have to do is to ask the town watchman to find me. Oh yes, and I managed to track down that Moon Codex I told you about. It will be valuable for your book about Mayan culture. It's unique and things being the way they are the Indians would let it go cheap. Getting it out of the country might be quite another matter.

I gave a good deal of thought to the argument Lazlo raised here. In the intervals between the Eastern travels of the early fifties and the months spent in describing them, a good deal of work had gone into the book about Guatemala. Now I was inclined to agree that perhaps too much had been devoted to a vanished past and too little to the tumultuous present. This was one of those occasions when the Land of Eternal Spring put aside its smiling mask. A fresh experience seemed essential to restore to my account the balance between past grandeur and present ruin among what was left in this mountain enclave of the great Mayan people.

Accordingly I took my decision and packed to go. I told Ribas and Juan Ripoll that our maritime excursion would have to be postponed, arranged an extension on my lease at Ses Estaques and, having promised my friends that I hoped to be back either in the autumn or the spring of the coming year, I set off.

Chapter Seven

GUATEMALA WAS GETTING over its thirteenth revolution of this century when I arrived. I spent the night at the old Palace Hotel where the Indian girls who waited at table still went barefoot because the tourists liked it, and wire-mesh dating from the last revolution but one still covered one of the windows. There was a breakdown in communications and it took two buses to reach Huehuetenango where I hoped Lazlo would still be living. They had an old-fashioned system in use in the town which I much liked, and which worked very well. Nobody had a fixed address but the municipality employed a man to go round with a drum and shout out the name of the person you happened to be looking for. This I engaged him to do, and a few minutes after he started his banging and shouting, Lazlo came into sight tagging at his heels. He was so changed I would hardly have recognised him. He was very thin and had become more Hungarian in appearance than before, like one of those sad fiddlers playing in a café on the Danube waterfront in Budapest.

There was a glum sort of cantina in the square, where our neighbours at the next table were a couple of dog-faced policemen with an Indian tied up with a rope.

'Where's Lena?' I asked.

'Down in the city,' he said. 'She couldn't take it here any more.'

'What happened to the finca?'

'A long story. I'll tell you about it in a moment. You had the right instinct about that place. Remember we were in two minds when you left, but in the end we decided to take the chance. I've told you all this in my letters.'

'There have been long gaps in the correspondence. I suspect some of them didn't arrive. So what happened?'

'You remembered that what worried us about it was the child-labour thing. Our first idea was to cut it out altogether but then the parents began to turn up asking us to keep them on, so we put up the minimum age from eight to ten and reduced the working day to nine hours.'

'Which made you unpopular with the finca owners.'

'Yes, I was unpopular. I told you, I'm seen as a crypto-communist. Well, to cut a long story short, a police investigator came up from the city and the finca was intervened, as they put it, or in plain English, confiscated.'

There was an outburst of nearby laughter and I risked a glance at the next table from which came the evil odour of an illicit liquor called boj. This was available only to the police. A child beggar had chosen this moment to approach their table on his knees and was kicked away. The policemen drained their glasses and one tossed some dregs in their prisoner's face as they made ready to go.

'Hell, isn't it?' Lazlo said.

'What makes you stay here?' I asked.

'Nothing I can do about it. I'm under local surveillance, and also subject to curfew; I have to be in the house by six.'

'Given up all hope of the finca, then?'

'And of this country,' he said. 'The Embassy is doing what it can. We have to raise the necessary to fix the investigation and buy ourselves exit visas.' He glanced over his shoulder. 'Never can be quite sure someone doesn't understand English in a place like this. I wanted to ask you about the book. The one about this country. How's it going?'

I made a face. 'It drags on,' I said. 'I took on more than I bargained for.'

'There's a lot of history in it, you told me.'

'A lot of it, unpublished letters. Holographs. There's still quite a backlog to get through. It'll be nice when I can stop reading old Spanish.'

'But you still think it worthwhile going as deep as all that?'

'Perhaps a little less than I did. The trouble is I've put five years or so into it, off and on. I hate to think of the wasted effort.'

'Ever thought of making two books of it – one history and the other about what's happening now?'

'I don't think I could face it, and I don't think it would work.'

'This place makes me nervous,' Lazlo said. 'Let's go and sit in the gardens.'

The gardens were on the far side of the square, a pleasant place full of the flowers that grew like weeds in the beneficial climate, and bright birds squawking in the trees. The child beggar from the cantina hobbled across. He was blind in one eye and I gave him a few cents. 'Notice how few wear national costume these days,' Lazlo said. 'They don't want to draw attention to themselves.'

'It's part of the ongoing process,' I said. 'Remember the missionary who used to buy up all the blouses with the copulating horses and burn them? He used to go to a Zutuhul village and pay twice what a blouse would fetch in the market and toss it into the fire. Remember the free handouts of Mickey Mouse ponchos and skirts?'

'That is nothing,' Lazlo said. 'I don't believe you've the slightest idea what's happening.'

'I can see for myself,' I said.

'Not all of it,' Lazlo said. 'I'm not talking about folklore. This is something that's happening out of sight. Since the Arbenz business the Indians are seen as a problem. Arbenz gave away a few hectares of wasteland and that started the panic. The Americans got rid of Arbenz but they couldn't get rid of the ideas and the thing's become an obsession. They've suddenly noticed that fifty per cent of the population of the country are Indians. Three millions out of six. So they've decided to act.'

'You mean as before. Sterilisation campaign. Take out the troublemakers.'

'Not this time. This is the real thing. They're going to cut the Indian population by half.'

'They can't ,' I said. 'There's absolutely no way they could get rid of a million and a half Indians.'

'They wouldn't dream of trying it. A great deal of thought has gone into this. They've had population control experts over from the States studying the problem, and now they've come up with the solution. The proposal is to stop half the Indian population from being Indians.'

'And how will they do that?'

'Give them the experience of living like a white. At least that's the intention. Most of them live on the tops of the mountains. They're half-starved and their children are half-starved or they're sick much of the time. Trained psychologists are going to be sent up there to tell them what miserable lives they lead and how good it is to be down in the lowlands. The grown-ups get clothes and the kids are given cough mixture and sweets, and they're persauded to come down and see what it's like in one of the new voluntary collaboration centres that are going up all over the place.'

'And they collaborate? Almost certainly, yes,' I said.

I looked up. Two small ragged Indian boys stood there watching and seemingly discussing us. 'Aren't they referring to us as ghosts?' I asked.

'They are. The long ghost, you, and the short ghost, me. How did you know?'

'I remember from last time. Your servants always used to call you and Lena the ghosts.'

'That's right. It's said in the nicest possible way. We are ghosts, just as dogs are dogs and cats are cats. Physically we're less attractive than animals. They're sorry for us, just as we are for them. We're both of us underprivileged from the other's point of view.'

The boys moved on.

'So these collaboration centres are some sort of trap?' I asked.

'Inevitably. It's part of a five-year plan referred to in the papers as Operation Rescue. Eventually local centres will be expanded into Ideal Villages.'

'As in Vietnam?'

'As in Vietnam. Inmates will dress as whites, work regular hours for wages, drop all their ridiculous customs, be allowed to ride horses if they want to, and sell their votes for a dollar a time in local elections.'

'A dazzling prospect,' I said. 'But apart from the voting hasn't it all been done before, starting with the Jesuits and their whippings with prayer?'

Lazlo had taken a paper from his pocket. 'We still have friends,' he said. 'Somebody slipped me this on the quiet. It's strictly confidential. When you're at the bottom of the human rights league most government reports have to be. This is about "Operation Rescue", which is sensitive. There's some tedious stuff I won't bother you with, but then it goes on to spell out what it proposes to do about Indian classlessness. It is to be abolished.' He read from the paper, ' "The operation envisages settlement and civilisation by the immediate creation of five social classes." '

'Hold on a moment,' I said. 'You're pulling my leg.'

He waved me aside. ' "Of these three will elect to be employed in traditional husbandry, leaving two to be occupied in domestic economy, maintenance work, and guard duties. Democratic ideals are linked to basic religious instruction, with the speedy elimination of outmoded credences and shamanistic rituals." ' He stopped. 'Why are you laughing?'

'I really don't know. It's far more sinister than funny.'

'You'll be relieved to know that regional art won't be completely suppressed. It goes on to say that it is appreciated that there is a market among foreign visitors for souvenirs produced by tribal artisans, and that this is of economic significance. The National Tourist Board will therefore be sponsoring the sale of what they call articles of this kind, although approval will only be given for selected ethnic designs. No doubt they've got their eye on those blouses your missionary used to burn. You can be sure your copulating horses are out. All this comes under the heading, "A Way Forward for Primitive Peoples".'

'It used to be genocide. At least it's only ethnocide now.'

'And I wouldn't even be sure of that,' Lazlo said.

'Are any of these voluntary collaboration centres already in business?'

'Yes, a number. And now comes the great surprise I've had in store for you. The finca has been turned into one.'

'My god,' I said. 'I thought you had something up your sleeve. Any chance of seeing it?

'We have to be a bit careful. I don't see why we shouldn't.'

'What about your surveillance thing?'

'Curfew's over by six and I check in with the police at six-thirty. There's a change of route. It's up the Pan-American by bus again, but this time we have to go to San Rafael, and pick up horses there to ride over to the finca.'

'Can we do it in the time?'

'Twelve hours is OK unless the bus breaks down. That's something I don't even want to think about.'

The local rule was that, by associating with anyone under surveillance, you automatically came under surveillance, too. You were also not allowed to spend the night under the same roof as someone subject to curfew, a frequent hazard and taken very seriously in Guatemala. I stayed at the local hotel, and was up with the whole country at dawn. Lazlo called for me five minutes after he'd reported to the police, just across the square. At six forty-five, with extreme punctuality, the bus going north to Ixtahuacan set out up the excellent Pan-American Highway, and once again I tried to decide just what the subtle and elusive ingredients in this landscape were that made Guatemala, so drenched in blood and sorrow, the most beautiful country in the world.

Our fellow passengers were either Ladinos or Indians, the Ladinos carrying their worldly possessions in single bundles. Despite the clandestine affinities of blood, these people held themselves wholly apart and while occupying the tight narrow benches in such a vehicle, spared no effort in both cases to avoid the slightest physical contact with racial half-brothers and sisters.

There was a wait for the horses at San Rafael. I had visited the town before, and I found it was now both richer and poorer. Capitalism had spread up through the high valleys of the Altiplano. Chiqui's bar, which supplied the horses, had once been a matter of adobe and whitewash; now there was a front by the road painted with huge 7-Up bottles and the claim *Apaga La Sed Al Punto* (vanquishes thirst instantly) in letters two feet high. The Indian girls in the street market wore tartan kilts, and a photographer put local boys into Lone Ranger outfits to take their pictures.

When the horses were ready we set out for Santa Maria, and it became immediately clear from the landscape that there was money in circulation. They had steamrollered broken-up rock into the road surface and the peppery red dust of old was no more: corrugated iron threw back its headaching reflections where palm thatches had been stripped away. The owners of the small coffee fincas now built their houses with mahogany planks, and the electrified fences round their property carried, for the benefit of illiterates, cartoons of a fence-scaler in the instant of electrocution. The position of the finca of old was only to be located by recognition of the low hills surrounding it. Even here there was a difference, for the hill-tops as we remembered them were always blackened by slash and burn cultivation. Now they were verdant with fresh growth. Where the small slum-like Indian village of Santa Maria de la Sagrada Concepción had once been, there stood a large featureless building which reminded me of a pavilion in a major trade fair. This was part of a complex enclosed in a higher fence than we had seen before. Although it was too far away for the details to be picked out, a placard was fastened to the fence, and I had little doubt that this one too illustrated the fate of those who attempted to enter or leave the complex other than by the main gate.

A man appeared from nowhere to take over the horses, leaving us to ring the doorbell under the banner which said Centro De Voluntaria Colaboración, and almost immediately the door opened, and a small man stood there, hand outstretched.

'Señor Rodriguez? Mr Anderson?' It was quite clear that he was expecting other visitors, and we explained who we were and what we were doing there, which in no way affected the geniality of his manner. 'I'm Richards, Plantagenet Richards of Operation Rescue,' he said. 'Two other gentlemen were coming to see me, but I guess something's holding them up. Why don't you just step inside? Maybe you'd like me to show you round.'

'That would be very kind of you,' Lazlo said. 'We'd certainly appreciate that. I used to own the old finca here. Lost it at the time of the Armas trouble. We happened to be in Huehuetenango and someone told us we ought to take a look at what you're doing here, and, well, I guess my curiosity got the better of me.'

Richards listened, nodding. 'Understandably,' he said. He turned his head to smile at each of us in turn. 'I never had the opportunity of seeing the original finca myself, but I was shown photographs of it, and you'll find that a certain amount of change has taken place.' He gave a soft laugh.

Apparently, he had only just taken over. We were shown into an office which he said he proposed to move around a bit. The fine jaguar skin on the floor had been left by his predecessor, and he disapproved of the slaughter of protected animals. Nor did he much care for the collection of scowling or simpering Indian masks with which the outgoing co-ordinator had sought to decorate the walls. The replacements, stacked in readiness, were large photographs of the attack on the original finca by the fleet of bulldozers that had helped to transform it into the Centre of Voluntary Collaboration.

The telephone rang and Richards picked it up. 'Yes, yes, I understand,' he said. 'It's quite the normal thing. We'll be seeing you shortly, then. My visitors,' he explained. 'Tyre trouble at Heuhuetenango. Well, that certainly gives me a little more time to show you what we're doing here. Afraid I'd have to persuade you to spend a day with us to be able to show you the whole operation. Do the best we can in what little time we have.'

Access to what Richards called 'our little enterprise' was through a steel door at the back of the office which slid open on the pressing of a button. We walked through and found ourselves at the top of a gentle slope, and below us was laid out a miniature town. It was stark white and as regular as a military cemetery. From where we stood we looked straight down a street lined with white box-like cabins, each with a door and a single window, and, so far as we could make out, surrounded by a low, spiked fence.

'We amuse ourselves by calling this Fifth Avenue,' Richards

said, 'and naturally that little plaza at the bottom had to be Times Square. Rather childish of us, but quite a bit of US aid went into the scheme so you have to forgive the self-advertisement.'

A group of Indians carrying metal sprayers fed from tanks strapped on their backs hurried past. They were dressed in grey denim pyjamas and were a little hunched, as if walking through a low tunnel. Richards grinned happily.

'That's the squad from the KP roster. They go round disinfecting the chalets every day.'

We made approving noises and Richards said, 'You must have had problems in your time, Mr Papas, the way the old buildings were and the well-known Indian indifference to dirt.'

'The main problem was money,' Lazlo said. 'Indian likes and dislikes came into it too. I tried to put in concrete floors but they wouldn't have them. It had to be earth floors so that if a kid was sick in the night or anyone couldn't bother to get up and go to the yard where they kept the pigs they could just make a hole, and there you were.'

'And you could do nothing about that?' Richards said.

'I had no back-up,' Lazlo told him. 'I didn't want to push it too far. The only people they are afraid of are the police.'

'I ought to tell you we feel we have a mission to accomplish here,' Richards said. 'Those who have studied these Indians say that they cease to mature after the age of twelve. There is an intellectual gap between puberty and old age. What you have is a child in a body that grows older.'

'In some ways, I imagine, not a bad thing,' I said. It was a remark that Richards did not appear to have heard.

We moved on to look over the vast communal kitchen hall, with no sign of life beyond several denim-clad figures that slipped in and out of doors. We saw the dispensary, the clinic, the hospital, the undenominational church which also smelt, slightly, of disinfectant, and a children's playground with swings.

Richards said, 'It's a disappointment that you're seeing the town when it's kind of half-empty. Because it's mid-morning the work-force are down in the plantation, and they have to keep the dormitories locked up.'

A key was found for a family chalet: doll's-house tables, two chairs, blankets folded army-style, mosquito-net hanging from a peg and a mirror on the wall. For the first time Richards showed something other than satisfaction, in this case with an Indian version of graffiti on the mirror's surface. 'Pagan symbols,' he explained. 'I'll have someone clean that off.'

'Where are all the children?' I asked.

'Down on the plantation,' Richards said. 'The women go there to be with their husbands. It's something we don't care for but we can't stop them. The children won't leave their mothers.'

'So they don't use the playground?'

'No,' he said. 'Actually it's not in use. Indian children don't play like ours do. The fathers never grow up, but the kids are adults as soon as they can stand on their two feet. Kind of strange isn't it? They have no sense of play. The guy who put in the playground certainly boobed.'

Someone called to him. 'Excuse me a moment,' he said. 'I'll be right back.'

'The feeling I have is the operation isn't working out quite as hoped,' I said.

'I get that impression too,' Lazlo replied.

Five minutes or so passed and Richards was with us again, but something had changed. I caught an unmistakable whiff of whisky I could not remember ever encountering in Guatemala. Suddenly I suspected that Richards, as often happens, was a depressive with a smile, but now the persistent smile was no more.

'Talking of what we have to offer,' he said, 'we just don't seem to be reaching them with incentives.' The corners of his mouth were turned down. 'Trouble is, if they have a blanket to sleep on and a couple of handfuls of maize a day, why should they care?'

'Ever tried them with a fiesta?' Lazlo asked.

'They're not interested if they can't drink, and that's something we can't permit. To give you some idea of our problem, I'm going to ask you to take a glance at the articles on display in the store. We have entered into a legal contract by which our voluntary collaborators are paid in scrip. This way quantity buying enables us to supply all requirements at the equivalent of half the cash price they'd be charged elsewhere. You'd suppose these guys would be fighting to get through the doors to take advantage of the arrangement, but you'd be wrong.'

We followed him on a tour of inspection of the piled-up shelves, of the three hundred-plus items including sateen neckties, zipper wallets, plastic flowers, tin trays painted with snowscenes, imitation watches, imitation rattlesnakes and Guatemalan flags.

'They don't want to buy them,' Richards said. 'They don't even look at them. Now I'll show you what they really go for.'

We found ourselves in a room containing nothing but hundreds of mirrors. There were large mirrors, medium-sized mirrors, and mirrors the size of large postage stamps. All the mirrors were in atrociously coloured plastic frames. 'We do our best to put across the idea of quality,' Richards said. 'One of those small introductory mirrors you see there has a scrip-value of only ten cents, and we explain to them that the coating starts to flake off after a few days and that they have to go up to scrip-value of maybe a dollar to acquire a lasting possession. We offered to take old mirrors back for a trade-in and some of them fell for the idea. We told the store-clerk to keep the best lines in the background and try to put over the scarcity-value angle, and I guess that seems to work too. There are a few cases of families with five or six mirrors, but there it stops. It's all they want. Ninety per cent of the stock we bought in is left on our hands. The people who pay my wage-check', Richards said unsmilingly, 'are looking for customers with a houseful of furniture who sit down to tenderised steak on Sundays. Maybe not right now, but in the long run.'

'Which is never likely to happen with your collaborators,' I suggested.

'Don't quote me, but not in my opinion. No. They'll go on working their asses off, with nothing at the end of it.'

It was a U-turn that took my breath away, then suddenly I noticed the stagger. Egged on by the whisky, it was as if something inside him had broken loose.

I risked a question. 'How do they come here in the first place?'

'Are you kidding?' he asked. 'You must know. Everyone knows. They've no choice. They're sent here with a gun at their heads. Tell you something else. Stupid as they are, in a way I like them. We squirt vitamins into their maize posole and they put on weight. But remember, this is their last chance. In this country, life is cheap. You won't find anywhere it's cheaper. While they're in this place they stay alive.'

'What am I to understand by that?' I asked.

'Don't tell me you don't know what's going on in the villages?'

We did not, and nor in all probability did anyone else from the outside world – including Richards himself – except in the vaguest of ways. It was only years afterwards, having studied the testimony of the 23-year-old Rigoberta Menchu (later to be awarded the Nobel Peace Prize), that I understood the martyrdom of the Indians of Guatemala. A vast tragedy spread through these mountains but only Rigoberta saw what happened and survived to tell the story. In Chajul, twenty miles from where we stood at that moment, the army had 'punished' villagers believed to have supported the call for the return of their ancestral lands. Indians in all the neighbouring villages had been rounded up and brought in to witness the fate of the 'malcontents'. Attendance was compulsory and the Indians were warned that those who stayed away would receive the same treatment.

Rigoberta's teenage brother and her mother were among the group sentenced to death. Her brother had been tortured for sixteen days, and finally blinded. Hardly recognisable as a human being, he was then burned alive with the rest of the Indian prisoners, while Rigoberta looked on. 'After the fire went out,' Rigoberta writes, 'the bodies were twisting about . . . they kept twitching. Rigoberta's mother's torture went on for three days. 'They cut off her ears, then they cut up her whole body bit by bit.' She was still alive when they threw her under a tree to be eaten by the dogs.

This was several years after our visit to Santa Maria, but as we were to discover, the atrocities were well under way. Richards, softened by whisky, repeated his lack of animosity towards Indians, adding that he did not understand them. 'Something about these guys reminds me of bees – or is it ants? They stick together all the time. No way you're ever going to turn them into individuals able to make a separate rational choice.'

'And is that a bad thing?'

'For them yes, because it gets them a bad reputation. They're liable to fall for any crazy ism going around, and then they all go in together. It makes people kind of nervous about what could happen if you gave them half a goddam chance.'

I spent a few days with Lazlo in Huehuetenango and the nearby area of the Cuchumatanes mountains, after which he was released from police supervision and we went down to Guatemala City together.

'What are you doing about the Moon Codex?' Lazlo asked.

'Nothing,' I said.

'You're very wise. They're asking two thousand dollars and hardly any of it's been interpreted.'

'It wouldn't be useful in any case. I've changed my mind about what I want to write.'

'I'm glad about that,' he said.

It turned out that Lazlo and Lena were going to be stuck in the country for an unspecified time while they tried to obtain exit visas, and we said goodbye at the airport before I boarded a plane for Miami.

Back in London I settled to rewrite most of the book about Guatemala I'd been dickering with for years. All the research went by the board, and the glossary of archaic Spanish so painfully put together ended in a 'may come in useful' corner of the cupboard where it would be quickly forgotten. In the end I wrote a novel about my stay among some Indians of the Altiplano who were to be 'settled and civilised' in a place like the Centro at Santa Maria.

Chapter Eight

DURING THE EARLY months of 1956 I worked on the novel that became *The Volcanoes Above Us*, eventually delivering the manuscript to Jonathan Cape with a separate note. This said no more than, 'Here's the book you wanted about Nelson.' Stunned by the belief that I'd taken him seriously, Jonathan opened the packet only to find himself confronted by an account of Indians and revolutions in Latin America. It turned out that, once he had taken a grip on himself, Jonathan was pleasantly surprised.

I was invited to Bedford Square, and the customary lunch followed. All was as before: the waxworks emplacement of William Plomer, Daniel George, Jonathan and myself, the faint odour of carbonised meat as the housekeeper advanced with the stew, the cuckoo clock signalling the hour for lunch to begin. Jonathan congratulated me warmly on the book, which was only the second he had read about Latin America, and which he admitted presented it in a new light. A toast to its success was drunk in wine sent by a friend of Jonathan's who had a vineyard in Provence. It tasted slightly of the camden tablets with which fermentation is suppressed.

There was some reference to that year's sojourn in Eastbourne, but it was perfunctory and half-hearted. Since my last lunch at Bedford Square Jonathan had been made a widower for the third time, and now recalling the details of what must have been a sentimental pilgrimage, he was suddenly convulsed with sobs.

Part of the subsequent success of the novel was probably due to the fact that Jonathan twisted the arm of his friend Cyril Connolly, who normally only read non-fiction, but who in this instance chose it as the subject of his leading review in the *Sunday Times*. It was a bright moment for the firm at a time when sales had been a little disappointing, Jonathan said.

Some useful time was spent with Michael Howard on minor reorganisations of the manuscript for which he took time off to attend to although engaged at that point in his major work on the history of the firm. A number of completed chapters he showed me offered a fascinating insight into the cut and thrust of the literary world plus an inside account of the manoeuvres, some of which were astonishing to me, of an adventurous and aggressive publisher.

Hype in publishing may have existed before his time, but he brought it to a fine art. Deciding to put Katherin Mayo's *Mother India* on the map, he sent an advance copy to every member of Parliament and sold 300,000 hardback copies. Sometimes he could be devious. Spotting Mary Webb's *Precious Bane* as a potential winner, he first negotiated an advance on royalties of £100, then, having noted that the story was set in Shrewsbury where Stanley Baldwin had been brought up, engineered the PM's 'discovery' of the book. Baldwin's enthusiasm was reported back to Cape by his spies, as was also the PM's intention to speak in praise of *Precious Bane* at a dinner for the Royal Literary Fund. Mary Webb's four previous books had met with little success but it was clear to Cape at this juncture that they might now have a future, for he promptly approached the original publishers and was able to buy up the rights for small sums. In the first year of its publication *Precious Bane* had attracted little attention, having only earned two thirds of Jonathan's hundred pounds. Then Baldwin, in one of his rare oratorical passages, called it a masterpiece, and it became a bestseller overnight, while the four previous near-flops shared enough of the limelight to become commercially viable. Fame and fortune for Mary came too late. Royalties were beginning to pile up to which she had no instant access and to which Cape refused anticipatory release. She remained short of cash and her appeals for loans were turned down. Jonathan refused to see her and his deputy Wren Howard put her off and got his face smacked. By this time her health was failing. She was reduced to keeping a flower stall on Shrewsbury market, and with her books selling by the thousands – as they continued to do for many years – she died in near poverty.

Among Jonathan Cape's many literary associations had been the truly extraordinary and profitable one with T. E. Lawrence - Lawrence of Arabia – with whom he had remained on intimate terms for a number of years. I had read *Revolt in the Desert* and as much as I could manage of *Seven Pillars of Wisdom* - books which had transformed the fortunes of the firm. Through my friend at Routledge I knew something, too, of Lawrence's life while serving as Aircraftsman Shaw of the RAF for a daily pay of 2/7, at a time when he was negotiating deals of thousands of pounds for the publication of his books. By the time of the lunch at Bedford Square Lawrence had been dead for fourteen years yet I remembered only too well the headlines in the national press when it was announced that the manuscript of 'the greatest work of literature since the Bible' had been lost – left behind in the taxi carrying Aircraftsman Shaw to Bedford Square. Could this, I wondered, have been part of the greatest edifice of publicity ever erected in the history of publishing? Another version of the lost manuscript story was that it had been left in, of all places, the waiting room of Clapham Junction station. As soon as it was diplomatically possible to do so, I tackled Daniel George on this matter, and although he gave me no reply, I was left to interpret a secret smile.

Cape and Lawrence spent much time in each other's company and there were certain areas of similarity in their characters. Both men had a taste for austerity. The leader of the Arabs (and personal friend of Winston Churchill) professed to enjoy life in an RAF barracks. Jonathan Cape travelled third class by train or slow steamer, lived largely on Irish stew, and although thrice married once spoke in my presence of being troubled by the carnality of sex. Lawrence pretended to enjoy poverty and, shortly before the publication of *Seven Pillars of Wisdom*, wrote asking Jonathan about the possibility of taking on reviewing jobs to help out his army income, which had increased to 3s. 9d. per day.

The book was bought by the whole nation, made the firm's fortune and presumably Lawrence's too, although no information was disclosed about this. It runs to 672 pages on excellent paper, is poetical and sometimes biblical in style, contains three photographs of the author and can still usually be found in the libraries of substantial houses. A suspicion remains that few readers soldiered on to the end of this recital of the minutiae of a military campaign in the desert. Borrowing a copy recently I found that, characteristically, many pages had been left uncut.

By this time, Michael Howard had reached a point in his book when he was exposed to the grinding labour of sifting through correspondence exchanged over the years with some of the most difficult of Cape's authors, and was rapidly becoming sick and tired of them as a species. He was now thoroughly bogged down with Malcolm Lowry who, in spite of his exceptional gifts, had suffered from what Michael believed to be an extreme form of megalomania. All Lowry's life and work, he said, was characterised by excess. Having a friend who knew Lowry well, I had to agree with this. Authors in this particular category were almost perpetually drunk, went in for wretched sexual affairs, spent years writing long and intricate masterpieces and, worst of all, innumerable letters.

Lowry published a single book with Cape, *Under the Volcano*, involving everyone engaged in its production with endless problems. Daniel George was given the nominally final manuscript in 1947 and worked on it off and on for two years before it could be sent to the printers. The book is roughly about booze and sex among American expatriates in a small Mexican town overlooked by a volcano, but suddenly the author pulls himself out of this simple and recognisable scene to go off on a sea journey described in huge and tedious detail.

It was Daniel's job to excise this literary tumour from an otherwise moderately healthy body of work. It was left to the directors to face the ensuing wrath. His intervention produced a letter from Lowry running to sixteen thousand words of critical analysis, and I was shown the enormous bundle. It was one of the thirty-odd letters received from the author, several being more than five thousand words in length. Nevertheless, the firm stuck to its guns and the truncated version came out in 1950. It was a great book with a touch of surrealistic madness about it that I immensely enjoyed. William Plomer thought it might have been better for Lowry to stick to poetry, although I found the outbursts of mania part of the charm.

Michael said, 'Lowry was only the most energetic of the correspondents. Look at these.' He was about to start on the last letters of T. E. Lawrence, written shortly before his death. I picked up two of the letters and glanced at a few paragraphs. 'If anybody needs money, it is surely myself, earning 3/9 a day with considerable effort and pain: but I would rather starve than earn another penny by any publication . . .' 'Thank you for sending the Liddell Hart book to the Air Ministry, and for not sending the bill. That kindness postpones my need of a translator by rather more than ten days. Actually I'll be full of money in March for they gave me a gratuity of £12. I have an income of 25/- per week, clear, and hope to live comfortably on that, without work until at least 1935.'

'Did you ever see him?' I asked Michael.

'Only once, when I was eleven. I went to see my father in his office, and he was there. He was very polite and serious, and talked to me as if I were grown up, and I liked that.'

*

In the mid-fifties business at 30 Bedford Square was on the upturn again after a temporary slump. The success of Ian Fleming's Bond novels had contributed to this revival of fortunes, yet Jonathan Cape was disconcerted by the author.

Fleming had been virtually forced on the firm by his friend William Plomer, with whom he had worked during the war. While Plomer was a poet, it would be fair to say that there were few writers who had more completely escaped the touch of the muse than Fleming. Yet there is little doubt that he became the narrator of the improbable adventures of James Bond with some regret, for at the time when he first peered out wistfully over the threshold of the literary world he had actually tried to persuade Edith Sitwell to collaborate with him on a study of the Swiss philosopher Paracelsus.

At Bedford Square he was seen as a brash outsider, and was thoroughly disliked by everyone except William Plomer. Jonathan Cape read only a few chapters of Fleming's first offering, *Casino Royale*, and none of his subsequent books, and would never meet the author. Wren Howard, Jonathan's partner, customarily referred to him as 'that bounder'. Michael Howard wrote: 'the book itself repelled me and caused me sleepless nights, for I thought that its cynical brutality, unrelieved by humour, revealed a sadistic fantasy that was deeply shocking, and that the book would do discredit to the list.'

I now knew Michael well enough for him to be able to express his doubts over the new acquisition. He was astounded but also troubled by Fleming's extreme self-confidence, and by his determination to involve himself in every aspect of his book's production. Although Jonathan Cape wished to have as few dealings with Fleming as possible, a remorseless and hair-splitting tussle went on – with Michael Howard acting as intermediary – when the contract for *Casino Royale* was drawn up. The spectacle of these two rich men scuffling together over trivial financial arrangements was engrossing if weird. Later in the contest, Fleming asked for sixteen free copies of his book rather than the six free copies an author customarily receives. In the end Jonathan was goaded into actually writing him a personal letter on the subject, in response to Fleming's suggestion that the question of the extra copies might be dealt with by a toss of a coin, on the basis of double or quits. This, finally, Jonathan agreed to under pressure from his co-directors, and Fleming lost. In a further letter Jonathan referred to his regret that the situation had to be decided in this manner, which 'goes entirely against my Quaker origins'.

The fact is that Jonathan Cape at all times avoided spending more than he had to. Those who worked in the conduct of his business were not overpaid. The celebrated reader Edward Garnett at first received £200 per annum, which was what a shop assistant might expect in those days, although lunch was thrown in. When I first met Daniel George, he was paid £400 but had to fork out for lunch. I certainly lost no face with Jonathan by asking for no advance against royalties at all, which for him may have been a unique experience.

My first meeting with Ian Fleming had been at the second of Jonathan Cape's two annual Christmas parties, shortly after the publication of *Casino Royale*. We drifted into each other in a far corner of a half-empty room and Ian greeted me with one of his frequent slightly-enraged smiles. The second party, he told me, was reserved for Cape's second-list authors, and I gathered that he saw this as another attempt to put him in his place. I assured him that it was an alphabetical arrangement, but with the efficiency that characterised all his endeavours, he had already checked on this possibility and pointed out two Bs and a C nobody had heard of wandering disconsolately among the sparse and unsuitable furniture in the room. Suddenly he pulled himself together and to my amazement told me he had just read *Volcanoes*, adding that he found it 'quite poetical in parts'. Much flattered by this, I would have liked to reply in kind. His reference to his own work was deprecatory, but I said that I had heard nothing but praise for *Casino Royale*, and was much looking forward to reading it myself. The unacceptable truth was that I had already made a start on the book, but had given up after the first two chapters, for although I was by no means shocked by what Michael Howard described as brutality and cynicism, the sheer improbability of this opus broke my spirit and deterred me from soldiering on.

It was curious that, while so much absorbed by mundanities, Fleming should have had a respect for poetry. 'Do you write poetry?' he asked, and I replied with regret that I did not. Someone had told him that I lived in Bloomsbury, he said, and he wanted to know if any of the old literary coteries still existed. Once again I had to disappoint him. We talked about Eliot and Auden. I told him my favourite poet was García Lorca. He surprised me be asking if I had read him in the Spanish, and I said that I had. After further discussions on such topics he invited me to lunch at the White Tower next day, where in a somewhat more discreet environment than the Cape party he questioned me about my travels in Central America and in particular Cuba.

After the meal we moved on to his office at the *Sunday Times* where he was foreign manager. He had a proposition to put – would I go to Cuba, he asked. 'To do what?' I wanted to know. To find out all I could about the charismatic revolutionary called Castro who had established himself in the mountains of that island, and to investigate the chances of his success.

Fleming had been in Naval Intelligence throughout the war, and it was quite clear in the course of the conversation that followed that despite his current occupation with a newspaper his links with Intelligence had not been severed, although his efforts in that field were now concentrated upon the Caribbean. It was evident that he had been able to come by the full details of my highly undistinguished army career in Field Security at the bottom of the Intelligence pyramid. Fleming said he was unhappy with information reaching him from the island, not only through our Embassy and the Foreign Office but from his own contacts, naming one of them as Edward Scott, a New Zealander, ex SOE and now editor of the English language *Havana Post*. He showed me Scott's most recent report. This said that the Castro rebels were confined to a small redoubt in the Sierra Maestra mountains, from which they showed no signs of breaking out. They were under constant attack by the Cuban air force, and with the United States solidly behind the Cuban dictator Batista, the end could not be postponed much longer. Fleming said, 'I simply don't believe this.'

I now discovered that Ian was a fanatical admirer of Ernest Hemingway, who had chosen to settle in Havana. He told me that he had read all his books several times, and believed that he had come to absorb Hemingway's distinctive style in such a way that he frequently wrote passages agreed among his friends to be indistinguishable from the work of the master. He was currently on his second book, *Live and Let Die*, containing, he thought, a number of instances that he called inspirational borrowings and he was looking forward to trying a few of these on me.

There was no reason why I should have attempted to challenge these comfortable self-delusions, but what was more disturbing at this moment was, in addition to Fleming's worship of Hemingway as a writer, his view of him as the supreme man of action and a champion of democracy. Who would be more likely than the agents he employed to know what went on behind the scenes in the Cuban conflict, Fleming asked. A way therefore had to be found for me to see Hemingway, but although he had already written to him he had received no reply.

However, Jonathan Cape himself was able to come to the rescue, for the two men had remained on affectionate terms since Cape had published Hemingway's first book. Cape still refused to see Fleming, so it was left to me to persuade him to write to Cuba and ask Hemingway to talk to me. This he agreed to do, and received a favourable reply. Jonathan's personal interests entered into this, for this was at a time when the whole literary world awaited news of Hemingway's latest book, which had been years in the writing. Of this, what was generally believed to be an excerpt, *The Old Man and the Sea,* had been published and acclaimed a masterpiece. The mission to Havana, then, was to be in pursuit of two separate goals, and during inevitable and lengthy delays caused by the necessity of arranging meetings with Fleming's various contacts in Cuba, I got to know the man a little better.

Above all I found Ian to be remarkably organised in every aspect of his personality and life, with the possible exception of his marriage. He was able to bulldoze Cape into letting him supervise the production of his own books, and to plan their production over the years. While doing his best to keep Ian at arm's length, Jonathan had contributed his unique skills in the matter of their promotion. Ian clubbed, dined and played cards with the newspaper proprietors, and Jonathan had the top reviewers under control. Thus the foundations of what is now called 'hype' were laid.

Many people, apart from his publishers, disliked Fleming, although I got on well enough with him, albeit while perceiving inexplicable weaknesses in the smooth façade. He seemed to have little regard for women apart from in their sexual role, and told me that he had only written *Casino Royale* 'to make me forget the horrors of [his recent] marriage'. I noticed that in the presence of women his conversation tended to be salacious, whereas at other times it was not. On three occasions when reference to some well-known person had been made, he had said, 'He is afraid of me.' The remark would be accompanied by a smile of quiet satisfaction, although I could not understand why it should please him to be feared. In our personal transactions I found him genial, expansive and considerate, and he was without a trace of pomposity. He had a lively, schoolboy interest in almost every subject, and was constantly ringing up friends he assumed to possess some specialised knowledge he could use in his books. I had once owned an old racing car and could tell him what it was like to race at Brooklands. Other friends might be asked the muzzle velocity of a .25 bullet fired from a Beretta automatic, or details of an Amazonian butterfly reported to impart a painful sting.

Despite our publisher's bad publicity, I had no objection to Ian Fleming as a person, and I agreed with his own view of himself as a writer: that he was mediocre. There was nothing I read in his books I could believe, and the more books he wrote the more an excessive fantasy took over. But the suggested mission to Cuba I found irresistible, partly because of my ardent admiration of the island, and also for the promise of an adventure I could never have brought myself to reject.

*

It was a Sunday in late December 1957 when I arrived in Havana. I was carrying several letters of introduction, including one to Edward Scott, who lived in the Sevilla Biltmore Hotel - rather splendidly, Ian told me – in the penthouse flat. Ian had asked him to reserve a room for me, which had been done, but there was a note from Scott saying that he had been called away to Pinar Del Rio and might be held up there for two or three days. I unpacked, took a quick bath, then decided on a short tour of the neighbourhood.

The Sevilla Biltmore was on the Prado, Havana's principal street, which even now at half-past eight in the morning was hugely active with strolling, loudly chattering crowds, and men smoking tremendous cigars. Among these were many American tourists, some of them behaving in an erratic fashion, and I was told by the man at the kiosk from whom I bought the morning edition of Scott's newspaper that most of them were drunk and would normally remain in this state over the whole of their weekend in Havana. It was a situation confirmed by the existence of a number of bars advertising in English 'Hangover Breakfasts'.

I carried on down to the port, where at this hour the Gallego shark fishermen who came here from Spain were bringing in their blood-lacquered boats, and then went on to the Malecón, the greatest sea promenade in the world. Here nothing had changed in the nineteen years since Ernestina and I had first stepped ashore. Once again I was overwhelmed by these flowering, scented spaces, the great grey, time-scoured walls glistening with their granite facets, the outrageous, thrusting femininity of the women, the playful arrogance of the men, the soft growl of Negro voices through the spray spattering over the sea wall, the rust-choked barrels of cannons that had last fired at English pirates, and the millionaires' seaside houses like wedding cakes turned to stone, and painted red, blue or yellow according to the political party their owners supported.

At the end of the Malecón I turned back and went to the Parque, and of course this, too, was unchanged, with its broken-nosed statuary, the children scrambling round on hands and knees in search of cigar-ends, the handsome pimps lurking in the bushes, and the imperious Negresses flaunting their beauty before the world.

In those days, Cubans wanted to lend or give me things. I found myself at the wheel of a fish-tail Cadillac pressed on me as a loan by a chance acquaintance who happened to like the English. I was made a member of the Jaimanitas Club, and watched aghast as waiters waded waist-deep into the sea carrying trays of daiquiris for club members who preferred not to leave the water. I wheedled myself into the good books of fishermen who took me out fishing at night with lights. Before they raised anchor they sacrificed a white cockerel to Chango – the Yoruba god of war – in such a way that it fluttered about for a while spilling brilliant gore on its plumage. 'But you're Spaniards from Galicia,' I protested. 'Yes, dear friend, but this is Cuba'.

*

Despite outward appearances, profound changes had taken place under the surface. Batista, a sergeant in his twenties in the old days – The Handsome Mulatto, he was called - had taken on and defeated the ferocious colonels of the old regime, but now Batista, too, was old, and had himself been defeated by success and the years; instead of laughing at his opponents he shot them and had filled the city with unmarked graves. One of the old reactionary officers, Enrique Loynaz, had actually survived, and not only that, he had become a general. By the greatest of good luck I had a letter of introduction, and next day was able to call on him, and he took me to see General García Velez, the other surviving hero of Cuba's War of Independence against Spain. Velez was an outrageous anglophile who had been ambassador to Great Britain for twelve years and had done his best, against considerable odds since his return to Cuba, to create for himself a typical West End of London environment. He was now ninety-four and believed the fairly sedate surroundings in which he lived might help him to last out to a hundred. With this end in view he had filled his flat with heavy Victorian furniture imported from England, and the room in which he received me had a complement of fringed lamp-shades, antimacassars and aspidistras, together with a small part of a unique collection of the *Edinburgh Journal*. Of these he said that he possessed every issue since the first in 1764, and they were piled round the walls, filling the room with an intense odour of paper under the attack of decay. His prize possession was the biggest pike I had ever seen, displayed in a case among rushes and simulated water. Velez, who admitted to being no fisherman, had bought this at an auction in Notting Hill Gate because it reminded him of one of his aunts. He smiled continually through the grey cobwebbing of his moustache, made a face in mockery of an aunt's disapproval remembered over most of a century, gesturing in illustration of his thoughts in a wholly un-English fashion with hands patterned with fine, blue veins.

The horrors of war had left Velez a pacifist, whereas Loynaz, despite a variety of wounds, had remained bellicose. The story of his most dramatic escape from death was clearly held ready for such occasions as this, and as soon as a mulatta in lace cape, apron and gloves had brought the Earl Grey tea, he launched into his account.

It was at Babinay in '98, in the last stages of the war. The Cubans already had the taste of victory in their mouths and the Spanish were preparing to sell their lives dearly behind a seven-foot stockade. Loynaz, who claimed to be a poor horseman at the best of times, was compelled now by iron custom to mount a white horse to lead the final charge. 'I could never jump,' he said. 'I landed on the horse's neck and one of the Spaniards brought down his machete on the top of my head.' At this point both Velez and I were ordered to examine the result. The skull had opened up, leaving a trough about six inches in length in the bone, the edges of which could still be felt through the skin. 'Three American presidents have felt that wound,' Loynaz said, 'Harding, Teddy Roosevelt, and I forget the third. I managed to scramble back into the saddle, holding my brains in with my fingers. They got me to the nearest house where a honeymoon couple had installed themselves, and I commandeered their bed. It was a month before I was on my feet again and I noticed a remarkable thing. Up to this time I had suffered from headaches all my life. Now they were gone. My doctor said that opening up the skull had made more space for the brains.'

It was now García Velez's turn. 'Do you think he'd like to see the album, Enrique?' he asked.

'I'm quite sure he would,' Loynaz told him.

Velez found a bunch of keys on a shelf and went into the next room. I followed Loynaz to the window, drawing the cool air into my lungs and with it the leafy sharpness that Havana breathed upon us. Space was short in the inner city, and white pigeons coating the window sills of the flat across the way were like packed snow. Far below, what looked like a toy ship flying innumerable pennants was squeezing through that sack of water known as the Bay into the narrow passage to the sea. We turned away and Victorian England took over again with the must of old magazines, and a tinkling musical box Velez had set in action.

The old man returned with his album, and displaced an aspidistra to make room for it on a low table.

'I inherited it from my ancestor Francisco Miranda,' Velez said.

'It's a piece of history. What'll become of it when I'm gone, I don't know. I've offered it to the National Museum, but they seem to be toffee-nosed these days.'

He opened the album just as Loynaz released a preliminary cackle. I found myself looking down at a wisp of hair as dry as hay stuck to the centre of a yellowed page over an illegible scrawl of faded ink. 'What you see there is pubic hair, one of fifty-one examples donated by the great ladies of his acquaintance.'

'What on earth made them agree?' I asked.

'It was a passing craze,' Velez said. 'It did a woman's reputation no harm to have had an association with a man of the standing of Francisco Miranda. All the women were after him when he came to London. He was sixty by then. An old man by those times.' Velez stroked the filaments of grey hair with a fingertip. 'This is La Perechola La Segunda,' he said. 'She was the greatest actress ever to appear on the American stage. Pay no notice to the message. It's a fake. She couldn't write. Nine out of ten of the women couldn't.'

Velez turned over several pages. 'Well, there it is. It's all much of a muchness. I don't often get the book out these days. It's showing signs of wear and tear.'

'May we see the greatest of the conquests?' Loynaz asked.

'You may,' Velez said. He fingered cautiously through the pages, then stopped. 'At least this one should be in a museum,' Loynaz said.

'It should. Where it could be properly looked after, before it's lost altogether.'

This time the writing was legible under the little ragged tuft: a splendid, arrogant K half-smothered in entwining curlicues. 'Catherine,' Loynaz murmured reverently.

Velez nodded. 'The Great Queen.'

'Apart from the remains in the Kremlin vault this is all that has survived of the body of Catherine the Great of All the Russias,' said Loynaz.

Velez agreed. 'Yes,' he said. 'You could say that.'

I expressed all the wonder expected of me, yet a lurking doubt remained. Shortly after Loynaz and I left we stopped at the next street corner to enjoy the slight variant in the previous bird's-eye-view over the city. A blond patch of sea under the walls of the Morro Castle shone as though powerful lamps had been lit in its depths. These days the castle served as a prison for Batista's many political opponents, and, as was now often the custom, a passing inbound ship sounded a derisive blast of its siren.

'So what did you think of the famous album?' Loynaz asked.

'It gave me a new view of people in the high places of the past. Do you think the Catherine part is true?'

Loynaz patted the cavity in his skull as if to confirm that his brains were still in position. It was a gesture that suggested he might not be sure of the facts. 'No reason why it shouldn't be,' he said. 'Miranda was forty-odd at the time, an absolute ram of a man. Catherine put up funds for his adventures and invited him to stay in Moscow. She was very lustful. Also, she was fifty-eight.'

A later chat with Velez contained no wounds or pubic hair. People, I said, were talking of the Castro revolt and its chances of success. What was it all about? This gave the General the chance to ride his hobby horse about the scandalous treatment Cuba – and he himself – had received at American hands at the end of the War of Independence, which he believed had sown the seeds of almost all the nation's subsequent troubles.

'The war was over before they came in,' Velez said. 'They dropped like vultures out of the sky to pick up the spoils. I and my troops were not even allowed into Santiago after the final battle with the Spanish. For six years the Yankees ran the country and snapped up everything worth having. You could buy a caballería of land for the price of two bottles of Coca-Cola. Hence Castro.'

'Why, hence Castro?'

'A lot of middle-class boys see Castro as their only chance of getting anywhere. This country is owned by foreigners. Don't ever believe Karl Marx has anything to do with it.'

'Isn't Castro a socialist, then?'

'We're talking of high school boys who can't be found nice white-collar jobs. Fidel started as a lawyer. He went in for revolutions because he only had ten clients and they were too poor to pay. Did anyone ever tell you how the present bother started? It was over an increase in bus fares. They put up the bus fares and this was the last straw. University drop-outs who refused to walk.'

This interview took place days after Herbert Matthews of the *New York Times* had been the first visitor to the Sierra Maestra and Castro's handful of revolutionaries. Matthews could count only twenty of them, but he took Castro's word for it that there were 'plenty more lurking somewhere in the background' and was much impressed. Fidel, possibly the greatest talker in history, talked him into the ground. 'Thousands of men and women are heart and soul with Fidel Castro, and the new deal for which he stands,' Matthews wrote in his paper.

I phoned Ian, mentioning in a roundabout way the possibility of a trip to the Sierra, which I described as a mountaineering holiday. By this time I had learned that Ruby Hart Phillips, the *New York Times* correspondent on the island, had had a hand in the Matthews interview, and I hoped that she might do something of the kind for me. It turned out that she shared Scott's office, but was also away. There was no shortage of undercover operators in this city, for another organiser of Matthews' trip happened to be in town at this moment, and an evening meeting with this man took place in the intensely informal surroundings of the coffee shop of the Sevilla Hotel. No-one would have dreamed that Havana was in a state of revolutionary ferment. The Castro agent, straight from the Sierra, made no attempt to check on my bona fides, or even my identity. While in the middle of what was supposed to be a highly confidential discussion, a shoe-shine boy grabbed my foot, put it on his box, started to rub polish into the shoe, and was completely ignored. The headquarters of the SIM special police was only 150 yards away, and possibly for this reason we were interrupted by a burst of sub-machine gun fire. We sauntered to the door, but saw nothing but running men in the distance. A stylish prostitute approached, bowed slightly and presented each of us with a nicely engraved card and withdrew. Years back, to commemorate a birthday, Batista had released five thousand canaries in the streets of the city, and now one of their descendants, disturbed by the gunfire, woke up in a nearby shade-tree and began to sing. Next to the coffee shop the hotel ran a bingo game. All the players were men, some of them with pistols outlined in their hip pockets, and none had bothered to move. A little team of boys who patrolled such hotels were picking up half-smoked cigars for exceedingly skilful reconstitution. The agent and I finished our business and he had a request to make. He was slightly bored with life in the Sierra, he said, and also a little lonely in Havana, which was not his home town. However, he knew of a good American gangster film showing at that moment, and wondered whether, if I had nothing better to do, I would consider accompanying him to see it. To this I readily agreed.

Next morning Scott was back, and we met in the coffee shop. His appearance came as such a surprise that for a moment I thought that I had picked out the wrong man. He was short and somewhat plump, with rosy cheeks, small blue eyes and the expression of a confiding child. He had been a champion boxer, but had put on weight. All Ian's friends asked sooner or later if James Bond was based on a character from real life, and the standard replay was that he was an amalgam of four actual persons, one being a 'toughie', who lived in Cuba.

So this was one quarter of James Bond. He read the letter of introduction very slowly, then folded it with great care and put it into the breast pocket of his shirt. In this brief delay I took in his small feet encased in brilliantly polished shoes, the gold fountain pen and the small, dimpled hands. Most importantly I noticed that in moments of concentration, as while reading the letter, his expression became wary and stern.

'Let's go and talk things over,' he suggested. He guided me to the lift and we went up to his flat, at the end of a long passage scented with wax polish and fine cigars. The door was closed to, but not on the lock. He pushed it wide and waved me through, and we passed into a kind of small anteroom, in which stood a quite naked Negress, who at first glance I took to be a statue in an elegant but lifeless pose. She presented a side view, and in passing I could not help noticing the goose-pimples produced by the chill of the air-conditioning which growled softly like the warning of a tiger from a thicket. Scott glanced at her in passing and then after a moment of hesitation we passed on into his office.

Of this incident I was later to wonder if he had simply forgotten the girl was there. It transpired that, like the Belgian writer Simenon, Scott believed frequent intercourse increased mental creativity and, again like Simenon, he kept a register with entries of several thousand such encounters over the years, accomplished wherever and however the opportunity arose. Occasionally there were embarrassments. 'No, Mr Scott, I didn't stop by last week to get your OK for the war-risk surcharge for your building. Surely you remember screwing me on Friday?' It was a compulsion he shared with J. F. Kennedy, who occasionally popped over to Havana for random excitements of the kind, and Scott had had the pleasure, as he claimed, of showing him round.

Scott ran over the contacts list again. 'Who have you seen?'

'The lot,' I said. 'All but Ruby Hart Phillips and Hemingway.'

'Hemingway?' he said. 'But why Hemingway?'

'Because Ian thinks that he and Castro may be working together.'

Scott omitted a low-pitched, bellowing laugh. 'Hemingway of all people,' he said.

'There's some story that he met Castro when he was hunting in the mountains.'

'The only mountain Hemingway hunts in is the Montana Bar. Hemingway is a burnt-out case. Any time you want you can see him in Sloppy Joe's. His friends bring him king-sized prawns. He chews them up and swallows the lot, shells and all.'

I was already beginning to suspect that Ernest Hemingway was a waning star. Jonathan Cape's new American partner, Robert Knittel, was married to the film star Luise Rainer who did not conceal her dislike of him. The American humorist S. J. Perelman had published a piece in the *New Yorker* describing the two men's encounter in Africa, where Hemingway had made it clear that the only thing that interested him about Africa was the availability of the local girls. Scott's intense dislike of the great man stemmed from an incident that had recently taken place at a party given by the British Ambassador in celebration of the Queen's birthday, at which Ava Gardner had appeared on Hemingway's arm. In a moment of high spirits the actress had taken off her pants and waved them at the crowd. Scott, who saw himself as a confirmed patriot, objected to this insult to the crown. In the wrangle that followed Hemingway, known for his bellicosity, threatened to thrash Scott 'within an inch of his life'.

'Next day,' Scott said,' I sent him a formal challenge to a duel.'

My feelings showed in my expression. 'Don't laugh,' he said. 'This is a serious matter.'

'Do people still fight duels in Cuba?' I asked.

'They do. Frequently. Right now they have a couple of victims mixed up with the student revolutionaries in the city morgue. Now that's a place you should take a look at some time.'

'Do you think Hemingway will accept?'

'No, I think he'll back down. Anyway, in case he doesn't, how about being my second?'

'Sorry,' I said. 'It would make a good story, but nobody would ever believe it, so what's the point?'

I spent the next day working out the arrangements for the journey to the Sierra with Vaquero, the Castro agent who liked to see gangster films. Scott seemed to want to impress me that his talk of duels was not to be taken lightly, and he took me up to a private shooting gallery in the form of a long room extending the length of the building of the offices of the *Havana Post*. The far end of this had been fixed up with an arrangement of the kind that might have been used in a fair booth, in which playing cards were clipped to wires in a way that allowed them to move laterally at varying speeds, and intermittently to jerk up and down.

Scott produced two strange and sinister-looking pistols that used liquid carbon dioxide to propel the bullets, and were not quite silent in use. He set the cards in motion, bobbing and ducking on their wires, and, one following the other, we took aim. 'Let's see you shoot out a few pips,' Scott had said, but I failed to do so, and so did he.

'Pst ... missed it again. Pst ... this isn't my day. Pst ... not again! I don't believe it. Pst ... I'm not altogether happy with the way these fit into the hand. May have something to do with it. Hang on while I slow the thing down.' Neither of us even hit a card. I expected no better of myself, but for someone who was a quarter of James Bond it was not good enough, and it did occur to me that it might even be as well for him if Hemingway did turn down the challenge.

*

Acting on instructions, I took the plane to Santiago, the most unspoiled of all colonial Spanish provincial towns at the eastern end of the island. As I came in to land, it appeared as a complex child's toy of houses like coloured boxes, parks, promenades and churches, scattered through the fields. There had clearly been an upsurge in rebel activity since Matthews had been there, for within minutes of our take-off from Havana the co-pilot came back excitedly to point out a cane-field fire. This was a new form of protest that infuriated the Cuban communists whose policy all along had been to work with the dictator as far as possible, and thereby to squeeze what small concessions from him they could.

At Santiago the dragon of wealth had been confined to its cavern and this beautiful city was still made up of perfectly proportioned wooden houses, built often by the ancestors of those who now lived in them, in the most unerring taste. In lifestyle, culture and taste the city was completely separate from Havana and longed to free itself from the domination of the capital. Nevertheless, Havana had succeeded in imposing its rule, and perhaps this had been all to the good, for since those early days Santiago had never been able to afford the development that would have ruined it. Aesthetically, everything fell into place under a mantle of gracious poverty. It was early evening when I arrived and I made for the cool of central park where the lamps in their elegant Victorian standards glowed palely among the trees, and the small ceramic-tiled benches were S-shaped so that you almost faced the person with whom you shared one, and with whom by local custom you were expected at least to exchange a few words. They seemed to be occupied largely by grey-haired intellectual old Negroes.

'Tell me, sir, what is your opinion of Emmanuel Kant?' my neighbour wanted to know, after which our conversation veered off in the direction of religious belief. 'Do you agree with St Paul that we shall rise from the dead?' In the background children were exploding fireworks, and well-behaved pigeons strutted up to peck respectfully at our toes in the hope of the reward of a few grains of the corn that many of the regulars who came here carried in their pockets.

Santiago was famous for its clairvoyants, in particular one called Tia Margarita, and as arrangements had been made that I should spend the night in the town, and I had time on my hands, I went to see her. Someone had told me that one person in three in Cuba, regardless of colour or social status, was a secret adherent of one of the cults introduced by the Negro slaves, and Tia Margarita, high priestess of Chango, was said to be consulted by Batista himself.

She proved to be a comfortable-looking middle-aged black woman of compelling humour and charm, living in a small surburban house with a garden full of sweetpeas, attached to the usual straw-thatched voodoo temple. Women of her kind were to be found in every town in Cuba, combining in their operations all the exciting mumbo-jumbo of horoscopy and divination with the real social service performed in solving personal problems of all kinds, and in treating the sick from a repertoire of herbal remedies.

Tia Margarita ushered me into a chamber cluttered with the accessories of her trade – the skulls of small animals, the withered bats and the dusty salamanders – gently kicking aside the live piglets and cockerels that would provide the material for future sacrifices. A faint culinary odour suggested the preparation of her celebrated remedy for nervous tension – a thick soup made from the bones of dogs. I added my contribution – a pair of dark spectacles – to the homely offerings, which included roller skates, tubes of toothpaste, and a jar of Pond's Cold Cream, stacked under the war-god's altar. I noted the framed autographs, offered in gratitude by famous personalities – senators, baseball-players and motor-racers – who had come here with their troubles. Everywhere in Latin America one encounters these wonderful old spoofers who at least teach people how to put up with life.

The mild, maternal eyes scanned my face, and her expression was one of slightly puzzled amusement. She expected to be called upon to demonstrate her speciality by forecasting the exact date of my death, instead of which I asked her what the people of Santiago thought about the war, and its likely outcome. If that was where my interest lay, she said, who better to discuss the matter with than Chango himself – surely the final authority on all such matters – who spoke through her mouth at seances held at the temple every Saturday night? Unfortunately this was a Monday, and when I asked Tia Margarita for an off-the-cuff opinion as to the way things up in the Sierra were likely to go, she was oracular and obscure. 'Chango says victory will come to whom victory is due,' she said. Still, something came out of the interview, because Tia Margarita went into a kind of mini-trance, lasting perhaps ten seconds, then said that the war would be over in a year – which, give or take a few days, it was.

Even in the short time I was in Santiago, warlike activity took place. From the roof of the hotel in Cespedes Square the night sparkled distantly where Castro partisans had gone into the cane-fields to plant candles, their bases wrapped in paraffin-soaked rags. There was gun-play every night, usually when revolutionaries took on the police, but on one occasion when Castro's 26th July Movement and the communists decided on a shoot-out. By custom, the first shots were fired precisely at 10 pm, giving the citizens the chance of a quiet stroll in the cool of the evening before the bullets began to fly. With a half hour to go, and all the street lights ablaze, the promenaders began to stream out of the square and make for their homes, where they clustered at their doors like gophers ready to bolt for the shelter of their burrows when the shadow of an eagle fell upon them. Then, as the cathedral clock struck ten, all the lights went out, and the streets were cleared for battle.

The agent Vaquero came to the hotel early next morning to confirm that everything was fixed at Manzanillo, which was the nearest point to the Sierra Maestra before the climb into the mountains began. He hoped to be back in Havana in a week or two, he said, and looked forward to meeting me again. I took the bus that stopped at Manzanillo on its way to Havana and after an hour or so the first slopes of the sierra came into sight. This was cattle country, and I watched cowhands riding stirrupless after skittish gambolling cows, their legs dangling almost to the ground. Clouds blown up from the horizon streamed like bubbles across the tin-plate sky. One of the passengers was carrying a sack of pineapples. He chopped four or five of these into chunks which he handed round, and soon juice was running down all the jaws in sight.

Manzanillo, just like Santiago, was full of colour, with yellow and deep blue paint slapped over the houses, and the forest of the sierra showing over the pink roofs of the single-storey buildings. The bus-stop was at a bar called the Cantina of the Parrot, and there was a beautiful macaw in a gilt cage hanging over the door. This was the bar in which my contacts were to wait. One of them was to stroll across and say, 'Do you happen to have a light?' The answer to this was, 'Sorry, I just gave up smoking.' Instead, when I got down from the bus, three soldiers closed in on me. They were much more polite than I would have expected. A sergeant asked me to open my suitcase and went through it in a civilised and almost apologetic fashion. After a moment of fumbling he pulled out a khaki shirt. This I had bought at Millett's army surplus shop in Oxford Street only a few days before, having chosen it for its light-weight material and unusually large pockets. It was now clear to me that security had been much tightened up since Matthews had passed this way.

'This is a military shirt,' the sergeant said.

'No, not military,' I said. I explained to him that it was made of very light material for a hot climate, and he agreed. 'Here it is hot,' he said. The trouble was the colour. 'This colour is only for the military,' he said. 'For other people it is not allowed.' He liked the shirt and did not see why it should not be allowed. The matter would have to be discussed with an officer who was away but would come soon. In the meanwhile he would have to take charge of my baggage, and suggested that I might go and make myself comfortable in the bar.

We had been joined by a sympathetic man who had ridden up on a chocolate-coloured horse. He was a natural onlooker, and whenever I or the sergeant spoke he nodded agreement, and after a moment he fiddled in a saddle-bag and presented us both with a thin, black, twisted cheroot of a kind made locally. We left the sergeant to stand guard over my suitcase and went into the bar where I ordered Hatuey beers and a plateful of beans for my friend, and the man who owned the place who kept up a muttered conversation with himself, shifted the electric fan so that it would blow on the back of my neck. The macaw started to screech and through the door I saw some children poking at it with a stick, and the owner ran out and chased them away.

We sat there for an hour, sipping beer and cuffing away the big blue flies, then the officer drove up in a jeep and the sergeant showed him in. He, too, was polite. He held the shirt up to the light and whistled softly at its quality, and told me how sorry he was to be obliged to confiscate it. He examined my passport and a letter from the *Sunday Times* and asked me what I was doing in Manzanillo, and I said that I had been interested to see the place. 'A bus leaves for Havana in a half hour,' he said. 'There are no more buses today. The hotel is closed for the emergency. A policeman is travelling with the bus who will see to it that you arrive safely.'

When I boarded the bus half an hour later we shook hands. 'This is a nice town with a fine church and an interesting old prison. Please visit us again when you can,' he said.

Back in Havana a call came through from Ian Fleming.

'How's it all going?' he asked.

'Fairly well,' I said.

'Do you think I was justified in my point of view?'

'Yes,' I said, 'This thing is not going away. It's going to get a lot bigger.'

'Have you talked to the writing man?'

'Not so far,' I said. 'Scott takes a poor view of him. He seemed to think there wasn't much point.'

'Never mind Scott. Do your best to see him.'

I assured him I would, and Fleming said that he had just read *The Old Man and the Sea* again and was more convinced than ever that it was a masterpiece. He had the book open by the telephone and read me a favourite passage. I agreed with him that it was superb but could not see that this literary skill had any bearing upon the judgment of a political situation. 'People say he keeps out of politics these days,' I said, 'but I'll go on trying to have a word with him.'

A letter from Hemingway arrived saying that he had heard from Jonathan and that he would be pleased to see me. It was written in a small neat hand, and there was a certain formality about it that held me at a distance. The next day he sent a car to pick me up, and I was driven to his converted farmhouse, La Vigie, in the hilly outer suburbs of the city. The privacy of this retreat was protected by a high fence over which hardly more than the roof was to be seen. A gate closed the approach road, and this was secured by a heavy chain. When we stopped the driver got out, thrust a huge key into the padlock and let us through. I got out and wandered a short way along an uphill drive to the house, little realising that with each step I came nearer to the threshold of an experience which was to change my outlook on life, not instantly but slowly over a period of time, in a most fundamental way.

I was free of the taciturn chauffeur, the high, forbidding fence, the heavy padlock and chain, and about to enter the presence of a being of a heroic, almost legendary kind, who had reconstructed the literary architecture of the twentieth century, and had justly been given its highest award – the Nobel prize. Not only that, it was Hemingway who had had the courage and the vision to come out in support of the Spanish republican government when it was under attack not only by Spanish rebels but by troops sent to Spain by Mussolini and by Hitler's Luftwaffe, which first practised on Spanish territory its techniques of mass destruction. He had pleaded with the English who had invented 'non intervention' to realise that their turn would be next, and even by that time he was a big enough man for his warnings to be at least listened to, if not followed. Now as I walked up to the door, the driver at my heels, the great moment had come.

The driver pushed open the door and shoved me through into a narrow passage with another door at the end. I tapped on this and a growl came from the other side which I took to be an invitation to enter. I did so and found myself in a bedroom. Hemingway was seated on a bunk bed. He hauled himself to his feet and turned to face me. He was in his pyjamas and I was bewildered by what I saw. Hemingway had remained for ever young in my imagination, boisterous and vigorous – a moving spirit in the never-ending fiesta of life. This was an old man, slow-moving, cumbersome and burdened with flesh. The room was lined with bookshelves, and many bottles were stacked within reach of the bed. He mumbled a belated welcome and went to find the drinks, moving slowly under the great weight of his body. To my great surprise he poured himself a tumbler of neat Dubonnet, half of which he immediately gulped down. Above all it was his expression that shocked, for there was an exhaustion and emptiness in his face: the corners of his mouth were dragged down by what might have been despair, and his eyes gave the impression that he was trying to weep.

Two objectives of this visit were to be kept in mind, the first being Jonathan Cape's hope for the imminent delivery of the book Hemingway had been reported as working on for several years, but a cautious reference to this subject provoked something close to an outburst of fury. A wasted and watery eye swivelled to focus on me with suspicion. What did I want? What had I come there for? 'Is this an interview?' he asked in the coldest possible manner.

Something in this scene reminded me of the riveting episode in *For Whom the Bell Tolls* featuring Massart, 'one of France's great modern revolutionary figures', now Chief Commissar of the International Brigade, a 'symbol man' who cannot be touched, and has come with time to believe only in the reality of betrayals. With infallible discernment Hemingway had described this great old man's descent into pettiness, and now I was amazed that a writer who had understood how greatness could be pulled down by the wolves of weakness and old age should – as it appeared to me – have been unable to prevent himself from falling into this trap. How grotesque, but how sad, must have been his appearance at the embassy party with Ava Gardner on his arm.

I hastily assured him that it was nothing of the kind, trying to explain that I was no more than a messenger from a very old and devoted friend, his enthusiastic English publisher.

Humble pie produced the reverse of the effect desired, and Hemingway now embarked on a tirade over what he saw as

Cape's parsimonious handling of the publication of *The Old Man and The Sea*. 'They didn't want to spend money on it,' he said. To make sure the American edition had a good dust-cover he had paid for a first-class artist himself, but the English version had been done on the cheap and lost sales as a result. At this point someone rattled at the back door and he lurched towards it with an outcry of irritation to suppress the female twitterings that came through.

Scott's challenge now came up. 'Do you know this guy? I hear you've been seen around with him. Is he a friend of yours?'

'I had an introduction from London. I've seen him a few times.'

'He's been built up as some sort of dead-eye Dick. You think that's true?'

'I've no way of knowing,' I said, 'but I doubt it.'

'Take a look at this,' he said. He handed me a copy of a letter he had written to the *Havana Post*. I read it. He had taken note, he said, of a challenge to a duel made by the paper's editor, Edward Scott. This he had decided not to take up in the belief that he owed it to his readers not to jeopardise his life by its acceptance.

'Dignified?' he asked.

'Very,' I said.

'Give me your frank opinion. What do you feel about this business yourself?'

'I wholly agree with you. The thing's absurd. Even if this is Cuba, it's the twentieth century.'

'Right,' he said. He nodded vigorously, smiling for the first time in the course of our meeting. 'That's the way it is,' he said. In view of the macho posturing for which he had become famous, I was astonished that he was prepared to give this publicity to what many of the paper's readers would see as a loss of nerve and of face.

As there was now nothing more to be done for Jonathan Cape, only Ian Fleming's interests remained to be served. But before Hemingway's opinion could be consulted on the chances of Castro's success his attention was diverted to something about my appearance, until now overlooked. I was dressed in the second of my pair of army surplus shirts, which, worn with grey, seersucker trousers, had aroused no interest in the streets of

Havana. 'Where did that shirt come from?' he asked. I told him and threw in the story of the small *contretemps* at Manzanillo, but he was by no means amused.

'What do you expect?' he asked. 'There's a rebellion going on here. You're carrying a uniform around – OK, you're probably a rebel. These guys are getting tired of being shot at. You have to see it through their eyes.' *You have to see it through their eyes.* This was from the man who had championed the cause of the underdog in Spain, and what was happening here was worse than anything Franco had done.

There was no avoiding it. Ian's question had to be asked. I took the plunge. 'How do you see all this ending?' I asked. 'Can Castro pull it off?'

Comrade Massart's cautious, watery, doubting eye was on me again. 'My answer to such questions is bound to be that I live here,' Hemingway said.

In my letter to Fleming, I wrote, 'There was something biblical about the meeting with Hemingway, like having the old sermon on the vanities shoved down your throat in the middle of whatever you happen to be doing with your life in the workaday world. They give funny names to the buses in this town and there's one that runs past the hotel that says *We just ran short of greatness*, which just about sums him up, although perhaps understating the case. This man has had about everything any man can ever have wanted, and to meet him was a shattering experience of the kind likely to sabotage ambition – which may or may not be a good thing. You wanted to know his opinion on the possible outcome of what is happening here. The answer unfortunately is that he no longer cares to hold opinions, because his life has lost its taste. He told me nothing, but he taught me more even than I wanted to know.'

*

By January 1959 Fidel Castro was in Havana, and I, too, was back. A single incident revealed the mood of a public intoxicated with the champagne of victory. Castro addressed the crowd from the palace terrace and as he began to speak someone released two white doves, one of which flew up and alighted on his shoulder. I could never find anyone who disbelieved this story, offered everywhere as a portent of the biblical kind. I, too, although I missed this sign from heaven, was astounded in my own way. Village boys, grabbed up and put into uniform as the rebels advanced, had taken over the city's marvellously tessellated pavements to play marbles. I stopped the taxi and got out to watch, and to listen to the nostalgic click of a marble striking an alley, bringing pleasant memories of a game I had no idea was played outside British shores. Dismissing the taxi, I walked on, passing young soldiers playing their guitars, then listening to the twitterings of Batista's canaries in the trees. The streets were scented with lilies. I made for the Parque Central where I suspected the *guarachas* would still be hurling their criticisms in verse (although probably toned down on this occasion) at the heads of those in authority. Whatever had happened I was certain that in the best possible way this was still the Havana of old.

It was a month since the rebels had taken over, but Havana was still full of bearded warriors – surely the politest who had ever carried a gun - who bowed civilians through doorways, waited at the back of queues and rushed to help old ladies with their parcels. Such was the current of civic enthusiasm that even long-standing opponents of the revolution fell into line. Ruby Hart Phillips, who had doubted Castro's sanity in the past and quoted in the *New York Times* the opinion of a Boston psychiatrist describing him as an outstanding case of schizophrenia, was won over. 'As I watched Castro I realized the magic of his personality,' she wrote. Edward Scott shifted the stance of the *Havana Post* slightly to the left and was photographed wearing his Dale Carnegie smile in the presence of Che Guevara. The new regime had turned out less puritanical than he had feared. He was a little sad that bingo, to which he was addicted, should have been included in the blanket disapproval of gambling, but had soon located clandestine operators of the game to whom he was happy to lose a little money.

Although it had so far been unsuccessful in its attempts to undermine the capital's renowned appetite for pleasure, a certain Calvinism was nevertheless in the air. The guardians of public morality moved cautiously to the attack. Those citizens, for example, who insisted upon displays of drunkenness in public places were not arrested but trundled off to centres of disintoxication, and prostitutes who drew too much attention were packed off for short courses of re-education. A drive for literacy was on. Socialist newspapers suggested to the public that they should study more and pray less. Church attendance went down, and the public rooms of such hotels as the Sevilla, where I had checked in once again, were emptied of hotel guests and crammed with docile students, mostly middle-aged, learning to read propaganda posters and cope with the paperwork created by a socialised regime.

I went to see General Velez and found him as hale and cheerful as ever. The year had passed off well with the exception of a break-in by a band of demoralised soldiers in the last days of the Batista retreat. These had done no damage but had stolen his stuffed pike. Pigeons had got into his flat while he was away and eaten his aspidistras. And now the great news – he had received a letter from the Ministry of the Interior announcing that he was to be created a Hero of the Revolution. With this had arrived a large bunch of lilies which by their perfume quite suppressed the soft, melancholic odour released by his collection of *Edinburgh Journals*.

'There is to be a victory parade,' the general said, 'in which I am expected to take part. A state landau will be provided and my friend Loynaz tells me that in the absence of one's wife on such occasions, a stylish young lady will be included in the carriage. I am now ninety-five and a half,' he said, 'and I have rejected the suggestion as preposterous.'

Watching his expression I believed that Loynaz's reference to this matter might have set off pleasant memories. Moments later, inevitably, he went in search of the famous album.

Two of the liveliest and most charming thoroughfares of Havana were side streets of the Prado, a short distance from the Sevilla, and it was perhaps to be expected that these, in which the majority of the best whorehouses were located, should have been named Virtudes (Virtues) and Animas (Souls). Part of the definition of a brothel in this city was that it provided beds, and in anticipation of a crackdown, the establishments in Virtudes and Animas sought to protect themselves by ceasing to do this. Instead it became normal for them to offer the clean, bare rooms, each containing curtained booths, hospital-style, with notices saying 'A respectful silence is solicited'. In the *salon economico,* sexual activities were *en pie* – standing up (time limit fifteen minutes). The second *categoria mesa* put into the booths tables previously employed for a variety of games. Agents of the Brigada Sociál occasionally called to check on this scene and departed after a nod, of tolerance if not of approval.

The demand for casual sex on a more sympathetic level continued to be satisfied largely by the numerous laundresses employed by the leading hotels, most of whom worked a 12 to 14-hour-day for extremely low wages. The villain of the piece was the old-fashioned *guanabera* shirt with its innumerable pleats and twenty-four buttons, and a statistic in the official newspaper, *Granma,* claimed that 6,000 girls in the capital alone were kept hard at it laundering them every day. A high percentage of these helped to make ends meet by surreptitious and diffident sexual activities which could hardly be termed prostitution. Any solitary male checking in at one of the leading hotels such as the Sevilla could expect the discreet approach by a male member of the staff mentioning that certain of the hotel's laundresses were on offer. 'None of your bedizened harpies, your honour. These are honest girls straight from work, in the smocks they wear, and the smell of the soap still on their bodies.' Scott claimed, although I did not necessarily believe him, that it was adventures of this kind that had attracted JFK when he slipped away to the island for a weekend.

All the cars that had been tucked away out of sight during the emergency were on the streets again. Following Scott's suggestion, the information people sent a flashy chocolate-coloured Cadillac with a horn that played the first bar of 'Colonel Bogie' to take me for a quick glance at socialism at work. An English-speaking guide born in Miami was provided and our first stop was at a building in the suburbs, once a school, but now with a high fence round it and poster picture over the door stating with assurance, 'Together we face the future with confidence'. We were shown into a room in which a number of men in their early twenties sat at desks scratching away at copy books under the eye of an instructor. All present wore military-style uniforms, and nothing showed in these students' expressions except a kind of frowning concentration with whatever they were writing.

'Buenos dias, companero,' the guide said to the instructor. 'I have brought an English friend to see how socialism is working with you today.' Turning to me, he said, 'This re-education centre is part of an experiment in which we bring about reform without repression. No-one is compelled. Participation is regarded as a privilege.'

'By them?' I asked.

Oh sure. Does that surprise you? In the new Cuba we are all learning new lessons together. My friend José here is teaching these men but he is learning at the same time. It is a privilege for him.'

'It's a refreshingly novel way of looking at it,' I said. 'What are they in for?'

'Living on immoral earnings,' the guide said. 'What also is new in our method of teaching is that José himself has been sentenced for this thing. He has spent one year in the Isle of Pines. He has good qualifications to teach now his life is changed.'

'I can see that. What is he teaching them at this moment?'

'At this moment he is teaching them self-criticism. When they have finished their written work those who wish to do so may discuss their progress with the class. In this way the level of auto-criticism may be raised.'

'Why are some of them wearing red stars?' I asked.

'This is to signify that they have offended more than once. The number of stars indicates the number of times the offence has taken place.'

'In one case I see three. Isn't that discouraging?'

'Not at all,' José said. 'His self-criticism is now very strong. We have all learned from him.'

He was a man with haunted melancholic eyes and a nervous twitch that widened his mouth slightly at intervals of about ten seconds. 'Sir, will you be staying in Havana long?' he asked as he followed us to the door.

'Unfortunately, no,' I told him. 'Not long.'

'A pity,' he said. 'I should have liked you to put a few questions to the students now, then perhaps talk to them again in a month's time.'

'That would have been interesting.'

'It is self-criticism that is interesting. It is not easy to learn this unaided. This can help all of us even if we commit no offence.' He smiled thinly and shook my hand. 'Anyone can benefit from these courses and they are easily arranged.'

On our way back we pulled up at a single-storey building plastered with propaganda posters, and climbing some steps I found myself at the edge of what might have been a large, badly maintained swimming pool from which arose an odour of stagnant water, decaying vegetation and mud. The guide waved at it in what seemed a surprisingly proprietorial manner. 'May I tell you, sir,' he said, 'this island grows nothing but sugar-cane. Some tobacco for cigars too, also rice – but not much. This is mono-culture and it is our ruin.' He turned his back on the water and the dank vegetation and threw up an arm in a gesture of hopelessness. 'Half our people work in cane-fields. For three months they work and then what must they do? They sit down – forgive me – on arses. They are hungry for food. Their children are crying. At least that was in the past. What I am to tell you now is we are saved. You will ask me how is that? And I tell you the answer – by tomatoes.'

I followed him through the door into a small room where he picked up a shallow basket holding five tomatoes and held it out for my admiration. 'These tomatoes I have picked yesterday,' he said. 'Tomatoes from water. This is hydroponics. Science of future. Today I show you five tomatoes. Next year we are exporting them in thousands. This is diversification. Next year we have a frog farm on the way.'

'But do they eat frogs here?' I asked.

'We have to look ahead to the way things are,' the guide said. 'Now they don't eat but no-one must say they can't.' He took a sheet of paper from his pocket and held it out. 'Here is leaflet on the subject,' he said. 'This tells us frogs contain maximum nutrition as well as being delicious when cooked right. The government says frogs are good for us and frogs are what we shall eat.'

The carnival mood of the capital lasted a month or two, till the slow and almost imperceptible tightening of food supplies warned that the holiday might be drawing to an end. The country had been too busy with war to devote enough energy to the cane harvest upon which, at the bottom, everything depended. With less cash to buy imports the prospect of tomatoes grown in water and casseroled frog could not be altogether ruled out. The government developed a craze for 'intervention', as nationalisation was called. When this was at first applied to such generally unpopular institutions as banks, the outcry was muted, but it became a different matter when small businesses of all kinds were submerged in the craze. At this time, for example, the best restaurant in Havana was run by a Chinese. Originally an astrologer in the service of Chiang Kai-Shek, he had done so well he had fled the country with diamonds tucked away in various parts of the body. From the sale of these the restaurant took its beginnings, offering a variety of culinary masterpieces that even managed to be cheap. It was explained to the owner of the Jade Pavilion that the revolution was opposed to luxurious foods, and from that time on all his dishes would be based on chicken with either beans, rice or chips. Shortly after the owner committed suicide and the place closed down.

My last day with Scott – and in Havana – was packed with activity. He was in a good mood because his powerful competitor, the *Diario de la Marina,* had overstepped the mark in its publication of so-called revelations about Castro's sex-life, and with that the brief honeymoon with the capitalist press had come to an end. Scott, who was careful to keep out of the political arena, had nothing to worry about, and we set out for the Colon cemetery. Laid out like a town, with streets and squares and a little park, all for the dead, this was an extraordinary place. What Scott proposed to show me was an avenue, strictly out of bounds, in which were located the tombs of the very rich. These took the form of the dignified miniature villas of the kind built by the richest of millionaires. Scott had the key to one of them. It possessed a lift, air-conditioning, a telephone, and a projection room for the showing of home movies, and so convinced were the family concerned of the reality of resurrection and even of its imminence that the fridge-freezer bore a notice recommending the intervals at which perishable food-stuffs should be renewed. The furnishings, intended to be sumptuous, were in poor taste and the reproduction Ingres pictures seemed to emphasise the pleasures of the flesh. Until recently, Scott said, these tombs had been used to store almost all the world supply of drugs, by the celebrated Sicilian gangster Lucky Luciano, now in custody and awaiting deportation.

From the cemetery we moved on to the Cabana Fortress where the much-advertised trials of war criminals were in progress. They were held in a large hall that might have served as a church, for entering it I breathed in the remnant of a stale, churchy odour, which dispersed as we moved forward in search of seats into the depths of the building into which so many persons were crammed. Most of those occupying the rows of benches were relatives of prisoners. A number were women with young children. Spaces had often been made for them to lie down, and some were asleep. Scott attempted to take photographs but was dissuaded by gestures of disapproval from adults in the vicinity. The place was surprisingly quiet, and despite the provision of microphones I had to listen intently to follow the details of what was going on, especially when prisoners under examination replied to questions, as they usually did, in a low-voiced, hesitant fashion. Two small birds fluttered continuously under the roof.

Numerous atrocities had been committed by Batista's army and police in the course of the war. Nevertheless, on the threshold of victory Castro announced that the government of free Cuba would reject a policy of reprisals and indiscriminate vengeance, but that the people's justice supported by courts of law would be unflinching and swift. In the chaos of collapse and defeat most of the important torturers and killers had fled the country, leaving only the criminal small-fry to be rounded up and brought to trial. Such was the savagery of many of these men that even the examining judge sometimes showed signs of being startled by what he heard.

José Cano, aged eighteen, was charged with 'homicide with atrocity'. He appeared younger than his age, had a chirping treble voice, and sometimes risked a doubtful smile.

Judge: Cano, it has been stated by the witness Bonet that he was present when you stabbed Sanchez through both eyes. Do you deny this?

Cano: No, your honour.

Judge: Then you admit to murdering him?

Cano: I didn't murder him, your honour. I couldn't have. He was already dead with a bullet through the neck. With respect, sir, the custom of the country people when a man has been killed is to put his eyes out, or maybe just stick a knife in them. If you believe in Chango you'll do this, otherwise the spirit can still see you and you'll be haunted.

Judge: According to the testimony of Alfonso Galau, who examined Sanchez's body in the mortuary, he died of knife thrusts. There is no mention of a bullet wound. I reject your story.

Someone sitting nearby sighed loudly but otherwise the silence was unbroken. Another murder committed by a young soldier was under investigation. This time it was Gregorio Gonzalez, aged twenty-two, charged with the murder of a woman of seventy-three.

Judge: Why did you enter this house in the first place?

Gonzalez: Two fugitives had taken refuge in it. They fired at us from the window.

Judge: And having broken down the door, what happened?

Gonzalez: There was an exchange of shots and we killed both of them.

Judge: Did you kill the child also?

Gonzalez: No sir.

Judge: Two witnesses have testified that you personally murdered Maria Gallardo, a grandmother, with two shots in the head. Why did you do that?

Gonzalez: I was ordered to execute her for military rebellion by Sergeant Cepa.

Judge: But how can a woman aged seventy-three engage in military rebellion?

Gonzalez: That's a question I can't answer, sir. The sergeant decides what is military rebellion and what isn't.

My impression of Gonzalez was that he was a cunning fellow who set out to appear stupid in the hope of shifting the blame from his shoulders to those of the sergeant, but he was unsuccessful in this, for both he and José Cano were found guilty and sentenced to death. Gonzalez shrugged his shoulders and Cano shook his head as if in disbelief, apart from which neither showed any sign of emotion. There was a brief outburst of weeping which came almost as a surprise in these remarkably calm and subdued surroundings, and a middle-aged woman with two children was hastily led from the court.

Wandering with Scott later through the stone entrails of the Cabana Fortress we found ourselves in the Zona Social where *campáneros* of mixed rank wearing scrupulously pressed uniforms mingled in an atmosphere as sedate as a vicarage fête, sipping delicately from small coffee cups, and smilingly discussing the past achievements and future promise of the new order.

Scott had made some allusion to the possibility of meeting someone in this place, and while he was scanning the faces in the vicinity something like a hush fell. Heads were turned in a nearby group and conversation was broken off, as a tall, thin, uniformed man came into view. This was the man Scott was to see, Herman Marks, the executioner, who had rung Scott's office and asked for the meeting.

Marks clearly knew Scott by sight. A hestitant smile came and died out, leaving flecks of saliva at the corners of his lips. I noticed his hands trembling slightly, the ordinary face of a man who does extraordinary things, and the butt of the biggest pistol I'd ever seen sticking out of its holster.

He thanked Scott twice for coming. 'I know it's a bother,' he said, 'but it's something I sure appreciate. It kind of hurts when people question your sincerity. I mean, you're liable to begin to ask yourself, for Chrissake why am I doing this? I don't see I'm called upon to justify an essential service I'm performing on behalf of the community. Not least when I can assure you one hell of a lot of forethought and effort goes into it.'

'How did you, an American, come to be with the rebels, Herman?' Scott asked him respectfully.

'You can say I was attracted by the ideals of the revolution,' Marks said. 'I guess I felt I had to do something to be of use in some way. Before I came out here I worked in the accounts department of Macy's and I had this feeling I needed to get involved in a cause ... Tell you something, though, Edward, too much paperwork comes into this. Most of it is paperwork. Well, I guess I have to drag myself away. I'm on call in a coupla minutes.'

Whenever I could I attended the political rallies held in the Plaza Civica. Not only to pick up titbits of political news but for the sheer pleasure of listening to Castro talk. In my opinion he was the greatest orator since Demosthenes, and I much enjoyed the faintly hypnotic effects of these entertainments. Castro's interminable speeches contained frequent quotations from Burke, Rousseau, Juvenal and even Shakespeare, and were liberally seeded with wisecracks and jokes. When I inadvertently mentioned my admiration in the hearing of Enrique Oltusky, a member of Castro's inner circle, I was promptly sent a large collection of Castro's printed speeches. It may also have been the reason why I was thereafter allocated a place as near the podium as it was possible for a foreigner to get. It was a concession that had disadvantages. A speech of Fidel's normally started at round about 10 pm, and could last until well past midnight. For an audience packed like sardines and unable to leave until the end, this could foster painful emergencies. On one occasion when I was present Fidel commented on a growing restlessness in the vicinity of the podium. 'I see some of you are becoming fidgety,' he said. 'I would recommend drinking less in advance of such occasions as this.'

On my last attendance at a Plaza Civica rally I took the Boston psychiatrist along, and although I warned him of this problem he felt sure he could manage. In a recent article published under his name in the *New York Times* he had mentioned that Castro frequently appeared in public wearing two watches on his wrist. It was a habit, he believed, that could reliably be taken to indicate that a crisis was on the way. Sure enough, on this occasion there were the two watches, and he said jokingly someone should ring Washington and tell them to put the air command on alert.

It was certainly a time when relations with the United States were at a low ebb. Nevertheless Fidel was on exceptional form and was much amused to be able to describe attempts on his life, all of them ineffective, and all of them absurd. He loved to display at these meetings the apparently innocent objects that contained lethal devices. These included a hollowed-out pack of cards firing a poisoned dart but with a range of only a foot or two, and a dog that would blow up when patted. On this occasion he told the crowd about an exotic sea-shell, also containing an explosive charge. Several had been left on the sea-bed in an area where he was accustomed to go snorkelling. 'I happen to know something about shells,' Castro told the guffawing crowd. 'These came from the Pacific. We can raffle them if you think it worthwhile.'

Now, with the crowd really with him, he turned to his political views. 'They say I'm a communist,' he told them. He held up a bulky edition of *Das Kapital*. 'I've read just a few pages of this book,' he said, 'and I must finish it some time.' Some of them took this as a joke, but others were worried. I looked round for my psychologist friend to get his views, but he was not there. He'd neglected my warning in our visit to a bar before going to the meeting, and I could only conclude that he'd been under pressure and had made his escape.

Thereafter Cuba and the United States drew rapidly apart. The Cuban Agrarian Reform Law expropriated land holdings in excess of 3,000 acres and the American United Fruit Company possessed almost one hundred times this limit. Compensation was rejected and an American trade embargo was imposed, with crippling effect. To survive, Cuba was forced to turn to Russia for its oil, but in doing so Castro was obliged to declare that he had become a communist. Eventually the fiasco of the failed US-sponsored invasion of the Bay of Pigs took place. It was preceded by a purge of all suspect foreigners living in the country, and

Edward Scott spent some days in prison before they put him on a plane for England. The story was that a CIA agent, parachuted in and picked up by the police, had been found to be carrying a list of useful contacts, of which Scott was said to be one. He had left his life behind in Cuba, and after this disappeared from sight.

Chapter Nine

I BECAME TIRED OF London, although by no means tired of life, and although Dr Johnson's celebrated views on this subject might have been reasonable when the milkmaids were still milking their cows in Drury Lane, I cannot believe his enthusiasm would have been rekindled by a revisit to his old haunts in the immediate post-war. For several years I lived in Orchard Street overlooking Selfridges where windows opened on traffic noise obliterating all other sounds. It must have been in 1959 when Selfridges began the expansion of their food department just across the road. A substantial area of their premises was to be rebuilt, in preparation for which equipment that can hardly have changed in design since the Middle Ages went into action and existing walls were knocked down by a huge metal ball swung at the end of a chain. This was done rapidly but many weeks were required to drive piles deep into the London clay to support the weight of the huge new building that followed. Once placed in position, the pile was struck a tremendous blow by a steel driver, which had been hoisted aloft by a chain for some fifty feet before its release. The shock-waves of the concussions occurring at intervals roughly five minutes apart caught up the flimsy building I inhabited in such a way that it regularly gave an upwards jerk of possibly a twentieth of an inch. Work went on for twelve hours a day, starting usually at 7 am, and after a month I decided to move.

It was about this time that I learned through my solicitor that I had long since been divorced according to Mexican law and that my ex-wife had forthwith taken a husband. I therefore married Lesley, an old friend who had been helping me to organise my books. We decided to look for a house in a calm area of the countryside with reasonable access to the capital. I have always believed that, despite evident disadvantages, the attractive life-styles of the past were frequently protected by abusive governments, the malarial mosquito and bad communications. It was this last factor that drew my attention to East Anglia where the London and North Eastern Railway held would-be commuters at its mercy with the slowest, dirtiest and least reliable trains – not only in this country but, short of the Balkans, probably in any other part of Europe. A prime example of this brake on the loss of the charm of the past was the London–Colchester line. No urban dwellers in their right mind ever considered migrating to Essex, in consequence of which house prices were about half those south of the Thames. By way of compensation, also, I found main roads quiet enough to drive on, and lanes along which I could stroll for hours on end without being passed by a car. Fish still swam in unpolluted streams, and the woods and glades were full of the songs of birds. Among the more unusual animals were a number of abandoned cats, transformed into efficient hunters with the lean, muscled bodies of their ancestors and narrow heads. Prospecting for a house I surveyed slovenly flatlands littered with the shacks that slum-dwellers of Latin America might have knocked together overnight. It was to the sour poetry of these landscapes that I was most attracted, even more so to settlements where they reared chickens and sold car spare-parts by the sticky wildernesses of the esturial rivers of this county. Had I been here to write about Essex, no landscape could have been more suitable or inspiring, but most of my writing was to be dedicated to overseas experience, so I continued my search in other directions.

In the end I found a house to suit on the edge of the Essex plain where the rise and fall of the land began. A few patches of ancient woodland remained, and there had always been enough money about to provide tidy villages and the occasional thousand-acre estate with its big house and those who supported its activities submissively but without servility. Our house – The Parsonage – had been up for sale, cheap, for two years and no-one had wanted it. You couldn't live in a place like Finchingfield without a car, for there was only one bus a day to the nearest station eight miles away, and, as was to be expected, a high percentage of the villagers had never visited the capital.

The house was the oldest in the neighbourhood, technically a medieval hall-house, and a builder who had worked on the restoration of local churches pointed out what he believed to be thirteenth-century bricks. A precursor of this building is described in the Doomsday Book as the 'priest's house opposite the church'. In the period of its recent abandonment tiles by the hundred had showered into the garden, calling for the replacement of the roof, and beetles of a rare kind continued to live on what sustenance they could derive from oak beams which might have been five hundred years old. The builder scraped and tapped around the holes they had left, then examined the powdery detritus left by the chewing of ancestral beetle-jaws at the time, perhaps, of the Wars of the Roses. 'They're still there,' he said, 'but why bother? Whatever you do this house will outlast you and a few generations of your descendants.' He held a nail against the wood and struck at it with a heavy hammer, the nail bent but left no more than a mark on the beam. He was also the local undertaker, lured easily by his profession into sardonic philosophising on matters of time and eternity. At a later stage in our happy relationship he mentioned that what remained of attractive churchyard plots had been spoken for but there were always ways of stretching a point when it came to a good friend.

In the large garden cats, descendants of those previous owners had left behind, roamed among the chin-high nettles; and a collection of species roses had become an Amazonian thicket. On the day of my arrival, a flood left by the turbulent rivulet at the bottom of the garden was subsiding and a snipe prodded at the uncovered mud. There were snipe, too, in the ditch separating the garden from that of the adjacent vicarage. Primroses by the thousand, uncultivated snowdrops and the occasional spotted orchid grew undisturbed under the yews in the vicarage glebe land. Close to the vicarage itself a magnificent grove of these trees screened the view of the pond by which the Puritan divine Stephen Marshall had sat to compose his sermons, with the red kites of his day swooping on his ducklings, and reminding him of the devil snatching up souls.

The area was rich in wild life, favoured by a stream grandly named the Pant River running through the garden, the water meadows and a number of dense thickets in the vicinity. Little attempt had been made to look after either my garden or the large garden of the adjacent house, and much of what once had been neatly clipped hedges with even an occasional attempt at topiary had been stifled by the natural growths of the area, greatly to the benefit of birds and butterflies, and the occasional badger or fox. The bird population, shortly to be cut in half by the introduction of pesticides, was exceedingly rich and varied, and included what must have been the last of a family of Butcher birds, which have since become extinct in this country. These continued for several years to nest in one of our thickets, in which – to the astonishment of friends taken to see them – they established their larder of food surplus to their immediate requirements, such as moths, caterpillars and even nestling birds, which they impaled on the thorns.

The builder, chiselling away at suspect wood, drew my attention to the only vestige of the presence of the previous occupant – a pair of frames containing stained and faded prints of what appeared to be Tudor dignitaries. He had heard some story, he said, of the important people who had once lived in the house, although he had no idea who they were.

I found this surprising. The house consisted of a hall and four ground-floor rooms, five bedrooms, and an attic into which servants would have been crammed in earlier days, although the window was blocked up and the room had evidently remained unused for many years. It was the kind of dwelling a priest, or subsequent parson would have occupied in a reasonably prosperous living, although outstandingly unsuitable for the accommodation of a peer of the realm in any period. Upon examination these two dignitaries turned out to be Philip Howard, the first Earl of Arundel, and his son Thomas. A Catholic convert eventually beatified by the Pope as 'a renowned confessor and martyr', Philip comes out rather as a kind of holy madman. Having openly confronted Elizabeth I on a number of occasions and fallen under suspicion of intriguing with plotters, he was committed to the Tower for undertaking the celebration of a secret Mass and twenty-four hours of continuous prayer – for the Spanish Armada's success. For this he was tried for high treason and sentenced to death. The sentence was not carried out as he was eventually taken ill after dinner and died in a manner suggesting that he had been poisoned.

Meanwhile, Philip's son Thomas was born at the Parsonage, where his mother Anne had been ordered into close confinement by the Queen. The Second Earl of Arundel grew up to be a great and in many ways extraordinary man, who relinquished his family religion to become a Protestant 'out of natural leanings to a simple and unadorned ritual'. He has been described as a gruff scholar, who managed to offend Charles I, among others, by his forthright manner and the plain dress he insisted on wearing at court. Nevertheless, after two periods of house restraint and a brief spell in the Tower, he was back in favour and of all things appointed general of the force sent against the invading Scots. It turned out that although he knew a good deal about art he was weak on military strategy, and as a result he was easily defeated, with the temporary loss of Newcastle. Recovering from this setback, he was advanced to the lord high stewardship of the Royal Family, and sent in this capacity on a diplomatic mission of extreme importance to the Austrian emperor in Vienna. His report on this venture produced a shift in foreign policy, for thereafter France substituted for the house of Austria as England's most valuable ally. Thomas Howard was also to become the greatest of English collectors of antiquities. He kept agents in Italy, France and Greece to buy for him the best of whatever treasure was brought to light.

His mother Anne's incarceration at the Parsonage was a strict one and when the Queen learned that she had received a visit from another Howard, Lady Margaret Sackville, a messenger was sent with the order that she was to leave next morning. Anne had some fame as a practitioner of fringe medicine. In a book published locally in the twenties it was reported that medicinal plants of great rarity raised by her from seed still flowered on the steep slopes of the churchyard hill, and in sheltered nooks of the lane leading to the house. Of these I have found no trace.

My arrival in Finchingfield in the early sixties coincided roughly with the abrupt ending of an era. The village had suffered in the past from the poor-laws and the plague but otherwise things remained much as they were. Thirty years earlier, the majority lived in chocolate-box cottages with a short walk, whatever the weather, to the garden dry-drop. Next came the Elsan, and then, with a row of sterile and monotonous-looking council houses, the first bathrooms. The Second World War, followed by labour shortages, snuffed out the last ashes of feudalism, but otherwise the class structure remained inviolate. A week or two after settling in, I watched the local hunt in action, charging like a mounted Mongolian horde through the villagers' gardens and flowerbeds, and disposing of the surplus of village cats.

Yet although the social displacement was a gradual process, the environmental disruption was more sudden and absolute, causing me to toy with the theory that wars are the greatest promoters of change. The determination to survive and to conquer in war provokes resourcefulness and ingenuity superfluous to the needs of society in times of peace. The post-war years witnessed a deterioration of flora and fauna which accelerated with the introduction of defoliants developed during the Vietnam War. The Americans had created these products to remove the jungle which sheltered their enemies. Once hostilities were at an end, fairly simple variations of the formulae employed (which in early versions simply destroyed all vegetable matter) allowed selectivity to be achieved and developed. Farmers could annihilate the weeds growing among crops. Wild plants of any kind rate as weeds for some farmers, even in the case of orchids of great rarity. Publicity has been given to instances where government protection has been extended to 'areas of special interest' only resulting in their immediate treatment with lethal spray.

Such sprays protected crops from both the competition of weeds and attack by insects of various kinds. Mortality was spread indiscriminately, claiming not only thrips and weevils, but also butterflies, moths and bees. Gardens and fields were then littered with small poisoned corpses which proved a deadly diet to birds and hedgehogs that fed on them. Owls were among the first to go, and a succession of brown owls inheriting a hole left repeatedly vacant in our horse-chestnut died in most cases within weeks of beginning their tenancy. Death by poisoning was followed by death from starvation. Suddenly the swallows ceased to nest under village eaves. The year of our arrival the swifts had practically to queue to pass through the gap giving access to their nests in the attic. Three years later none remained. Worst of all, the skies of Essex emptied of their larks. My children, born within yards of a river and a pond in the garden that supplied the village with water in times of drought, reached their teens before sighting a frog. It seems almost incredible that in the heart of the English countryside a whole summer can pass, as sometimes it does now, without the cuckoo being heard.

*

Oliver Myers arrived on leave from the Sudan where he was now teaching at the University of Khartoum. This was the latest in a long series of appointments in an Islamic environment, and by this time he had admitted to spending more than half his adult life within hearing of the call to prayer. The tropical years that seemed to have faded the blue eyes had also calmed the defiant tan of a young Westerner who challenged the sun. Instead there was a pastiness in his appearance of the kind to be observed in desert Arabs who are careful to cover all they can of their skin. When he had occasion to remove his tie, a talisman in a tiny ornamental satchel dangled in the opening of his shirt and he wore a silver bracelet like a hand-cuff engraved with runic scratchings. His habit of dropping a word or two of Arabic into a sentence caused him to be taken for a foreigner by those who did not know him. Although for me these small exaggerations only served to underscore the basic Englishry of his personality.

He listened with hardly concealed excitement to the Arundel story and the account of the banished countess who treated local distempers with potions and salves, and left a legacy of exotic herbs in the village hedgerows. I waited for him to assure me that I had been drawn to this house by the intricate contrivances of fate, but to my disappointment he failed to do so.

I mentioned that an old gardener, who still did a little work for me had removed an unwanted gate-post in the thirties and in so doing had uncovered a cache of undamaged but empty Roman vessels, subsequently sent to the Colchester museum. There was something strange about this story, for why should the Romans have bothered to bury empty pots? When I had put this question to the old man, something closed in his memory like a door. It had all been a long time ago, he had said, although in other areas his power of recall proved acute. Standing roughly where the gate-post had been, the gardener and I looked down on the vestiges of a moat, now perhaps only eighteen inches deep, although in his boyhood he had watched the struggles of a cow that drowned at this spot. There had been one other find in the course of his digging, a Roman toga pin, only the second one of its kind recorded. This had been on show in the village museum, as I confirmed, until stolen during the war. It was clear, I told Oliver, that there had been a substantial Roman presence in the area, for a Mr Coverington, an amateur archaeologist who had previously lived in the house, had carried out a cursory investigation of a sizable Roman villa two hundred yards away, which still remained largely undisturbed under a farmer's field upon which potatoes grew. By custom and temperament the villagers preferred to avoid disturbance by those in search of souvenirs of the distant past. When a mosaic floor was unexpectedly revealed under the floor of a neighbour's kitchen, the tiles covering it were hastily and silently replaced.

Having listened to these stories, Oliver called for a spade and we dug deep into the nettles of the herbaceous border, recovering a large number of pottery fragments at varying depths. These were duly confirmed as being of Roman production, although none was otherwise of the faintest interest and, having been piled up respectfully out of sight, they were ultimately forgotten.

Oliver insisted that pre-historic artefacts, if any, would be found down by the river. This flooded in both spring and autumn, and with the subsidence of the floods little islands of gravel and pebbles appeared in the bed. Oliver found these a rich hunting ground, assuring me that worked flints of a vigorous tool-making industry were scattered everywhere. The best of these brought cries of astonishment and delight in Arabic – a language remarkably suited to outbursts of emotion. Several shoe-boxes were eventually filled with the collection, although not a single one corresponded so far as I was concerned with anything recognisable as a stone-age tool. Oliver explained this as due to the large number of rejects involved in the production of an acceptable result, which as a valuable possession would not have been left lying about.

It was clear that it was the house itself that impressed Oliver most. He preceded a tour of inspection with a rough sketch in his notebook showing the relation of the building to the points of the compass. In the visit that followed, the placement and dimensions of the rooms were studied with the kind of professionalism he probably devoted to an Egyptian tomb, and I noticed that when he entered a bedroom he hushed his voice slightly, as if unwilling to disturb the sleep of an important person. 'Very much of an atmosphere,' he said at one point, and I gathered that this was not intended as a reference to the faintly stagnant odour of antiquity lingering in corners upon which very little sunlight fell.

'So many generations have come and gone,' he said. 'There's something I can't quite define about the place. The feeling it gives me. Do you know what I mean?'

'It's old and it's rather dark,' I said, 'and it has got a history.'

'I'm not sure that it's entirely that,' he said. 'Do you ever experience happenings you can't account for?'

'Not personally,' I said. 'The bedroom doors burst open once in a while at night. It's supposed to be a poltergeist thing but I put it down to the fact that nothing fits very well in the house.'

'Poltergeists,' he said. 'Interesting. I wanted to talk about that.'

'This is the heartland of the poltergeist,' I said, 'and from what I'm told they seem to be practically everywhere. It's not only the villagers. Even the commuters suffer from them. Two of my friends who write bestsellers and one who's an RA called in priests to have their houses exorcised. They don't do anything very exciting. Just bang doors and throw the furniture about.

Once in a while someone reports seeing a woman in what they always call an outdated costume who promptly vanishes.'

'Ah yes, but they're ghosts.'

'Of course, but they're around by the dozen, too. The lady who comes in once a week ran into three at the same time in a local pub when she was seventeen, and our post-lady tells me she sees them once in a while on her rounds, but not often.'

'So it's an everyday thing in this part of the world? They take it for granted.'

'Just about that.'

'And you never have any inexplicable experiences in this house?'

'None at all.'

'Nor even in your friends' houses either?'

'No,' I told him, firmly, 'there aren't any poltergeists when I'm about.'

'And what do you put that down to?' Oliver asked.

'The people of my father's spiritualist circle used to say that where the spirits were concerned I weakened the power. Perhaps that goes for all the poltergeists, too.'

'I forgot he was a medium.'

'It was an environment I spent some years in as a child. It wore out my capacity for belief.'

'I suppose it's to be expected,' he said sadly.

'The members of the circle used to talk to their loved ones on the other side – as we called it – and sometimes they got a message back. When they did it reminded me of a couple of lines scribbled on a holiday postcard and sent home by someone who is bored with the place he finds himself in.'

'And did you ever receive a message from the other side?' Oliver asked.

'Yes, once only, from my brother. We were very close and we always had a lot to say to each other. He was a brilliant musician. At the age of seventeen he was in an orchestra and I asked him if he still played Bach sometimes on his violin. He didn't seem to know what I was talking about. All he could say was, "It's quite nice here. I read a bit sometimes and go for walks." I asked him if they rode bicycles where he was, but he didn't reply, and the medium said the power had given out. This was all about what my mother used to call heaven, but they made it sound like Broadstairs out of season.'

Oliver shook his head. 'I'm afraid a certain amount of chicanery tends to come into these things. More's the pity. It tends to discourage genuine investigation.'

He spent a disappointingly peaceful night in the bedroom in which Anne Arundel probably slept during her enforced occupation. I should much have liked to have been the means of a confrontation with what was evidently a speciality of the neighbourhood but not a door burst open and not even a bird scuffled in the rafters. Next day I made enquiries as to the possibility of tracking down a phenomenon that would have made his holiday memorable, but alas, like the Morris dancers who turned up without warning on the village green, poltergeists gave no advance notice of a performance. My three affected friends had dealt with their disturbances as they might have an attack of dry-rot, and now all was silent. Queer things were rumoured to go on in two or three of the other larger establishments but their owners preferred to keep quiet about it in case their houses were ever put on the market. Poltergeists, I learned at this time, showed a preference for spacious surroundings, and no case was known of one taking up residence in a council house, or a red-brick terrace dwelling dating from the last century, of which there were a number to choose from.

Oliver was due to return to the Sudan in a few days, and with so little time to spare I was only able to locate a single case of a poltergeist in the area. This was a small, basically equipped country cottage rented by a young couple of my acquaintance while in the process of looking round for more convenient accommodation. They were quite agreeable to our inspection of this, but it would have been pointless, for poltergeist activity is notoriously unaccountable and sporadic, and there is very little hope of arriving at a location precisely at the hour when one happens to be active. In this case the girl's father was more than happy to speak of his experiences while staying with the couple in their house. The poltergeist did all the trivial and pointless things that poltergeists do: shunting the furniture around at night, messing with the pots and pans in the cupboards, and even – some poltergeists have moved with the times – fiddling with the house's electrics, and switching the television on and off. Having paid some months in advance for the tenancy, the young pair looked round for ways of abating if not putting an end to the nuisance and succeeded at least in improving the situation by giving their poltergeist the name Fred. Under this down-to-earth appellation it could be appealed to, and remonstrated with, at least to some extent. This may well be a commonly used device, for in an article on the subject in the January 1995 edition of *Essex Countryside* magazine, the author mentions that the poltergeist in The Rose and Crown Inn at Thaxted is called George, while the Greyhound in the same town has more or less domesticated a ghostly presence under the name of Tich.

Most readers will remain unimpressed by the accounts of such goings on that appear with a fair degree of regularity – particularly in the Essex press. Yet social standing, education and intellect seem to offer little protection in encounters with what some accept as the supernatural. Friends who had been at public schools and universities were even more ready than the average intelligent villager to fall back on exorcists when the furniture began to move of its own accord. I could think of no more striking example of this appetite for belief than the case of Oliver, who had devoted his life to the exact science of archaeology yet was prepared to believe that the desert sites in which he worked were haunted by afreets appearing among the sand dunes as capering points of red light.

*

In addition to his qualifications as an archaeologist, Oliver had put in a year at an agricultural college and was knowledgeable about gardens, so part of his leave before returning to Africa was devoted to helping me re-plan certain areas of mine. His hope was to be able to introduce formal aspects, including flower-beds laid out in classical style, a little topiary, a fountain with nereids, and possibly a piece of damaged Greek statuary the Museum might be induced to let go at a reasonable price. Nothing, alas, came of these possibilities, for this was the last time we worked or shared such fantasies together. He had complained of mildly disturbing symptoms in the chest, and soon after this, while I was out of the country, he died of a heart attack. Oliver was as close in my affections as a member of the family, and his loss was a sad one indeed.

Formal gardens are anathema to birds and wildlife in general, so what remained – although in dilapidated condition – of the tidiness of close-sheared hedges and trim arboreal shapes, had to go. The impossible ideal at the back of my mind was the environment in which the various species have adapted themselves over the millennia. From this point of view, the least successful habitats were the shrubberies of suburbia.

Fortunately, my distaste for regimentation was encouraged by the grounds of the large and pleasantly forlorn-looking vicarage, with which I suspected no-one had bothered much since Stephen Marshall philosophised on religious topics by the side of his pond. The evidence was that no member of the current vicar's household ever ventured as far as the magnificently overgrown area down by the river, and I was not surprised when the vicar himself admitted that he had not even realised that this was included in the area under his control. At first sight this was chiefly notable in early spring for the thousands of snowdrops and aconites carpeting the ground under the yews. Later I took an interest in the great variety of birds crammed into thickets from which one year two Canada geese emerged with their young. The trees, the dense undergrowth and the immediate proximity of the river offered irresistible attraction to birds, and in the year of Oliver's visit a German ornithologist at work in the neighbourhood reported the presence of a long-eared owl and – a great rarity – a grasshopper warbler, which I sighted once or twice: a tiny olive-green bird slipping as inconspicuously as possible through the tangled undercover.

The time had come when it was clear that all the remaining unexplored spaces in Finchingfield would sooner or later attract the fatal attention of a developer, and that even the vicarage garden itself might not escape. With this prospect in mind it was Oliver's suggestion that the best hope of protecting the habitat of rare birds would be in an approach to the Diocese of Chelmsford with all the support of prominent church members and the vicar himself. This was done and an agreement was reached by which I took over the area, which would always remain a bird sanctuary.

The river was bordered by water-meadows upon which the village sheep had been grazed since before the Conquest, yet these meadows were under attack. My first view of the village had been from the footpath leading to the Norman church over this spread of green fields. It provided a stunning insight into the grace, even the spirituality, of mediaeval planning at its best. Nothing here distracted the eye from the purity of a scene which never failed to inspire its moment of delighted surprise.

The council had decided that this was to become a vast car park surfaced with thousands of square yards of concrete, which in deference to aesthetic considerations would be coloured green. The river, curling gently through its sedges, was to be girdled in cement, and widened at one point to form a balloon of water surrounding a cement-bound artifical island with pinioned ducks by way of further decoration.

The council had announced that this was a take-it-or-leave-it situation. Nevertheless, a meeting was called in the village hall with a function merely to approve. There followed an extraordinary confrontation which convinced me that I had grossly underestimated the powers of discrimination of village people as well as the spirit and tenacity with which they would defend their opinions in a contest of this kind.

The fury aroused by the ugly pasquinade of the water-meadows was extraordinary. Up until this moment I had believed these people to be sapped by resignation. Now suddenly, when things had gone too far even in a rural situation where dissenting voices are heard only in the last extreme, there was a rare outburst of fury. I learned on this occasion how excellent village taste could be. It had clearly been assumed they would be delighted by the Disneyish fantasy to be imposed upon them. Instead they yelled their detestation in an uproar I would never have believed possible in this traditional 'God bless the squire and his relations' setting. It is to be remembered that this was a rebellion. There was still a whiff of feudalism in this village where back in the twenties the Lord of the Manor's steward stood at the church door to note the name of any farm servant who skipped attendance, and who would lose a day's wages from his weekly pay packet as a result.

Once again the villagers must have suspected that something was about to be taken from them by the rich, and such was the public hubbub that whatever decisions had been taken by those in authority were promptly reversed, and the village was rescued from defacement. The concreted river, the artificial island and the captive ducks were out, but there was no doubt that predatory eyes were still on the site and that the farmer who owned the meadows would sooner or later receive a compulsory purchase order, and be told to remove his sheep.

I took counsel on this matter with neighbours, learning that the only way these meadows could be positively protected was to devise some commercial purpose to which they could be officially designated. Continued grazing by sheep would be rejected as being too casual as compared to a settled commercial operation upon which a bank loan could be raised. Tree-planting, it turned out, came under the umbrella, but it was required that they should be grown for a profit, which ruled out most of the kinds giving pleasure to the eye. The recommended 'profit' tree was a fast-growing poplar. Joining forces with a neighbour, I therefore bought the meadows from the farmer and planted them with uninteresting poplars, convertible after twenty years into several million matchsticks. This was perhaps half a victory, for even though the water-meadows were no more, there would at least be grass under the trees.

The great battle faced by any such village possessing features of scenic, architectural or historical interest is for the preservation of its identity and style. If it is within fifty miles or so of London commuters will be attracted, most of them well-off by local standards and the houses built for them will feature urban amenities but lack charm. A certain decadence is promoted by wealth, involving building complications of an unsuitable and frequently pompous kind. Red-brick walls replace hedges, stables are built, and in one local case what appears as a fairly accurate copy of a Norman barn has been added to a Tudor house.

The attraction of Finchingfield, which draws pilgrims from London to its centre for eight months of the year, is of all things a pond. Over the green and across the water there is a view of a hillside miscellany of houses of all sizes, shapes and colours, dating perhaps from the eighteenth century, but it is the pond, not the houses, which is the thing. As many cars as can be squeezed into the area form static lines each weekend. Some of those who are brought in them may get out and stray a hundred or two yards up into the village, but the pond always fetches them back, and many prefer not to leave their cars and appear not to take their eyes off the water.

To someone like myself who has spent long periods in the East, there is something about this scene and mood that is tremendously familiar. For the short length of their stay these people (many of whom return over and over again) appear to have fallen under an Asian influence. They sit in their cars, or stand to watch the water, all of them facing the same way like orientals in search of a mystic experience. In India pilgrims would have been drawn to this nondescript patch of water by legends concerned with a divine king or a god. Here there is nothing, no legends, no history, no creative essences in the water that cure sickness of body and mind. In India the pond would have been ringed by hucksters, half-naked holy men smeared with ashes, epileptics, sellers of fake jewels, amulets, charms, saucers of scalding food, cow's excrement for the treatment of illness, and a god with an elephant's trunk and multiple arms. The Indians would have been there for the water, too, but they would have waded into it, sluiced it over every part of their bodies, even drunk a little, their faces imprinted with huge joy. For them this would have been a holy place, where nevertheless you went to have a good time. Religion, at least in the East, was spiced with entertainment. In the village, the beneficiaries of the silent, almost biblical congregations are the ducks that assemble here, too, in the certain knowledge that they are about to be fed. They are all of them wild, as many as fifty glossy, energetic mallards at a time. These, combining inherited experience with the most delicate avian sensitivity, not only take their tribute of food without a trace of nervousness, but raise their enormous broods of ducklings in the village gardens, often preferring a site within feet of a door. Such sagacious animals have no objection to establishing a relationship with their tame counterparts. Mallard drakes come winging in to fall upon any farmyard duck they can take by surprise, such matings producing offspring which must cause the farmer surprise by eventually taking to flight. Many of them, like their Aylesbury mothers, are pure white, and there are few more splendid sights on a summer's day than that of these brilliant albinos overhead, soaring sometimes to become no more than a powdery scintillation in the high sky.

The poplars were sprouting vigorously, but wildlife suspicious of change rejects plantations, and I never saw a bird's nest in a poplar. Nevertheless, animals in retreat from the new farming procedures took refuge in the recently acquired glebe-land and began to spread from it into the garden, where much of the disorder they appreciated was made available. I welcomed, for example, the ordinary stinging nettle – a sensitive plant which responds to encouragement – and grew a half acre of it, upon which butterflies were invited to feed. At some point the Water Board washed its hands of looking after the river, enabling me to anchor in position tree-branches that had fallen into it, thus helping with the nesting problem of moorhens and providing a perch for the occasional kingfisher. Odd blackthorn seedlings were carefully looked after, and transplanted to a position where they would grow into a thicket.

Having tended my nettles and blackthorns and cat-proofed the boundaries, I was now lord of an acre of promising wilderness. In the second year of these reforms the garden resounded with birdsong in a countryside that had become largely mute; and I could sit back and enjoy the result.

Chapter Ten

WAY BACK IN the days of Gordon Street, immediately before the outbreak of war, Ernesto would occasionally receive visits from his countrymen straight from Sicily, who sometimes appeared to have given him no notice of their intended arrival. It would thus happen that he was sometimes away. According to the social protocol of the Mediterranean island, it was incorrect for the wife to entertain them, so there were instances when I was hastily summoned by my mother-in-law to do the necessary honours. The Sicilian visitor would be seated in the drawing-room, one of Ernesto's ornate chairs placed at his side ready to receive his hat. Next, according to the schooling she had received, Maria would rush off to lay a tray with coffee and wine, after which she would follow me into the room. These encounters were ritualistic in the extreme. I would enter, bow and announce myself, give my name and, speaking Italian, define my relationship with Ernesto, concluding by begging the guest to make himself at home. With that the man would smile his gratitude and only then pick up the hat, previously held on his knees, and place it on the chair.

The conversation that followed could have been taken from a pre-Hugo phrase book but was brief and to the point. I was happy that it should be so, for although my Italian was going fairly well, I had not yet come to grips with certain recent changes ordered by Mussolini. The old Roman form of address, *voi*, in which the second person plural was employed, was to replace use of the third person singular, *lei*, which he found effeminate. Nevertheless all Italian expatriates stuck to *lei*, and I was forced to do the same. There was a further complication here, for whatever the dictator said, most Sicilians had continued to use *voi*.

Having thanked the visitor for his kindness in making the call, I explained my father-in-law's absence, and then asked after his health.

Nodding gratefully, he would place his hand on his heart and say, 'I can't complain.'

'And the family?' In Sicily as in most of the Orient, you do not ask after a man's wife even if she is well known to you.

'We arrange ourselves – living in hope of better times.'

'You are from Palermo, Signor Volpe. How are things there now?'

'In Palermo, Signor Luigi, there is good and bad. Nothing changes.'

'And that,' I would say, 'Signor Volpe, is roughly the same here.'

I suspected that almost unconsciously I was beginning to adapt myself to a Sicilian environment, for such a meeting no longer struck me as unusual. In this case what was a little different was that in his youth Ernesto had been banished from Italy, although I was never informed why. There was something about these men whose hats were treated with such reverence that made me suspect that they were emissaries from the old country, carrying information about which natural curiosity made me eager to know more. But hardly a hundred words had passed between us on this occasion before the visitor got up, recovered his hat and, excusing himself, slipped away.

Ernesto was very much a private man, who preferred to watch life from the background, and to avoid ostentation and display. After we had lived under the same roof for a year or two he persuaded me to accompany him to a tailor in Conduit Street who fitted me out with a dark grey suit of good cut that would attract no notice. His only criticism of me following this small interference was that my voice was too loud. All the Corvajas conversed in soft voices that were unlikely to be overheard. 'Before you speak, think,' he used to say, 'then if necessary remain silent.'

The house was a quiet one. All the doors shut with a soft but decisive squelch on rubber insulation through which no sound could be heard. Despite Ernesto's distaste for public display it was richly furnished with gilt furniture, painted ceilings, and no dark corners existed in it anywhere under batteries of lamps and their thousands of candlepower of light.

Against this background, with its echoes of a mysterious South, it was inevitable that a kind of obsession with the enigma of the Mafia grew upon me. Two decades had passed since the great bomb had just missed the house at Gordon Street with its silent doors, its vociferous gramophone playing nothing but Puccini, its ceiling after Michelangelo, its staring owl and its rickety chickens kept as pets, and much had returned to dust. And now, dressed in a Marks and Spencer off-the-peg grey suit, I set out for Palermo where I hoped to complete the material I was gathering to write a book about perhaps the most powerful secret society of all times.

I had an address through which I hoped to be able to contact one of the small Sicilians who had visited Gordon Street. Also, my friend James McNeish had been in Sicily recording its rapidly disappearing folk-music for the BBC, and had recommended me to see Mauro Di Mauro, editor of the prestigious left-wing newspaper *L'Ora*. I arrived on the scene too late, for a week or so before, Di Mauro had popped out of his office to buy a packet of cigarettes at a nearby kiosk, and was never seen again. Instead I saw his assistant, Marcello Cimino, who took me under his wing to the extent of giving me access to the archives of the newspaper and the many grim secrets they contained. We then travelled round the island together, talked to numerous people living in the shadow of the Mafia terror, and spent a short time in Partenico with Danilo Dolci, a Sicilian teacher who led the non-violent peasant resistance to the Mafia. Of this stay a representative incident was the experience of a woman volunteer in this organisation who had arrived from England that day. For some reason her taxi had dropped her a hundred yards from the town centre, and she had been instantly obliged to step aside in the narrow lane to avoid a body deposited there. My journey with Marcello was followed by several successive visits to the island which served to cement a friendship only terminated by his death in 1992.

Back in London I met the American humorist S. J. Perelman, who travelled whenever he could in the Far East and felt obliged in consequence to read my books about Indo-China and Burma. Having much in common, we saw a great deal of each other and I showed him a chapter or two of the book I was writing, to be entitled *The Honoured Society* – this being the mafiosi's description of the secret organisation they served. Sid Perelman thought that William Shawn, editor of the *New Yorker*, would be interested to see this and he took the first instalment back with him to the United States. Shawn had a reputation for personal exclusiveness that could be equalled only by a Byzantine emperor. He enjoyed the privilege of a guardian secretary who was herself accessible only to writers of established reputation. Sid's entrée into this magic circle was due only to having known the great man back in the days when Shawn had been a jazz pianist in the Village. But even he took care never to address Shawn by his first name. Shawn read my piece and must have shown excitement for Sid telephoned me to come to New York as soon as I could. I arrived three days later and Sid was there to take me to the *New Yorker* office where I found Shawn – a rubicund, smiling, almost excessively polite little man – at a desk as big as Mussolini's in a huge silent cavern of an office. To me it was astonishing that so much power should have come to rest on the shoulders of a man who was outwardly so meek. The interview took five minutes and Shawn asked me to go back to Sicily and finish the book for the *New Yorker*, mentioning what seemed an unbelievable fee for its publication in the magazine.

In the summer of 1963 I returned to New York where I delivered the completed manuscript to Shawn's secretary, whose surroundings of isolation and grandeur almost matched those of her employer. Early next morning Shawn telephoned me at the

Algonquin Hotel, where all *New Yorker* contributors were supposed to stay. He invited me to lunch, served at the famous round table, and I was subjected to a somewhat awe-inspiring phenomenon. After a short outburst of generous praise for the book, Shawn had nothing more to say. He seemed uncomfortable and after a while I became aware of the beads of perspiration rolling down his cheeks. I found that I was sweating too. After an agonised effort I managed to break the silence, and things slowly became easier for both of us. Later Sid Perelman said of this alarming episode, 'I should have warned you. It happens to everybody. All you have to do is to pitch in and keep talking.' On our third meeting I managed this with total success.

The Honoured Society was serialised virtually in its entirety in six issues of the *New Yorker*. Shawn had stipulated that no mention should be made of the Mafia's extremely powerful American ramifications. Nevertheless the magazine was in trouble with the Sicilians, who claimed they had been libelled, and I found myself under attack as soon as copies reached Sicily. Gavin Maxwell had written an exciting book called *God Protect Me from My Friends*, dealing with the life and death of Salvatore Giuliano, the most intelligent and resourceful bandit of all times, who with a couple of hundred outlaws had run rings round army detachments sent to Sicily to get rid of him. Now Gavin rang to warn me, 'You have succeeded in libelling Prince Alliata in exactly the same way as I did. I fought the case and lost it and have been caught for massive damages. If it comes up you'd do better to settle out of court.'

Both of us had quoted the same newspaper report that claimed Alliata had offered the bandits sanctuary on his estate in Brazil. To quote this in an Italian publication was not libellous in Italy, but in England, strangely enough, it was. In a matter of days the feared writ dropped from the sky and I fell back, just as Maxwell had done, on the legal firm of Rubinstein, celebrated for their expertise in this particular field. I was seen by Michael Rubinstein who had handled the case for Gavin Maxwell. He looked me over doubtfully and told me that the man I should have to face in court was a Prince of the Holy Roman Empire, a man of impressive presence and of international standing, fluent in English and persuasive in any language. 'The judge was knocked sideways,'

Rubinstein said. 'Gavin Maxwell comes from a notable Highland family, but Alliata made mincemeat of him.' Rubinstein studied me again, in my imagination shaking his head. 'Do you think you could do better?' he asked. I told him I thought that was unlikely. 'I don't think this should go to court. This man seems potentially generous. If you offer to pay his hotel bill in London he'll probably let you off.' And this is what happened.

In addition to the *New Yorker* serialisation, *The Honoured Society* was translated into fourteen foreign languages, with the notable abstention of Russian, and I was told by Professor Evashova of Moscow University that this was because in the Soviet Union non-fiction works were not regarded as literature.

Four years after the book's publication, an internationally publicised Mafia trial in Palermo took place. This set a precedent in that not only were Sicilian mafiosi in the dock but visitors from the States alleged to have entered Sicily with the object of strengthening the collaboration between the two countries in matters of organised crime. Three of the accused had American and Italian dual nationality, but six of the visiting Americans had managed to escape.

All previous Mafia trials had followed a simple pattern of failure, collapsing because witnesses either refused to give evidence or retracted statements made to the police as soon as they were put in the witness box. It had been announced that this would not happen in this case, and that reluctant witnesses could expect to be hauled off to prison for contempt of court. On 14 March 1968 the trial finally began. It was a gala occasion, Southern-style, in celebration of the impending triumph of justice. There were street cordons of granite-faced armed police, stampeding pressmen and entranced crowds waiting for the arrival of the cortège from the prison as if for a religious procession, and carrying banners and images.

The *Sunday Times* sent me to record these extraordinary happenings, and I arrived at the courthouse to find that I was awaited by a photographer organised by some unspecified Sicilian contact. He was a small, gleeful, impish individual – the only person I have ever met to describe himself as 'a man of

himself with implacable enemies, and in July
as recovered riddled with bullets.
usso had fought head-on battles, and his end in
been seen in Palermo as a certainty. Boris
parison was an intellectual, a diplomat, who
lerated working arrangements with his oppo-
him the Pubblica Sicurezza had held its own,
things could hardly be said to be better, they
worse.
9, while taking his usual morning coffee in a bar
oris Giuliano was shot dead by an assassin who
ape. His funeral was celebrated in a way that
ny people of Palermo may have been grateful for
otection he had been able to offer them. He was
th the extraordinary civic accolade, far greater
received in his lifetime, of *Cadavere Eccelente*, with
ntury only six Sicilians had been honoured, and
he grave in a hearse drawn by twelve horses.

respect'. I could only conclude that this he really was, for despite the notices forbidding photography, Lo Buono wandered openly round the courtroom photographing the men in the dock, witnesses and finally the presiding judge himself, admonishing him sharply when he closed his eyes, 'Look at me, your Honour.'

It struck me as extraordinary that a number of the famous criminals in the dock, some of whom were said to have been in custody for as much as a year, should sport impressive sun-tans and be dressed in the smartest of outdoor fashion. Of this phenomenon Lo Buono said, 'Do not believe everything you are told, Signor Luigi.'

Within three days the trial showed signs of languishing. The most important of the accused failed to appear in court on grounds of sickness, and most of those who did were shown to have led exemplary lives. Several were known for their association with leading personalities of the church. Two had sons training for the priesthood. Another had paid for the building of an orphanage. John Benventre, one of the alleged Cosa Nostra chieftains (he had studied for holy orders in his youth), was head of a charity organisation famous throughout the United States. Vincenzo Martinez, also in charity, had lost an arm and been decorated for valour in the war and reminded one newspaperman of an 'aloof and splendid Coriolanus'. Addressing the court on 'the eventual triumph of virtue', he said, 'Surely we are all agreed that a quiet conscience is a man's dearest possession,' whereupon a mumble of approval spread through the court-room to reach its furthest corners. On 25 June all of the accused were cleared for lack of proof.

It was evident within days of the trial's opening that it would end as it did. With time on my hands I called on Colonel Giuseppe Russo of the Carabinieri, advertised in the press as having been sent to Sicily to carry out a conclusive war on the Mafia and to see to it that the accused men were not able to slip through the fingers of the police once again. He was an out-and-out northerner, tall by Sicilian standards, with a brusque manner and a dislike for the island he made little attempt to disguise. His office betrayed a liking for military order of a severe kind, with handcuffs – made to his own design, he confided – used as a paper-weight on his desk. He described the Mafia as 'an oriental conspiracy fostered by local interests', saying that he proposed to finish it off. Describing the methods he had in mind, he said, 'Take the case of Frank Coppola.' (One of the three American Cosa Nostra chiefs to have been discovered in Italy.) 'The custom here is to carry out arrests by night, to avoid public humiliation, which is just what I have in store for these people. I sent two men for him just at the time when the neighbours would be up and about to see what happened, and they chained him up and dragged him away. It gave people a chance to see he's no bigger where the law is concerned than any other man. You can forget about him. When crooks like Coppola lose face they're done for.'

Boris Giuliano, Chief of the Pubblica Sicurezza of Palermo, was next on my list. He was pleasant and informal and it came as a surprise that he should speak English fluently with a marked London accent. He explained this by telling me that for two years after taking his degree he had worked as a waiter in a restaurant in Frith Street, Soho – 'illegally', he added with a touch of quiet pride. As it happened I knew the restaurant well and often ate there. It was celebrated among its regulars, including myself, for its escalope milanese, admitted at a time when food was in short supply to have been made with horse meat, so well prepared as to be preferred by many to the standard version employing veal. Giuliano claimed to have remembered me from those days, having trained himself as part of an intended policeman's skills to keep a record of faces. This interview went off so well that that evening he called on me at my hotel – alleged, he said, to belong to a Mafia consortium and thus providing the best Palermo had to offer in the way of service and food.

Hostility between the two Italian police forces, as I had learned in the British Army in Naples, was traditional, and Giuliano was horrified although not surprised to hear from me Russo's story of the arrest. 'He's signed his own death warrant,' he said. 'They'll give the dust time to settle, then take him out. I give him five years.'

'So what would you have done?'

'I'd have turned up in a plain car, been polite and given him half an hour to get his things together. If a woman had been

around I'd have bo
Coppola I might hav
have to do what I'm
finger to have you s
'So what do you t
I thought he mean
like hussars in scarle
polite. 'It's excellent,'
that I was impressed
could leave my hire-c
'We have very little
snatching. No burglar
man to live in, becaus
'So can Russo smash
Giuliano scoffed at t
you can contain it, bu
members are among th
I saw Giuliano aga
exchanged sporadic con
from which I learned o
became clear that the Mafi
heroin. Their secret laborato
world supply, and it was di
stand on the sidelines and
occasion when Giuliano made
him for an hour or so at
Washington to confer w
previous visit had had to
Kennedy. He had put f
many Americans – that,
Commission, this had b
tions suggested the plot
subsequently wrote ab
Notwithstanding Gi
Russo would meet hi
incident, he actually la
hundred, nearly all o

thus surroundin
1977 his body w
In this cause h
this fashion ha
Giuliano by co
probably even
nents, and unde
and if at the er
were certainly
On 21 July 19
near his house,
was able to es
suggests that m
the degree of p
accorded in de
than any he had
which in this c
was carried to

Chapter Eleven

OUTSTANDING IN THE long string of tragedies engulfing much of the South American continent at one time or another since the Spanish conquest, was the near-annihilation in the late sixties of the native races of Brazil. It came as a surprise that this was brought to the notice of the outside world by the Brazilian government itself, which offered no excuses, and described with absolute frankness the dimensions of the tragedy that had taken place. Murder, said the government report, had been committed on a huge scale. No-one knew precisely just how many had died out of sight and beyond reach of help in the measureless depths of the forests, but it might have been half the Indian population. And who had slaughtered all these innocents? The government's own Indian Protection Service, the report confessed, by the employment of gangs of professional killers. The lands thus freed were then sold off, and the money embezzled by agents of the service.

In 1968 the Attorney General, Jader Figueredo, broke this news to the nation and the world, adding the information that the ex-head of the service, Major Luis Neves, was now to be tried for forty-two crimes, including several murders. A further 134 functionaries were charged with similar crimes, and Senhor

Figueredo doubted whether, of the Service's 1,000 employees, as many as ten would be finally cleared of guilt.

According to the reports, outright brutality of the old-fashioned kind existed alongside the most sophisticated methods of extermination. Professional bravos who normally shot the victims through the head or hacked them to pieces with machetes might be accompanied or replaced by men of science versed in the techniques of bacteriological warfare. Some tribes had simply disappeared. Once they had been there in the thousands and now they were gone. Sometimes figures could be supplied. Of the recently counted 19,000 Munducurus, only 1,200 were left. The Guaranies were reduced from 5,000 to 300. Decimation had left the Carajas with 400 out of 4,000. The Cintas Largas, estimated in 1966 to have totalled 10,000, had since been attacked by an overland force and from the air with their reduction to an estimated 500. The Government White Paper detailed an endless list of atrocities:

> The Maxacalis were given fire water then exterminated by the killers with machine-gun fire when they were drunk.
>
> The worst slaughter took place in Aripuana where the Cintas Largas Indians were attacked from the air using sticks of dynamite.
>
> To deal with the Beiços de Pau, an expedition was sent carrying foodstuffs for the Indians. These were mixed with arsenic and formicides. Next day a great number died, 'due' it was announced 'to an epidemic'. Most of the Tapaunas were wiped out with gifts of sugar laced with arsenic.
>
> Two tribes of the Patachos were exterminated by doctors giving them smallpox infections.
>
> Pioneers in league with corrupt agents of the Service issued clothing to the Indians impregnated with the virus of smallpox, and having thus eliminated them took over their territory.
>
> In the Ministry of the Interior it was stated that crimes committed by ex-functionaries of the IPS amounted to more

than 1,000, ranging from tearing out Indians' finger nails to allowing them to die without assistance.

These things happened during a period when the *Sunday Times* set out to gain ground over its competitors by an extended coverage of world events. The editor of the magazine, Peter Crookston, had liked my report on the trial in Sicily of leading mafiosi, and so he asked me to investigate what was happening in Brazil.

In Rio de Janeiro the co-operation I received was immediate and total, and there was no doubt that the daily airings in the press of the mechanisms of genocide were received with a degree of horror equalling the reaction in Britain or any other country. Huge areas had been emptied of their human population by the methods described, yet a scrutiny of the small ads revealed that 'cleared land' – meaning those areas from which any human presence had been removed – still fetched more in the market than those where the clearing remained to be done. Among these advertisements was one by Amazon Adventure Estates couched in poetic style with allusions to monkeys and macaws and the 'occult' glitter of gems in the banks of 'mighty rivers sailed by ships of the explorer Orellana'. A Brazilian deputy revealed that Prince Rainier of Monaco had bought a presumably cleared estate twelve times the size of the principality.

A single statement in the White Paper's panorama of catastrophe astounded me in a way more than all the rest. There had been half-hearted explanations rather than excuses for the Service's collapse based on starvation of financial backing and – in this colossal country almost the size of Europe – the demoralisation of underpaid agents faced with unthinkable isolation in their living tombs among the trees. An assistant secretary at the Ministry of the Interior spoke of the Service having to face 'the disastrous impact of missionary activity'. A journalist friend of his on *O Jornal do Brazil* took me to what was left of Bororos' Santa Critena reserve to explain what was meant.

The Bororos had been a great people celebrated by the account of the anthropologist Claude Lévi-Strauss who had lived among them for several years. Lévi-Strauss had been led by his studies to form the conclusions of structural anthropology, including the proposition that a primitive people is not a backward people and indeed 'may possess a genius for invention or action that leaves the achievements of civilized people far behind'. Writing of the Bororos, he said: 'Few people are so profoundly religious,' adding that they were obsessed by their relationship with the dead, a concern manifested – in the manner of the ancient Egyptians – in lengthy and most elaborate funeral rites. It is this excess of spirituality that gets the Indians of Latin America into trouble with the missionaries, who so often appear as the representatives of a material world. The Bororos, left to themselves and seemingly unable to part with their dead, bury them twice, and this custom is the emotional basis of their lives. In the first instance – as if in hope of some miraculous revival – the body is placed in a temporary grave in the centre of the village, and covered with branches. When decomposition is advanced the flesh is removed from the bones which are painted and lovingly adorned with flowers, after which the final burial takes place in the depths of the forest.

The American fundamentalist missionaries who had flooded into the country at the end of the war would have none of this, and were even able to have all such activities banned by law throughout Brazil. At this time only a single reservation maintained by the celebrated brothers Vilas Boas had been able to keep them out, and shortly before our arrival the Teresa Cristina Reserve given to the Indians 'in perpetuity' had been invaded by mobs of armed land-grabbers, with whom the missionaries had gone along. Thus their funeral rites were at an end, and with them, as it was to turn out, earthly pleasures of every kind. With the loss of their land the Bororos became instantly dependent on the missionaries, who forbade dancing, singing, smoking, and 'heathen' decorations of the body, offering in return a little work rewarded with handouts of food and clothing provided by charity organisations. By the time of our visit the reservation had become a typical forest slum. The Indians' cows had been sold off by the agents of the Indian Protection Service, and the Indians were reduced to the normal hard-times diet of lizards, locusts and snakes. The reservation, said my journalist friend, had been divided into two farms, one run with slave labour. On this there was a mill for crushing the sugar cane, and to save the horses they used four children to turn the mill. 'The missionaries,' he said, 'have raised no objections to these things. "We were sent here," they tell you, "to save souls, and this we are doing." They started a school here which the Bororos children were compelled to attend. My paper has published instances of the young girls being prostituted, and in one case even given away. When I protested to the head missionary, he said, "She has witnessed for Christ, and that is all that matters. She will receive compensation in Heaven." '

It was the testimony of Diego di Ribeiro of *O Jornal do Brazil*, and what I saw on the Santa Cristina reservation with my own eyes, that brought about the change in my attitude to these Protestant fundamentalists. Previously I had contented myself with emphatic disagreement, but from this time on I opposed, and there was nothing in my subsequent experience of these destructive sects that did anything to lessen this opposition.

No-one could have been more forthcoming in such lugubrious affairs than the upper echelons of the Brazilian police, and I was given immediate access to Federal Delegate Senhora Neves da Costa Vale, a slightly perfumed, sharp-eyed and elegant lady sent to Belen, close to Brazil's border with Peru, to look into the matter of the near disappearance of the Ticuna tribe. She told me that they had fallen under the influence of a missionary who convinced them that the world was about to come to an end, and that they would be safe only on the estate of one Jordao Aires. There the Indians were promptly enslaved, being chained hand and foot in such a way that some had become lepers with the loss of their fingers. She confirmed the existence of an island called Armaça where Indians too old or sick to work were concentrated by Aires to await death. One extraordinary aspect of this business was that a senior police official should have been obliged to use a missionary plane in order to reach her destination in Belen.

At lower levels the police fell over themselves to offer what help they could and I was whisked away by plane to talk to a hired gunman, Ataide, who had been awaiting trial for four years for multiple homicide. He was a small man with a wolfish triangular face and a deeply depressed expression shot through with occasional flare-ups of hope. Ataide had gained nationwide fame for spectacular and much publicised outbursts of remorse. He had participated in the overland expedition against the Cintas Largas and later allowed a priest to tape a confession of his involvement in the atrocity, parts of which he was happy to describe for the benefit of visitors such as myself. The attack, he explained, had been planned to coincide with the Indians' annual feast of the Quarap. This, lasting a day and a night, was a theatrical representation of the legends of creation (remarkably similar to our own) interwoven with those of the tribe itself, plus a family reunion attended not only by the living but by the ancestral spirits.

'As soon as we spotted their village,' Ataide said, 'we surrounded it and waited for the dawn when the Indians started to come out of their huts. I got the chief with the first shot from my old carbine and the fellows finished off the rest with their tommy-guns. I have got to say that I was all against what happened next. There was a young girl with a kid of about five yelling his head off. Chico, our leader, started after her and I told him to stop, and he said, "Our orders are to get rid of them all." We were both religious men and I said, "You can't do this. What are the padres going to say about it when we get back?" He shot the kid through the head, then he tied up the Indian girl, hung her head-downwards from a tree, legs apart, and chopped her in half right down the middle with his machete. "What was the point of that?" I asked him, and he said, "If I'd have left her in one piece all the boys would have been at her and discipline would have gone to pot. I'm the boss here and without me none of you bastards would ever get back." '

This interview took place in Cuiabá, capital of Mato Grosso. Along with Ataide, my police escort informed me, 1,000 criminals were awaiting trial there. The local lock-up only accommodated some fifty persons (all ages and sexes were kept together). So murderers galore on provisional liberty roamed the streets, and after the meeting Ataide was allowed to return to the sweet stall by which he normally made his living.

My investigation was inseparable from journeys to distant

places, conducted for the most part by buses through unending forest gloom and early floods. The President's report on the Commission set up to deal with the atrocities listed in lurid detail some of the felonies perpetrated by the Protection Service agents and the land-grabbers with whom they were in league. A case attracting particular attention in the press was one in which Indians in the 7th Inspectorate Paraná were tortured by grinding the bones of their feet in the angle of two wooden stakes driven into the ground. A husband and wife were singled out as having taken turns in this operation, but by the time I arrived they had vanished. 'We suspect a spontaneous public reaction,' a police inspector said. 'They had few friends. I do not believe we shall hear from them again.' Little more came out of this journey apart from a meeting with an agent who had been struck by a poisoned arrow. 'It is a poison that compels you to laugh,' he said. 'You laugh, then you scream, then you die. I did not die.' He was on a charge of setting fire to the cabin in which his aggressor had taken refuge, and in which he had burned to death.

A short break by the sea came as a relief from a blood-soaked environment and I went to Port Seguro, five hundred miles north of Rio de Janeiro, drawn to this place where the first Portuguese expedition landed four hundred years ago, leaving a scintillating account of the circumstances of a first contact between European adventurers and the innocents of the New World. The newcomers were enchanted by their reception, and Pedro Vaz de Caminha, official clerk to the expedition, noted in the minutest detail all the incidents of this encounter in a letter to the king that crackled with enthusiasm. By chance they had come ashore precisely at the spot where a number of village girls had been bathing, and, emerging from the water, they paraded quite naked on the beach, indifferent to the hungry stares of the Portuguese soldiery. Caminha was clearly on terms of unusual intimacy with the Portuguese monarch, for, as though taking by the elbow a crony from his home town, he launched immediately into a description of these ladies' private parts. The Indian girls, he said, were devoid of bodily hair. And although it was proper for all such letters to begin with a description of the climate and produce of the newly discovered country, such prosaic details were thrust into the background in this case while Caminha concentrated on those aspects of their discovery which interested both men most. 'Sweet girls,' he writes, overbrimming with enthusiasm. 'Like wild birds and animals. Lustrous in a way that so far outshines those in captivity they could not be cleaner, plumper and more vibrant than they are. Their genitalia would put any Portuguese lady to shame.' Such raptures are not to be wondered at bearing in mind the fact that in those days most Europeans rarely washed (a treatise on the avoidance of lousiness was a bestseller), and it was to be supposed that the Portuguese were verminous in the regions on which Caminha concentrated his attentions.

The Europeans were overwhelmed, too, by the magnificence of the Indians' manners. If they admired any of their necklaces or personal adornments of feathers or shells these were instantly pressed into their hands. In later encounters it was to be the same with gold trinkets, and temporary wives were always to be had for the taking. Encouraged by welcoming smiles, the bolder of the women came and rubbed themselves against the sailors' legs, showing their fascination at the instant and inevitable response that not even a doublet could conceal.

Indian generosity and lack of concern for personal possessions dazzled the newly arrived representatives of an almost fanatically acquisitive society. Carried away with enthusiasm, Caminha filled page after page with a catalogue of Indian virtues, before terminating the letter with the conventional recommendation of the times. All that was necessary to complete this image of the perfect human society was the knowledge of the true God. And since these people were not circumcised it followed that they were not Mohammedans or Jews, and there was nothing to impede their conversion. When the first Mass was said the Indians with characteristic politeness knelt beside the Portuguese and, in imitation of their guests, kissed the crucifixes that were handed to them. As discussions could only be limited to gestures the Portuguese suspected that their missionary labours were incomplete and when Pedro Alvarez Cabral's fleet sailed, two convicts were left behind to complete the natives' religious instruction.

Pondering Caminha's letter in a later century, Voltaire formulated his theory of the Noble Savage. Here was innocence – here was apparent freedom, even from the curse of original sin. According to Caminha's further reports and those of other early Portuguese arrivals, the Indians knew of no crimes or punishments. There were no hangmen or torturers among them, and no poor. They treated each other, their children – even their animals – with constant affection. It later became fashionable to deride Voltaire's theory, but since this is an autobiography I feel called upon to disclose my own opinions upon this subject, and I am persistently and increasingly of the opinion that Voltaire was right.

Making enquiries in the Porto Seguro area, I learned that a few descendants of the Indians seen by Caminha and his friends still lived on precariously in the neighbourhood. It turned out that a journalist on the staff of the highly respected *O Globo* covered this area and lived nearby and he immediately offered himself as a guide. These Indians, now named the Patachós, were well known to him and he had reported their misfortunes in his paper on a number of occasions. They had gone to earth in odd corners of their original land, Vicente said, until the late fifties when a doctor had been sent to vaccinate them by the Indian Protection Service. He had injected them with the virus of smallpox. This achieved the desired result, and the usable land left vacant by the epidemic was immediately absorbed into neighbouring estates. That this remnant had been left in the first place to struggle on as they did was a mystery, for they had been preyed upon by 'pioneers' and bandits of every description and ravaged by tuberculosis, venereal diseases, malaria and influenza. But they were tough and adaptable. They grew small quantities of excellent vegetables on clapped-out earth fertilised by their own excrement, which was devoid of odour, practised a little magic, made up herbal recipes for neurotic townspeople who visited them in secret, and at worst eked things out with a little prostitution and theft.

We went to look for them on a rat-scoured patch of land the colour of iron with a railway track running through. A few scarecrow figures came up out of the ground and moved towards us. Caminha's pretty girls might have been among them but it was impossible to tell their sex.

'They seem unnaturally dark,' I said, wondering if these Indians had managed in some way to come by a little black blood.

'That's dirt,' Vicente said. 'The nearest water's four miles away.'

'Why are they smiling?'

'They like us. Better not let them kiss your hands.'

An old man who was blind in one eye had appeared at the mouth of a cave and addressed us in broken Portuguese. 'Please come in, gentleman,' he said. 'My house is yours. The woman will bring you something to eat.'

'As you see,' Vicente said. 'They are very polite.'

My first meeting with Don McCullin took place shortly after I had delivered the enormous report on genocide in Brazil to the *Sunday Times*. Peter Crookston told me that in the meanwhile the paper had decided that it was essential to obtain the best possible photographic coverage, and that McCullin had agreed to leave for Brazil straight away. This delighted me for I had seen some of his pictures and regarded them not as mere photographic journalism but as high examples of photographic art. Don was in his twenties, and this was to be his first assignment of such magnitude, yet although he appeared understandably nervous, he showed abounding confidence. I was sure, as was Peter, that he would put everything he had to give into the job. I took an immediate liking to him. He said he hoped that we should be able to work together again, and intuition prompted me to assure him that we would, and that we would see a good deal of the world together. This proved to be the case, for a working collaboration and a friendship followed that has lasted to this day.

On this particular trip I was surprised that such a relatively inexperienced traveller, as he was at that time, should have shown himself capable of penetrating the most remote fastnesses of a vast and relatively unexplored country, and returning with certainly the most impressive collection of photographs to have come out of it. The most remarkable of them were studies of so-called 'unreached' Indians, in particular that of three Kamaiuras who had never seen a white man before. They were playing their enormous flutes, eyes closed in ecstasy. 'We speak to our gods with the sweet music of flutes,' one of them was able to explain through an interpreter.

Travel in these remotest of backwoods was possible only by missionary plane. At the insistence of the Brazilian Ministry of the Interior, one of these had carried Don to photograph what was left of the mounted Kadiweus – often referred to as the Indian Cavaliers. In 1865, the Portuguese Emperor Pedro II had appealed to 2,000 of their ancestors to save their country from invasion by the psychopathic dictator of Paraguay, and they had taken their spears and ridden naked, bare-backed and impeccably painted at the head of the Brazilian army to rout the invaders. For this they were given two million acres of the borderland in perpetuity. Donald photographed what was left of them, 'a pitiful scrounging band', he called them, led now by what appeared to be a grandmother on a broken-down nag, although she was only forty, and entitled as chief to wear a loin-cloth sewn with precious stones also donated by the Emperor.

At the Ministry someone had clearly blundered, for apart from their leader, all Don saw of the Cavaliers were a few sick and starving women and children who rode their skeletal horses each morning down to the mission house to beg for scraps. The missionary seemed indifferent to their plight. He was lost in a single all-absorbing task, the translation of Paul's 'Epistle to the Galations' into Kadiweu. He had given ten years of his life to this, he told Donald, and expected to finish the work in another ten years. 'Won't they all be dead by then?' Donald asked.

'Yes, they will,' the missionary agreed.

'Then what's the point of the whole exercise?' Donald wanted to know.

The missionary thought about this. 'It's something I cannot explain,' he said. 'Something I could never make you understand.'

The article 'Genocide in Brazil' was published in the *Sunday Times* in February 1969. At 12,500 words it was the longest piece ever to have been published in the paper, and such was the interest created that separate staff were required to handle correspondence and telephone calls.

The following are extracts from a letter from the Campaigns Department of Survival International, dated June 1995:

> Survival International is the only worldwide organisation supporting tribal peoples through public campaigns. It was founded in 1969 after an article by Norman Lewis in the *Sunday Times* highlighted the massacres, land thefts and genocide taking place in Brazilian Amazonia.
>
> Today, Survival has members and supporters in sixty-seven countries. It works for tribal peoples' rights in three complementary ways: campaigns, education and funding.
>
> It runs worldwide campaigns to fight for tribal peoples. Our campaigning forced the Brazilian government to recognise Yanomami land in 1992. In 1989, Botswana's government was forced to halt plans to evict Bushmen from the Central Kalahari Game Reserve within weeks of Survival issuing an Urgent Action Bulletin.
>
> Campaigns are not only directed at governments, but at companies, banks, fundamentalist missionaries, guerrilla armies, and anyone else who violates tribal peoples' rights. Survival was the first organisation to criticise the World Bank for its destructive projects. As well as letter-writing, we organise vigils at embassies, lobby those in positions of power (political or economic), put cases to the UN, advise tribes of their legal rights and advise on the drafting of international laws.
>
> Survival also plays a major role in ensuring that humanitarian, self-help, educational and medical projects with tribal peoples receive proper funding. A good example is the Yanomami Medical Fund, which succeeded in virtually eliminating malaria in some Yanomami areas.
>
> Since 1969, the 'developed' world's attitude to tribal peoples has changed beyond recognition. Then, it was assumed that they would either die out or be assimilated; now, their wisdom and experience are held in high esteem. Survival has forced

tribal issues into the political and cultural mainstream. This, perhaps, is our greatest achievement of all, but there are many barriers of ignorance, prejudice and greed which we must still overcome.

Chapter Twelve

OF OUTSTANDING INTEREST to me was the trip commissioned by Peter Crookston to study the predicament of the Huichols of the Sierra Madre of Mexico, who had come under the threat of invasions promoted by mining interests regarding them as little more than a nuisance. This turned out to be something of an adventure.

I had already spent several months of 1969 travelling in Mexico, and had run into a band of these rarely seen Indians – befeathered from head to foot and with bows in their hands – when a bus I had been travelling on broke down in the small town of Tepic. Someone told me the Indians lived at the top of the Sierra Madre, about nine days away by mule. They were carrying out some strange ceremony that had flowed into the road, with the traffic missing them as best it could. I got off the bus, made further enquiries and stayed in Tepic that night. Here I further learned that these were the only Indians north of the Amazon who had kept intact their tribal structure and most of their ancient customs, and that they lived in the highest valleys of the sierra where they had managed to keep up the resistance to the Spanish invaders until 150 years after the conquest had been completed elsewhere throughout the New World.

I was determined to know more about these people and was

directed to Padre Ernesto Loéra, the Franciscan in charge of the shrine of Zapópan, near Guadalajara, regarded as the Mexican equivalent of Lourdes. The shaman, or leader, of the Huichol people was persuaded to assist him as a healer during the annual festival. Loéra, an educated man, said the healing skills the shaman had demonstrated were phenomenal. 'Ramon Medina uses spittle and incantations to cure anything that doesn't call for surgery. Antibiotics don't come into it.' He urged me to track down Medina and persuade him to take me to the sierra. 'Don't forget the bodyguards,' the Padre said, 'also a good automatic rifle. They kill you as soon as look at you up there.' He added that he himself always made sure to take his trusty old Winchester repeater when engaged on his religious endeavours in the local mountains.

I had flown back to London and told Peter about the Huichols. A week later I returned to Mexico with the photographer David Montgomery, who certainly had little idea of what he was letting himself in for. Having started the ball rolling with Padre Ernesto, it was now only necessary to secure the blessing of Dr Ramos, head of the Instituto Indigenista, at first sight a somewhat austere if impressive figure seated behind an enormous desk beneath the double-headed eagle of the Republic. Dr Ramos looked at David's abundant hair and black shirt with pearl buttons, and asked in Spanish, 'Is he a hippy?' I replied, 'Absolutely,' and suddenly the Doctor's wary expression broke into delight. 'My daughter adores the Beatles . . . Of course you may go.' Ramon Medina happened to be in Tepic at that time, and an appointment with him at the Institute was fixed for that afternoon.

The shaman arrived punctually, a remarkable figure even in Tepic where there were plenty of Indians on the streets and not a few of them in bizarre regalia. He was a man of about forty with a small, brown smiling face and penetrating eyes. In his cotton shirt and trousers embroidered with deer, eagles and jaguars, and his wide hat decorated with pendant ornaments, he dominated the discreet environment of the Institute's office. He spoke a hundred or so words of Spanish that seemed enough to get by. We asked him if he would go to the sierra with us, and with Dr Ramos nodding approval in the background, he said, 'Of course,' adding that we could leave there and then if we wished. I told him we would like to depart on the first plane with free seats. As it happened, one was taking off at six the next morning, and it was this that we boarded. It proved to be a ramshackle single-engined aircraft piloted by a man who had only half his original face left. Several crash landings in areas where airstrips did not exist had resulted in extensive plastic surgery. Despite his notoriously great spiritual powers, the shaman some no more trust in providence than the Padre and some concern that neither David nor I was armed.

We landed on a tongue of tableland across a low precipice and bumped to a standstill. Here the pilot deposited us and, smiling a goodbye with one side of his mouth, took off. We were in the clearing of a forest of oaks, with orchids hanging like coloured ribbons from their branches. The shaman found an automatic pistol in the nest of feathers at his waist, held it out and I took it reluctantly. I cocked it but found that the trigger was so stiff that even under the pressure of both forefingers it could not be discharged. I handed it back and his smile saddened. He now explained that we must walk in single file, distanced from each other by about ten paces to reduce the likelihood of becoming eliminated in a single fusillade from behind one of the many huge boulders strewn about this landscape. With this began the least relaxed three days of my life, by comparison with which the equivalent time spent on the beach-head at Salerno in 1943 seemed relatively calm.

Eight miles away, a Catholic mission with which Padre Loéra had some connection had established itself in a Huichol village which it had promptly renamed Santa Clara. We made our way towards it, much slowed down by the desirability of giving suspicious boulders and trees a wide berth, and we reached the village after a trek of about five hours.

Set among dramatic scenery, the mission was staffed by a single priest, Padre Joaquin, with the support of a dozen or so nuns. Life here must have resembled that of an outpost on the American frontier at its wildest in the early part of the last century. Part of the mission had been destroyed by fire in an attack by the Huichols two years before, during which the nuns had kept up, as we learned, brisk and continuous rifle-fire from the narrow windows. The shaman slipped away quietly as soon as the building came in sight. He was known to be strongly opposed to the missionary presence and warned us that it would do our cause no good to be seen with him. However, we had been spotted from afar and Padre Joaquin received us coldly. Nevertheless we were permitted to sleep in an outbuilding, and although we made it clear that we had brought food with us, we were served by silent and unsmiling nuns with bowlfuls of *atole* – a sweet cornflour gruel – tortillas and a bean-stew; all of it delicious.

It was now early evening, with a resplendent sky full of toucans and parakeets, and soft lemon light. The little Indian girls in the care of the mission had finished their domestic chores and the boys had come down from the forest dragging wood on their sledges for the fires. What astounded me was that the Franciscans had allowed them to dress in Indian style in tunics embroidered with pagan symbols and gods that had assumed cavorting animal form. Some of the boys had brought guitars and Huichol violins, and we were treated to an enthusiastic serenade, which was accompanied by the girls' pentatonic humming.

The joyful atmosphere at Santa Clara was quite new to me. At best, mission camps – of which I have seen a number – are solemn places from which the elements of pleasure are firmly excluded. Here music and laughter were everywhere to be heard, and although a largely Welsh Baptist upbringing has left me unable to cope with religion in general, I realised how lucky these little Huichols were to have been taken into the care of the Catholics, rather than that of one of the ethnocidal Protestant sects. Only the shaman regarded this situation with gloom, insisting that the policy at Santa Clara was to encourage marriages between pure Indians and mestizos in the knowledge that the offspring of such unions would be brought up in the Christian faith and thus lost to the Indian community.

The night was exceedingly cold and we were awakened at about 3am by the intense surrounding activity. It was the Huichol custom to take a dip at this hour and the women were already in the freezing river. Such dousings, Ramon later informed us, fostered the sexual coldness much appreciated by the Huichols in their womenfolk.

The shaman appeared at dawn surrounded by adult Indians, and, selecting a spot just outside the mission boundary, began the lengthy and complicated ritual involved in helping the sun to rise. This was achieved with the aid of two wands with feathered ends, waved energetically while the shaman prayed in a loud, insistent voice. Slowly the mountain tops lightened, then glowed – a result acclaimed by general murmurs of relief.

Ramon had disquieting news. Four days prior to our arrival a Huichol living in the village's outskirts had been murdered. He explained that it had been no ordinary killing because of the ritualistic nature of the crime, which involved hanging the victim by a rope in which no knots were used. This showed that the murder was intended as a warning to the community. Such acts of pure terror in which robbery was not involved seemed to strengthen Padre Ernesto's theory that hired killers had been enlisted by the mining interests.

The shaman, who would clearly have been a prime target in a full-scale terrorist campaign, now seemed eager to leave Santa Clara and recommended a visit to San Andrea, the ceremonial capital of the Huichols where the annual festival was to be held on the coming Sunday. There would be archery, he said, music performed on ancient instruments, dancing, the drinking of great quantities of tesguino – the Huichol ceremonial beer – and even a bull sacrifice, to be paid for by a general contribution of several hours' work.

We therefore set out on another gruelling single-file walk, and some hours later San Andrea came into sight. It comprised fifteen stone-built houses enclosing a square. None of the houses was occupied, the shaman said, and the village served only as a meeting place for Huichol living in remote areas in the sierra, and for discussions of tribal policy, the punishment of law-breakers according to tribal custom, and fiestas of the kind we had come to witness. Of the promised fiesta there was no sign whatever. In the centre of the empty square stood a post to which, said the shaman, deflowerers of virgins were tied to be flogged. Under this the *topiri* – the village policeman who did the flogging – lay asleep. The shaman woke him and was told that the fiesta had been called off as a result of someone's unfavourable dream. Ramon asked for the *tatuan*, (the village headman) and the *topiri* told him he had gone off to look after his garden. He himself was tired after an unpleasant experience, he said. Being questioned about this, the *topiri* said that he had only recently been elected to his position, which offered no remuneration while imposing many onerous duties. As was the democratic Huichol custom, he had not been informed of his candidature in advance, and had only been persuaded to accept the nomination after a short spell of imprisonment without food. Huichol justice was immediate and stern, Ramon explained, and then, always eager to promote our journalistic interests, he asked if there were any prisoners available to be photographed. These, apparently, would be kept in stocks in a dark hole somewhere about the place. The *topiri* told him with obvious regret that there were none. If we came back in a week or two, he said, he might be able to help us.

David Montgomery was now in difficulties. He was extremely agreeable and accommodating, and had a notably equable temperament. He lived happily with his wife and produced photographs of outstanding artistic quality in a studio at the back of Victoria station, where he was assisted by a hard-working staff – all of whom, remarkably enough, were Mormons. From this stress-free environment he had allowed himself suddenly to be snatched away and dumped among the urgencies of the high sierra, where he had rapidly learned that life was held cheap. Now, surprisingly, we were to learn from the *topiri* that a murder had recently been committed in San Andrea, too. There are long delays between death and burial among the Huichols due to the many preliminaries required for the soul's successful entry into the after-life. The victim in this case had died from multiple bullet wounds, and had been wrapped in all the finery that could be found and strung up out of the way in as cool a place as possible under the roof rafters of one of the houses, where decomposition had long since set in. I was now obliged to ask David to photograph this scene, and although he made no demur he told me that he had never seen a dead body and was a little afraid that he might faint. I assured him that I would hold him up if this happened, and the photo was taken.

No sooner was this crisis behind us and we had returned to the centre of the village, than we were confronted with the spectacle of a grim-faced mestizo armed with a powerful rifle standing at bay while Indians who had appeared as if from nowhere closed in on him. Several of these held their bows at the ready. There was a general belief, shared emphatically by Ramon Medina, that this was a bandit who had been stalking us and followed us into what had appeared to him a deserted village. The man's rifle was taken from him, and the *topiri*, unwinding the sacred cord of office carried round his waist, tied him up. Messengers were sent to fetch the *tatuan* and the members of his council back from their fields, and a trial began. The intruder could offer no convincing account of his background, recent activities or threatening presence on an Indian reservation. In an attempt to rebut the charge of banditry he removed his shirt to display a wound like a purple mouth in the stomach – produced by the exit of a dum-dum bullet – and the tiny white circle in his back where the bullet had entered. He had suffered this a year before, he said, in an attack from ambush along the trail we had come down, but his argument that no man with such a wound could be other than innocent failed to impress.

A brief and perfunctory trial followed. The shaman called a verdict of guilty, with which the *tatuan* seemed unable to agree. The shaman had told us that should the case go against the man he was likely to be executed on the spot – shot to death with arrows. I warned David of this possibility, suggesting that the best thing we could do was to walk away from the scene as quickly as possible. But in ten minutes it was all over with the intruder released for lack of sufficient evidence – of which, as I saw it, there was none at all. He was given back his gun but as a concession to the shaman's objections the bullets were confiscated.

After that we set out on the hard slog back to Santa Clara, going as fast as we could because at all costs, Ramon insisted, we must be out of the sierra before dark. Reaching the Nautla Gorge where the Huichol idols are stored in a cave no white is supposed ever to have seen, we threw ourselves down to rest. The mission was only a half-hour's scramble down the mountainside, and already the sun had fallen behind the peaks.

By this time our relationship with the shaman had grown close and he chose this moment to create us honorary *compañeros* of the Huichol people, formally inviting us to set out with him on annual pilgrimage which would start in twenty-five days' time. For the sixth time Ramon would lead his people at the head of four captains, across mountain and desert for twenty days to Rial Catorce in the high desert of San Luis Potosí. We would march rapidly, he said, in single file, carrying nothing but bows, sacred tobacco, holy water and ritual implements, sustained on the journey by the virtue engendered by our own austerities.

Huichols regard peyote as deer that have transformed themselves by magic into sacred cactus, Ramon explained. The peyote would therefore not be simply collected during the pilgrimage, but hunted with bows and arrows, and would be prayed and sung to before being eaten. Then, renewed by the visions we had imbibed and with our faces painted with symbols of victory, we would set out again on the long march back to the Sierra Madre, sure of our reward of a long and good life.

This was the substance translated from the verbal surrealism of what the shaman offered. He took out the ballpoint pen he carried wrapped up with his pistol in his satchel and drew us as stiff little figures strutting happily through a forest of symbols towards Wirikuta, the sacred peyote country at the end of the pilgrimage. Now, in studying these naive sketches, I remembered the shaman's fame as the artist of the 'yarn-paintings', based upon votive offerings made at the Huichol shrines of which Padre Ernesto had collected a number of examples at Zapopán. We nodded, smiled and pretended agreement with the shaman's advance planning, and followed the adventures of the manikins representing us among the foxes, the giant centipedes and the enchanted deer peopling the deserts of San Luis Potosí we were to cross. If we found it impossible at such short notice to make our arrangements for the coming pilgrimage, the shaman assured us, the invitation could be renewed next year.

We went back to England, and my article on the Huichol

Indians appeared in April 1970. As the months passed, something I had almost dismissed from my mind reappeared and began to take on form and credibility and a kind of urgency. The shaman, I now realised, had half-opened a door to the purest of adventures. How could I possibly hold back? I wrote to him at Zapopán, and then care of Dr Ramos. There followed a long silence before the news reached me that Ramon Medina was dead – killed by persons unknown within weeks of our leaving Mexico.

Chapter Thirteen

Among those whose interest had been aroused by my article on tribal genocide in Brazil, was Tony Snowdon, who had worked for the *Sunday Times* as a photographer. Peter Crookston phoned to say that Snowdon would like to know if I was contemplating any more South American journeys, and if so could he come along to take the photographs. The arrangement would be a strictly professional one, and although Snowdon was at that time a member of the Royal family, no problem of protocol would exist.

The approach came at a time when I was planning a visit to Peru. I asked Peter if he thought that this was a country that would suit, and he rang a little later to say that Snowdon appeared delighted with the suggestion. Two days later Peter and I drove to Kensington Palace where Snowdon awaited us, and even at six in the morning I had the impression of a man full of enthusiasm. He said how much he was looking forward to our project and my feeling was that we should get on well together, for I much admired his photographic work, and more still the brilliant and original aviary he had recently designed for the London Zoo.

Peter drove us to Heathrow. It was a Sunday, and on the way Snowdon explained why he had particularly wanted to take this flight. Sunday, he said, was the day when people who were of interest to the press were least likely to travel, and such people, he had observed, did all they could to avoid early-morning starts. He was therefore unlikely to be bothered by reporters. In one respect Snowdon had done well, since the check-in area was virtually deserted. However, his baggage bore labels identifying them as the possession of the Right Honorable the Earl of Snowdon, and these were not likely to be overlooked. In a matter of minutes an excited young woman who was unmistakably a journalist bore down on us. Snowdon seemed to stiffen and change colour.

'Norman,' he said, 'could you possibly induce her to go away?' This, with what diplomacy I could muster, I declined to do. It was an embarrassing moment, and the first of a number of such confrontations.

At the check-in consternation reigned. We were down as travelling tourist class, as all *Sunday Times* journalists did, but our explanation failed to convince. Agitated conversations took place out of our hearing, before a senior staff member returned and said, 'It seems that the tourist class is full up, sir. In the circumstances could you possibly agree to up-grading? There will of course be no charge.' Snowdon fought a losing battle for the right to travel tourist before giving in. We took our first-class tickets, and then, as a foretaste of what was to come, were told that we would be boarding before the rest of the passengers and that 'the limousine' was ready to take us to the plane.

At Caracas a fuelling stop released us for a stroll in a first-class lounge decked out with tropical flowers with flies stuck to their stamens, and smelling slightly of decay. A bar was attended by a man dressed like a Venezuelan cowboy. They were serving snacks but as no English was spoken, Snowdon asked if I would order a lightly done fried egg for him. This I did, and he praised its flavour. Did I think he would have the opportunity to learn Spanish on the trip? he wondered, and I thought there would be hardly the time. He was eagerly looking forward to Peru, and had studied in advance the artistic accomplishments of the Incas, in particular their textiles which he hoped we would have time to see. I assured him that we would. Was I interested in textiles? he asked. I said I was, but I knew little about them, being stronger on ceramics. There was endless scope for study in both fields in Peru; but more than the arts it was the life of the Peruvian people that interested me. I hoped we would have time to visit parts of the country which had been bypassed by modern times and where many of the interesting customs of the past had survived. He agreed with me and said that if necessary we would make time.

We touched down at about 10 at night. I was surprised to find that, despite its proximity to the equator, Lima was both cool and misty. We took a taxi through empty streets to the hotel, which was grand in the old-fashioned style, and where we were received with dignity, but no special interest. The rooms reserved for us were well furnished in a heavy old-fashioned style. Each contained a large marble statuette of a lady who might have been Greek in the act of disrobing, and there was also a large painting of the divine eye spreading its protective rays. Snowdon had enquired at the desk if there were messages for us, and there were none. We could be certain that the telephone would not ring. The battle for anonymity had, it seemed, been won.

I was awakened by Snowdon rather earlier than I had hoped, and I was beginning to realise that he was the possessor of great physical energy, and quite clearly immune to jet-lag. At breakfast he was bubbling over with good cheer, and impressed and delighted by the decorative background of fruit, which was stacked up like an award-winning entry of a tropical harvest festival. We made plans for the forthcoming journey and I suggested a start might be made by an investigation of the Cuyocoyo area in the high Andes to the north-east of Lake Titicaca. It was the homeland of the Aymara Indians whose grandiose civilisation preceded that of the Incas. They had been enslaved over four centuries and were still fantastically exploited. I had been told that in remote mountain villages they were still compelled to carry priests in chairs and were publicly scourged for persisting in their ancient worship of Pachamama the mother-goddess, and Tio, the Devil, who is also – appropriately – god of the tin mines. Snowdon, full of agreement, and in no way discouraged by recent news of the emergence in the area of a guerrilla resistance known as the Shining Path, thought this was an excellent plan. Were the guerrillas likely to give us any trouble? he wondered. I thought not. My impression was that they had no quarrel with foreigners. And did I think that they could tell a journalist from England from Peruvian exploiters? I simply didn't know, but suggested that we might go there and take advice from the locals, and be guided by what they suggested, and that, too, he thought was an excellent idea.

By this time there had been few breakfasters and no-one had taken the slightest notice of us, but now suddenly I was aware that Snowdon was showing signs of unease, and this clearly was due to the presence of a man carrying a camera with a long lens who had drifted into sight at the far end of the room.

'What do you suppose he wants?' he asked.

'Probably the house photographer,' I said, 'taking holiday snaps for the guests.'

He seemed unconvinced. 'More coffee?' he asked.

'No, that's fine.'

He got up. 'Shall we go and look round, then?' he suggested.

There was not a great deal to see in the lounge and a view through the window of unexciting modern buildings in fog did not encourage immediate exploration of Lima. Suddenly Snowdon leapt to his feet and flung himself through a barrier of large, potted ferns through which a different cameraman had been trying to photograph him. As an expert photographer himself, he knew just what to do. The man held his ground, camera defiantly levelled, and Snowdon, taking him by the shoulders, oscillated his body violently backwards and forwards from the hips in such a way that the man could not focus on him. It was natural that this extraordinary scene should attract the attention of everyone in the vicinity and we were immediately encircled by spectators. An agitated under-manager came bounding into sight, the photographer was driven away and Snowdon retired, obviously upset, to his room.

Within minutes I was called to the phone. 'The British Embassy is on the line for Lord Snowdon, sir, and there is no reply from his room. Could you take the call?'

I found myself talking to Anthony Walter, First Secretary, who said that the ambassador had heard that Lord Snowdon was in

Lima, and wished, naturally, to welcome him, and also perhaps to suggest lunch.

It was at this moment that it first became apparent to me that our trip might not be as successful as I had hoped. I went to Snowdon's room. 'Do me a great favour,' he said. 'Please get rid of him.'

'I can't do that,' I told him. 'You'll have to talk to him yourself.'

'Couldn't you just say this is a strictly private working trip?'

Back to Walter, who said, 'I wish we could do *something*. Mr Morgan will be terribly hurt.'

I gave up and walked out of earshot, while Snowdon stated his terms. He would lunch with the ambassador and Mrs Morgan but he stipulated that this should be in some unassuming out-of-town restaurant where the party would avoid attention. Dress was to be informal. He himself would of course not wear a tie and perhaps Mr Morgan might care to refrain from wearing one, too.

It was clear that Mr Morgan took all this seriously, arriving at the appointed time in a large, open sports car which I felt sure he must have borrowed. He was attired in grey flannels and an open-necked white shirt, appearing to be not wholly at ease in these garments. Mrs Morgan, who was Bulgarian, had clearly decided that none of Snowdon's restrictions applied in her case. She was a fluttery, smiling, impetuous woman who had come dressed in rustling silk and an unmanageable hat. All heads turned as we passed through the packed and rumbustious streets of Lima, and when we were held up in traffic jams or by broken-down vehicles desperate beggars rushed with arms outstretched to implore our charity. An occasional glance at Mr Morgan's aloof profile helped to an understanding of the expression 'gritting one's teeth'.

The restaurant was – as required – small and acceptably remote. Several women had clearly been press-ganged into tidying the place, and, hiding their faces as we drew up, they made a flurried escape. It was a small room with a row of tables down each wall, and it was clear that a policeman lurking near the entrance would see to it that we were the only customers.

Now we faced the inevitable uphill conversational slog. Mr Morgan took on the subject of the performance by English cricketers somewhere in the West Indies, of which I knew nothing and cared little – as applied equally, I suspected, in Snowdon's case. This was followed by a desultory attempt on the ambassador's part to dramatise an account of the parlous state of the Peruvian anchovy-fishing industry. Mrs Morgan patched a gap in the conversation with her personal criticism of the sexual laxness of the Peruvian poor, which helped to inflate the numbers of those who could not be gainfully employed. It was following an attempt to keep this wretched conversation going, that she suddenly changed tack and dropped a clanger.

'Lord Snowdon,' she said, 'you will not know, but your children and mine attend the same school.'

The bleakness of the look with which this news was received did nothing to quench bubbling Balkan enthusiasm. 'At first I cannot say to you that your children were exactly popular. No, they were not liked, but after a while I think, as you say, they shook down. Now the pupils are saying, oh well, they are human after all.'

Back in the hotel the prospect of the evening meal loomed like a storm cloud on the horizon. I asked the manager, 'Do you expect photographers tonight?'

'I think they will come,' he said.

'Is there any way they can be kept out?'

'It is impossible,' he said. 'If we place a man at the door they will come through the windows. They are very persistent and they know all the tricks. A photographer will come in saying he is a plain-clothes policeman, and carrying an imitation police card. Or someone will say he has been taken ill and ask for a doctor. But the doctor is really a photographer and is carrying a camera in his bag. Nothing will keep these people out.'

'Don't you have a private room where we could have dinner?'

'I will show you,' the manager said.

It turned out that the hotel had an enormous basement banqueting chamber, only in use normally for the celebration of national festivals and for the reception of heads of state. It held thirty or forty tables and was illuminated by vast and elaborate chandeliers. At this time the furniture was covered by dust-sheets, but the manager lifted one of them to display the gilt and plush beneath.

'It would be difficult to prepare the whole of the banqueting chamber for Lord Snowdon's immediate use,' the manager said, 'but if this would suit we can certainly have a reasonable area ready. You would be private here, and if you approve we can send out immediately for some flowers to brighten up the place.'

Later that afternoon Anthony Walter from the embassy looked in at the hotel. It was to offer his services, he said, in any way that could possibly be of assistance in our journeying in the country. He was very affable and engaging. Snowdon, who had confided to me that in his view all ambassadors were twits, but clearly had no objections when it came to first secretaries, took to him, and by the end of the afternoon we were all on first-name terms, although the slightest of complications arose over Snowdon and Walter's possession of the same first name. It transpired later when we were joined by Walter's wife that her name was Antonia.

Walter, who almost certainly knew Peru as well as any Englishman, wondered if our visit might be made a little easier, and therefore more productive – without obligation of any kind, he stressed – by accepting a minimum of assistance and advice from the Peruvian government. There were parts of the country which he felt sure we would wish to visit which were virtually inaccessible to the private traveller. I brought up the Cuyocoyo area in which I was particularly interested, and he said it was a case in point: a place of endless fascination, temporarily out of bounds owing to the presence of guerrillas, although he knew someone in the Department of the Interior who was in a position to say yea or nay, and might be induced to say yea. Walter then went on to suggest that the ambassador might be agreeable to giving him a week or two's local leave, in which case if we thought he could be useful to us he would be happy to come along.

Tony Snowdon seemed to jump at the idea, but I was more doubtful. What I had had in mind and had suggested to the *Sunday Times* was something in the nature of an adventure. Our goal was to see virgin territories and remote peoples, and though it was possible that the Peruvian authorities could help us to do this, it also seemed possible that, either off their own bat, or as a result of direction from the Foreign Office, the Embassy would do all that was possible to make sure that Snowdon was not placed at risk.

Next morning it was quite evident that the idea of slipping unnoticed in and out of Lima was the stuff of dreams, for Snowdon's presence in the capital had already hit the headlines. It seemed probable, too, that the incident in the hotel lounge had made him enemies, as well as inspiring some inaccurate reporting. The newspaper described Walter as a bodyguard, while I started off as Martin Lewis, Editor of the *Sunday Times*, becoming thereafter an agent of the Secret Service. The newspapers found Snowdon either inaccessible and aloof, or aggressive. My worst fears about the degeneration of our planned adventure into a flavourless conducted tour seemed likely to be confirmed when Walter announced that he had booked seats for us in a plane to Cuzco. Although this was undoubtedly an interesting city, it had been the standby of geographical magazines for so many years that it would be difficult to say anything that had not been said many, many times before.

It was becoming clear, too, that there was a curious ambivalence in Tony's attitude to the general public. On the previous night, extraordinary zeal had been deployed by the hotel staff to re-inject life into the mortuary atmosphere of the banqueting room, with an enclave of tables set with shining cutlery, burnished glass and a vase with the disgruntled purplish flowers that were the best that Lima could provide. Nothing could be done about the special silences of a large empty room – which the on-off purr of the air-conditioning did little to relieve – or about the penetrating odour of dust. We had taken our seats and waiters came into sight, trudging as silently as assassins towards us over the thick carpet through the desert of sheeted furniture. Between us, the manager, hotel staff and myself had achieved an isolation of the kind that Tony was unlikely to have known before. Alas, it did not please. Next day we reached the top of the stairs and he seemed to draw back. 'Rather spooky down there,' he said.

'What's it to be, then? The main dining-room?'

'I think we should give it a try,' he said.

'Let's do that, then.'

The head waiter hurried to meet us. 'You want a corner, don't you?' I said to Tony.

'Oh, I don't know. Leave it to him.'

Moments later we were seated in the dead centre of the room. Occupants of tables in the vicinity were shifting their positions to get a better view, and an Instamatic flashed nearby.

At Cuzco we were met by Guillermo, the stout and genial head of the local tourist office, and a beautiful young assistant called Milagros (miracles). Two large cars awaited, the second containing two saturnine men in dark glasses and raincoats. (As we were later told that it was unlikely to rain in Cuzco for another five months, I assumed that the raincoats were intended to conceal sub-machine guns.) A score of photographers ran hither and thither like disoriented partridges in the background, and a policeman who wore a peaked cap pulled down so that nothing could be seen of his face above the end of his nose, blew his whistle continuously. It was at this moment that I felt the ball and chain fixed in position around my ankle.

We set off on a tour of the town with Guillermo and Milagros, our bodyguards and a handful of resentful pressmen. We were also accompanied by a number of Quechua women wearing a great variety of hats, among them a white topper. All were nursing mothers and we were informed by Milagros that they were there in the belief that the beneficial influences transmitted by obviously affluent whites would improve their milk. Guillermo bombarded us with colourless statistics about the size and weight of the stones in the ancient buildings we passed. Milagros leapt about, face ravaged and arms outstretched in an attempt to depict the death-agonies of the Indian leader Tupic Amaru who had been pulled apart by horses in one of the squares. The performance ended with a loud and convincing groan. It was, however, Snowdon who captured the Quechua ladies' attention. Tony was always ready to accept the advice of his friends, and he had been told by one of them, Michael Bentine, a native of this part of the world, that the high altitude of Cuzco might cause trouble with his breathing and he should carry oxygen equipment. This he did in the form of a tiny cylinder to which a mask was fitted. From time to time he took an obedient puff from this, and when he did so the Quechuas uttered small cries of delight. The white man was recharging his store of magic, which would certainly be all to the good of the milk.

It was a procedure that did not wholly avoid alarm in other quarters, for Milagros, who at the end of our visit was invited to dine with us, turned down the invitation as politely as possible. Guillermo took me into his confidence over the reason for this. 'She is afraid that Milord is taking aphrodisiacs.'

When we returned to Lima Anthony Walter met us off the plane and more plans of action were discussed. He told us that the Ministry of the Interior had confirmed that guerrillas were indeed active in the area upon which I had set my sights, and it would be imprudent to travel there without a military escort, which – reasonably enough – they were reluctant to provide. Instead Walter suggested a visit to the Callejón de Huaylas, a remote valley in the Cordillera Blanca, to the north.

Eighteen months earlier, the Callejón de Huaylas had been the scene of the greatest earthquake-plus-avalanche disaster in Peruvian history and it was only now that its fearful aftermath was beginning to be cleared up. In a number of towns in this 100-mile-long, densely populated valley every building had been destroyed, and in Ranrahirca alone, 30,000 people had been buried in a single instant under millions of tons of rock, mud and ice. Apart from the tragic spectacle this offered, Walter thought that the huge relief effort invited description, and mentioned that psychiatrists had been sent from all over the world to help cope with the psychological problems of thousands of victims of the catastrophe who had been driven beyond the limits of endurance by their sufferings. Disasters at Huaylas, he said, had occurred regularly throughout history, even being recorded by the Incas. Apart from spectacular loss of life, these terrible events had induced their own medically recognised form of neurosis, prevalent in people doomed to live out their lives waiting for millions of tons of ice to fall upon them from the skies.

An agreement was reached that we should go to Huaylas and that Walter would go with us. A permit was duly obtained, while the Ministry of Information supplied a car and driver. The first stage of the journey was on the Pan American Highway northwards from Lima, with a desert strip and the sea on one side and distant mountains building up on the other. Peru is a country of spectacular fogs, into which the road plunged almost immediately. The sun striking through produced weird colour combinations and hallucinatory effects. We plunged through the surface of a mock river. Fog in dispersion drifted away in osprey plumes over the sea, at the edge of which a wave carried a row of inert pink ducks towards the shore. The sand in between had thrown up strange white peaks, delicately chiselled by the wind, with mist hanging like fine lace from their spurs. Distantly inland, the driver pointed out the Hacienda La Madrugada built in the style of Brighton Pavilion, where until a year before a special version of the *droit de seigneur* had been imposed, personable young Indians being condemned to sleep with the aged mistress of the estate, who at the age of eighty-seven had still continued to exercise her sexual prerogative.

Three hours later we were in the suburbs of Chimbote, until lately a charming village by the sea, but now the world's largest fishing port – easily outdistancing any competitor in Russia or Japan – where 16,000 ex-peasants had become fishermen living in a wilderness of identical cubic shacks. Here, each year, ten million tons of fish were reduced to two million tons of fish-meal for export to all parts of the world. The terrible effluvium of the fish-mills of Chimbote can be smelt up to ten miles away and senior staff of the fish-meal companies visiting the scene of their operations are under orders to do so with gas-masks in place.

At Chimbote we were told that the road we had intended to follow into the Altiplano was not to be recommended so we turned round and drove south to Pativilca where we turned off the highway and began the climb into the Andes. Almost immediately we saw the first dramatic evidence of the disastrous earthquake of 31 May 1970. We were on one of the lateral roads of the great Inca Andean highway, which showed an almost brutal indifference to problems of gradient or terrain. Too often the view from the car windows on one side was an abyss, with the Fortaleza River curled like a bright thread at its bottom. The patches of maize and potatoes grown in these high valleys were continually showered by rockfalls from above, and those who cultivated them had been obliged to develop a technique of ploughing that involved constantly lifting the plough as the ox dodged to avoid the boulders.

The area of almost total destruction was reached under the pass at Huamba, a town which, through the munificence of some charitable organisation, had been rebuilt entirely in corrugated iron. Conococha, on the pass itself, was less fortunate. It had never been more than a street of wooden hutments, and these stood up only too well to the terrible earth convulsions that had rocked it like a ship in a heavy sea. Here, at nearly 13,000 feet and three hours from the equatorial desert of the coast, a mixture of sleet and rain was falling, and a great number of children with paeony cheeks and snotty noses came out in their soaking rags to watch us.

Two hours later, at the end of a marshy plateau, we drove into Huarez, capital of the great central valley between the two cordilleras, the Callejón de Huaylas. It had taken the full force of the earthquake and looked like a pigmy Hiroshima; an open space with not a single building standing where once there had been a colonial town with a population of 20,000. This clear space was fringed by the hutments in which the survivors lived, awaiting the day when a start would be made on rebuilding the town.

It was this earthquake, lasting less than half a minute, that set off the dire catastrophe that followed immediately. Within seconds of the shock one million cubic metres of ice broke away from the highest point of the glacier of Huascarán and, falling some thousand feet, detached another 24 million cubic metres. The avalanche, travelling at 250 mph, reached and buried Ranrahirca in one minute and forty seconds. Throughout history, all those who could do so have lived in Yungay, in belief that security was offered by a protective hill, yet this town, too, disappeared instantly from sight under some thirty feet of mud and rocks. When we arrived there nothing whatever remained to indicate the buried town's presence except the tops of four palm trees, still alive, protruding from the sea of debris covering its central square.

As there had been so few survivors it was hard to find anyone to talk to who had been in the vicinity at the time of the disaster but in the end we spoke to a group of Quechuas who had been to put flowers tied up in plastic bags over the spot where they believed their families to be buried under a great sallow sea of what could have been broken-up cement. The problem had been to recreate a phantom identity of streets and squares, and to decide where the dead lay in relation to them. Gradually, by agreement, a shadow town-plan had been worked out, and now on the surface of the otherwise featureless rubble there appeared orderly rows of little crosses, much like war-graves, except that here they were gathered in small clusters – in one case with as many as thirty over the spot where a particularly numerous family had lived.

The Quechuas described apocalyptic moments: first the rumble and roar of the earthquake coming in, with the sound of an express train in a tunnel; the earth heaving and plunging and shaking itself – then, seconds later, the screech of the oncoming landslide. One of the men had been saved with his young son because they had been out to look for strayed sheep in a nearby village. They had been flung to the ground, showered with earth and pummelled by flying stones. Uprooted trees had come crashing down around them and in a matter of minutes, as the great dust cloud went up (that over Ranrahirca had reached 18,000 feet), the day had gone dark. Hours later, after groping their way over landslides, round earth-fissures, and wading through floods produced by the damming of the Santa River, they reached the spot where the town had once been, to find their world at an end.

We stayed the night in austere conditions at Quiravilca. From this an ancient and narrow Inca road, with terrible gradients, unlimited blind bends and sickening views of rivers threading through abysses thousands of feet below, twists down to the coast. A notice at the entrance to the road warns the traveller by car on no account to attempt this climb before 11 am, by which time the fog had normally cleared, and the road had had time to dry. Walter beseeched us not to ignore the warning, and when called upon for an opinion the driver only mentioned in the most matter-of-fact way that his brother had gone over the top in the previous year. Tony told us that he had an appointment to keep down at Trujillo on the coast. Through lack of experience of the continent, what he did not know was that South Americans as a whole do not exaggerate in such warnings of danger. He wanted to push on, so at 9 am, over a wet road and through a light fog, we started the climb.

The road was steep from the start. Water dripped from overhanging ledges on to a black surface which glistened in places as if smeared with oil. From the outset our driver, Pedro, gave the impression of being almost excessively relaxed. He had the face of an Inca, with a forehead sloping steeply back in the admired fashion, and exaggerated by many loving mothers by binding a board tightly to the forepart of the cranium in early infancy. Walter, who sat in the front, was perturbed by the fact that Pedro never fully opened his eyes and occasionally let one hand drop from the wheel. When Walter asked him sternly why he never sounded his horn on bends, his reply implied that he felt that to do so called into question the arrangements of Providence. We came to the spot where his brother had lost his life, and stopped for a few seconds to peer down into the micro-landscape at the bottom of the chasm beneath us. He bowed slightly, smiled and said, 'He had completed his destiny.' Asked by Walter what had actually happened, he said that his brother had collided with a bus whose driver had fallen asleep. Did this often happen? Walter asked, and Pedro told him, not often, but sometimes. The high altitude made drivers drowsy, and in addition they were usually tired. It was possible to drop off sometimes for a second or two without running off the road. He had done it himself. At this point he mentioned a local custom by which passengers seated on the side of the car away from a precipitous edge often opened their doors on a bend to enable them to jump to safety in case of an uncontrollable skid.

From Quiravilca to Trujillo it was about eighty miles as the crow flies but the road wound through peaks which must have added half as much again to that distance. Buses managed to collect enough passengers in this tremendous wilderness to make the trip worthwhile, and there were more of them than I would have thought possible. On one occasion we were edging inch by inch past a crowded bus under the impassive stare of a dozen nursing mothers, pink-cheeked under their pantomime hats. Their menfolk had lashed themselves to the luggage racks on the roof. To our left we looked down on thousands of feet of vapour. 'Surely that driver is asleep,' I said to Pedro. 'No, sir,' was the reply. 'He is thinking. The eye of God is upon us all.'

Crossing the mountains had taken ten hours, for it was seven in the evening and pitch dark by the time we reached the coast road and the suburbs of Trujillo. This, I knew, was another occasion when the objectives of our Peruvian expedition, as planned, were to be pushed further from sight. Tony's presence in the country produced a degree of interest and excitement disproportionate, as he would have heartily agreed, to the importance of the happening. The fact was that this was a country where remarkably little occupied the press apart from the dismal merry-go-round of politics, an occasional coup or counter-coup, the stale old joke of projected reforms, religious and social news, the fluctuations of the stock market, horoscopes and lengthy obituaries. Now, at least, there was something new for the headlines.

Discouragingly, our stay in Trujillo had been scrupulously organised. A lunch had been arranged at the Golf Country Club. After that a display of local arts and crafts was to be followed by an equestrian parade led by a famous *rejoneador*, Hugo Bustamante, who would demonstrate the manoeuvres used in bull-fighting on horseback.

The situation at the Golf Country Club when we arrived was not promising. The exuberance of our hosts' welcome seemed overshadowed by preoccupation, and by the small crises that raged round them. It was whispered to us that a number of guests had turned up without bothering to be invited and that this had played havoc with the seating arrangements. Meticulous records of ancestry were kept in such Latin American towns, and a man with a forefather who had been included among Pizarro's licentious soldiery cannot be seated next to a man who has only made a lot of money or even, if he is enough of a snob, a great bullfighter. There was a problem, too, with the sun. The lunch was held in the club's gardens and when extra tables had to be brought they could not be squeezed into the limited shade, and some of the ladies could be heard complaining.

Amid these distractions, and momentarily unnoticed, Tony had slipped away to occupy a defensive position at one end of a bench, and called upon me to take the vacant seat on the other side. Asked why, he said it was to make sure that no woman could creep up on him and seat herself where she could be photographed. Such pictures, he said, were usually brought to the attention of 'his wife's sister'.

Next day we drove to Chanchan, the capital between 1150 and 1450 of the relatively short-lived Chimu empire, which spread through the deserts north of Trujillo to the borders of Ecuador. This city, the largest of all those of pre-Conquest South America, had come into being purely through technological discoveries in the area of irrigation. Previously the coastal peoples had lived well enough on the fish provided by this corner of the Pacific in superabundance; by way of dietetic variation in an area where rain never fell, wild potatoes could be dug out of the banks of the Mocha River. The great breakthrough happened when the decision was taken to dig canals diverting the water into fields, and what must have been many thousands of people got together to build a canal fifty miles in length across the desert to top up the failing water supply in the Mocha from the valley of the Chicama.

The Mocha area now became the market garden of North Peru and its huge and sudden affluence was reflected in this stunning city, an architect's dream of the day, and in some respects even of this day, too. It was designed and built by men of extraordinary vision and brand-new ideas. Geometry, supposed to have been invented in ancient Egypt, made its spontaneous appearance here and became almost a craze.

Development was carried out under the strictest of controls. Chanchan contains ten self-contained complexes, each based on a single model and a town in its own right. All buildings are symmetrical and rectangular and set precisely at right-angles to one another. The remnants of long straight walls still enclose its streets. These were decorated with monkeys and birds presented in an abstract woodland scene. Patches of this decoration that remain intact show no attempt at variation. The same animals and birds in the same frozen postures feature throughout.

Perhaps an enormous and unprecedented project of this kind, employing gangs of workers rather than devoted craftsmen, demanded standardisation. Chanchan was supremely functional, with every citizen correctly housed according to his status. There were no slums, this ancient city being enormously in advance in this respect of anything Europe of the Middle Ages had to offer. It was as devoid of excitement or surprise as a succession of identical concourses in an airport building. A citizen walking between these walls, with nothing to engage his interest but the same monkey, the same parrot, and the same bunch of leaves, must surely have preferred to stare straight ahead. A theory has been put forward that the straitjacket of architectural standardisation led eventually to decadence in the arts, the elimination of the individual masterpiece, and a sort of mass production in which, for example, a superb pottery head made to the order of a wealthy patron sits squarely upon the shoulders of one of a series of identical bodies.

In Trujillo we had been shown a famous collection of Mochica-Chimu effigy pots. Millions, possibly, of these ceramic masterpieces have been recovered from temples and graves, and there is no aspect of the potter's world that they do not portray. All forms of human and animal activity are registered: a female patient is visited by a doctor who, while examining her pelvis, caresses a breast. Another woman, naked, bends over a pot to wash her hair. A man smashes an enemy's head with his axe. Prisoners dragging what look like anchors are driven from the battlefield. A llama scratches its ear. Frogs copulate, a dentist knocks out a tooth, a parrot examines a newly hatched chick.

Sexual intercourse in its many varieties and every conceivable perversion is a favourite theme; the potters pried into every carnal secret with a searching eye for anatomical detail. Fellatio is scrupulously observed. Intercourse takes place between old men and young girls, and more remarkably between young men and old women. Three-in-a-bed situations are common. The Mochica-Chimu taste for sodomy was only curtailed by the coming of the Spanish Inquisition, and a famous pot shows a man sodomising a girl lying between her sleeping parents. What is extraordinary is that in this authoritarian, highly protective society, in which the death penalty was imposed for a number of crimes, such aberrations could escape even censure.

Before we left we were presented with a pot apiece. Mine took the form of a frog, dating from the period immediately before the Chimu kingdom collapsed under attack by the Incas. This fine animal, about six times life-size, has no part in the extreme realism of the Mochican potter's art. All minor physical details have been suppressed. The rugose skin has become featureless, polished hide, the legs have been hardly more than sketched in. What remains is halfway to an amphibious abstraction. There remains a face wearing a tolerant, quizzical expression and the slyest of smiles.

We arrived back in Lima in good time to fulfil an engagement upon which Anthony Walter appeared to set exceptional store. This was a visit to the most exclusive club in Peru. Walter told us that the secretary had added proudly that it was probably the most exclusive in the whole of South America, for it excluded positively anyone without an ancestor who had ridden with the small band of desperadoes who had destroyed the empire of the Incas, or was the possessor of less land than could be ridden round comfortably in three days.

My suspicion, going by something he had let drop, was that Walter was hoping to get a few paragraphs into the national press that would show Tony in a favourable light. I guessed that photographers would be kept out of sight for this occasion, and that any reporters allowed in would have guaranteed to make none of the usual references to what was rumoured to be an unsuccessful marriage.

Before setting out on this venture it occurred to me to consider with some doubt in my mind the way in which Tony had decided to dress. He had an almost obsessive preference for informality in the matter of attire. At this moment he presented himself in an open-necked sports shirt and tightly fitting, slightly flared trousers with a high waistband. This was his favourite outfit and had never failed to attract discreet glances when in the company of Peruvians who stuck to dark lounge-suits and club ties even in a desert environment. 'They can be extremely conservative in this part of the world,' I said. What was intended as a word of warning was lightly brushed aside. 'Can they?' he asked. 'Well, what of it?'

The Club Nacionál was located on the main street and had an unassuming entrance. Walter pressed the bell and I was slightly startled when the door was opened instantly by some kind of club servant with a face devoid of feeling or thought in a way that could have only been achieved by years of practice.

He was staring at Snowdon. Walter explained the purpose of our visit, and the man, still looking at Tony and speaking English with hardly a trace of an accent, said, 'Sir, you are not wearing a tie. I regret I am unable to admit you.'

Tony uttered a light, triumphant laugh. 'As it happens I was waiting for this,' he said. He pulled a scarf from his pocket and tied it round his neck. Nothing changed in the man's face. 'Sir,' he said, 'you are not wearing a jacket, I am still not allowed by the rules to ask you to enter.'

'I see,' Walter said. 'Well, this seems all rather unexpected. Is there someone I can talk to? Surely the secretary is available? We have an appointment with him.'

'I'm obliged to abide by the rules,' the man said. 'What I can do is to admit you to the club's sports area and I will arrange for someone to see you there.'

We exchanged blank looks. I was bewildered, as no doubt the others were, too. Had there ever existed a diplomatic precedent, I wondered, upon which Anthony Walter could draw for guidance as to how to handle an incident of this kind? And then a page boy was at our side indicating that we should follow him, and he led us out of the main entrance down a side-turning and back into the building again through a low narrow door.

For a moment all I could register was noise, but odour followed closely on the heels of this impression. We were in a huge room containing a swimming-pool, and a number of men in swim-shorts were chasing each other round the margin of this, hurling themselves or anyone they could catch up with into the water, with great, bellowing cries of pretended fury or of mirth, and constant use of the favourite Peruvian oath, 'I shit on God.' Every few seconds a high diver hit the water with a monstrous watery explosion that drowned for a split second the slap of running feet, the noise of horseplay, the oaths and the mocking laughter. The smell was of wet bodies, stale towels, chlorine and water.

A man in a tracksuit padded up, chewing with eyes averted. He grabbed a folded table and three chairs leaning against the wall, opened them up and nodded to us to take possession of them. Later he appeared with three cups of coffee on a tray. One saucer was full of spilt coffee and he snatched it away and splashed the coffee on the floor. He had placed the table against the wall next to a revolving door through which half-naked men came and went endlessly. Walter called back the man and asked him in a pause in the uproar if anyone knew that we were there, to which he replied, 'I haven't the faintest.' Five minutes, perhaps, passed while we looked at each other in silence, then Tony got up and left through the revolving door and we followed him.

We were to have spent an hour at most on this visit and the embassy had arranged that it was to be followed by a friendly and completely informal call – from which Walter and I had been excused – on one of the government ministers who was believed by the embassy to share with Tony an interest in the arts. This appointment Tony now decided he no longer wished to keep. 'I have a desperate headache,' he said to Walter. 'Could you possibly get in touch with the man and explain that I'm feeling a bit under the weather.'

We dropped him off at the hotel and drove on to the ministry. 'I have to admit I have a bit of a headache, too,' Walter said. 'I simply don't know what I'm going to say to the ambassador. It has been an appalling morning.'

'But does it really matter so very much whether he was shown round the club or not?' I asked.

'The trouble is that a member of the Royal Family has been snubbed. It's my job to see that things like this don't happen. I only hope and pray that this one doesn't get into the papers. Does he read them, by the way?'

'No, he asks me what they say.'

'And you tell him?'

'Yes, but I leave bits out.'

'Is he enjoying himself?'

'Most of the time. He seems exceptionally vulnerable to the kind of incident we've just experienced.'

'I wonder why.'

'I do too.'

I dropped Walter off at the ministry. 'Best of luck with the minister,' I said, and he made a face and shook his head.

Back at the hotel I found that the storm had blown itself out. We lunched in the centre of the main dining-room where Tony drew admiring glances and unhesitatingly agreed to autograph a menu passed to him by the waiter. So what had the upset been about? I found it mysterious that this intelligent man had been thrown so much off balance by the pinpricks of that morning. It had been a grotesque affair at the club, a scene from a play in the mood of *Waiting for Godot*, with a peer of the realm, a diplomat and a writer, hunched together, heads almost touching over cold coffee in a malodorous pandemonium, awaiting what? – the figment of a ceremony that had passed out of someone's mind. Surely this was less a cause for fury than a farcical memory to be put in store for the amusement of one's friends in years to come? Tony alternatively craved and detested the presence of others. He snubbed ambassadors and rebuffed hard-working pressmen. Our first supper in the hotel had been lugubriously consumed among the dust-sheets of a subterranean room, then suddenly and inexplicably next day we were upstairs among the Instamatics and the sycophantic smiles. What was to explain these violent fluctuations of mood?

Tony was the most intelligent, interesting and active member of the Royal Family, but even he may not have been wholly able to escape the syndrome consequent upon an over-long exposure to the inanities of palaces.

*

Most of the Latin American countries celebrated the feast of San Cipriano, patron of jugglers, magicians and the black arts, of which we had heard that something could be seen on the following night. In Salvador, Brazil, where the living came closer than elsewhere to the dead, it had been amalgamated with the day of All Souls, and was one of the most spectacular folk manifestations of the western world. But in Lima, we were assured, it was a hole-in-the-corner affair reflecting little of its impressive and rather sinister past. The voodoo performers of old had been wiped out by the police in combination with the Church. These were no longer secret, orgiastic meetings at which the gods of fire and water were worshipped. Here and there mediums in their trances still listened to the voices of those beyond the grave, but no-one any longer paid much attention to what they had to say. So in these days, was there anything worthwhile to be seen of the old carnival of death? we asked our driver, and he thought not. He had heard of a procession of devil-worshippers wearing masks in one of the remote barrios, he said, and he offered to take us to the place.

The slums of Lima were said to be the most extensive in Latin America and we made a cautious and difficult incursion into the labyrinth of shacks saturated with the shallow elation and deep melancholy of the poor. The lights of distant cooking fires and weak oil-lamps pricked through the gloom. With extreme care the driver skirted the banks of open sewers, young children mewed round us like kittens, boys beat drums, and the howling of dogs marked out a black horizon. There were no enchanters or processions here. We turned back into the town, finding ourselves immediately in a tiny, run-down square surrounded by tall wooden houses, and here, where the lights had come on again, a small but dense crowd had gathered to watch something that was happening, or had happened, out of sight from the car.

We pulled up and got out, pushing our way through to the front of the crowd where we found a boy of about twelve lying spreadeagled on the ground, and evidently unconscious. He had fallen, we were told, from the roof of the three-storey building under which he lay. A small, hushed murmur reached us from people commenting on this happening in an undertone, otherwise this could have been a church congregation. No-one moved.

I broke the silence. 'Have they phoned for a doctor? Is the ambulance coming?'

'No phone here,' a man said. 'No ambulance. No doctor.'

'Is the boy going to be left lying here? Why's nobody doing anything?'

'Nothing we can do. The doctors don't come out as far as this.'

It was only at this moment I realised that all the men had taken off their hats. 'We're here out of respect,' the man said.

Tony was looking over my shoulder. I picked the boy up in my arms. The crowd opened up for us and I carried him to the car. I was trying to hold him in such a way that his head was supported in case the neck-vertebrae had been damaged. 'We're taking him to hospital,' I told the driver.

It was a long drive through mean streets and under fogged stars. The hospital lay on the frontier of a development area with nothing in it finished through lack of funds, a bleak rectangular block among a thicket of pipes, wire and corrugated iron.

'No-one about,' the driver said. 'Very late. Maybe all gone home.' I sensed an undercurrent of relief. Nothing had to be done. He had been born in one of the slums where resignation was interchangeable with hope. We lowered the boy into the back seat where he lay snoring softly, and made our way to the door.

We rang the bell. A wan, dust-blurred light showed behind the window, there was a scraping of footsteps, followed by the clunk of a bolt being drawn, then a cautious face appeared in the opening of the door.

This, as the door opened inch by inch, we saw to be a woman dressed in a garment that was something between a nun's habit and a nurse's uniform. I explained what had happened and she shook her head. 'No-one here. Come back tomorrow,' she said, and was about to close the door when Tony pushed past her and I followed. 'This boy is dying,' I said. 'He fell from the top of a house.' She joined the tips of her fingers together, shook her hand violently, then drew an imaginary line in front of my face. 'Everything locked,' she said. 'Nothing we can do at this time of night.' She had set her teeth, and now thrust forward her jaw.

I translated this for Tony's benefit and he said in a loud voice, 'I insist on seeing a doctor. We will not go away until a doctor comes. Tell her to bring a doctor immediately.'

His words, clear and firm, had an immediate effect. The woman's clenched fingers opened, and her jaw muscles relaxed. When she spoke it was in a different and reasonable voice. 'It will take half an hour for the doctor to come,' she said.

'Go and get him,' Tony said. 'Tell him we are waiting here, and that he must come at once.'

There was no doubt that she understood, and that she had surrendered to an imperative that was not to be evaded. She gestured to us to fetch the boy from the car and by the time we had carried him through the door she was ready with a trolley, in which he was laid in such a way that she could support his head, while we wheeled him down a passage into what was unmistakably the casualty ward.

A single switch provided relentless illumination of our surroundings. It was clear that the ward had been instantly abandoned at the end of the working day and that the nursing staff, the orderlies and porters, and those who did the clearing up, had dropped everything and fled in a dash for freedom. Hair-clippings, bloodied swabs and the debris of food were strewn across surfaces of cracked tiles. A hosepipe like a moribund serpent curled across the floor, its nozzle in a shallow, pinkish pool which proved that a final sluicing-down had not been well done. A small man in a surgeon's coat came through the door at the end of the ward and approached us. He had a white, lightly tobacco-stained beard, and hands almost as small as a monkey's. He bent over the trolley, lifted an eyelid, and felt with a tiny hand for the heartbeat. His expression was kindly and concerned. 'Is unconscious,' he said in English. He shook his head.

'How bad is he?' Tony asked. 'Can you save him?'

'Is necessary an operation,' the doctor said. 'But first X-rays and observation. We cannot work in dark. When we have information, operation can take place. Now no radiologist persons, no specialist doctor.'

'So there's nothing whatever to be done?'

'Tonight nothing possible. This operation very difficult, only one specialist doctor can make this operation. Tomorrow at eight you may telephone for news. But now nothing.'

Tony was extremely concerned about this incident. We rang the hospital first thing in the morning but were unable to speak to anyone who could tell us what was happening, nor, for a while, to anyone who could even locate the patient. Some hours later we were able to speak to a doctor who could only say that no operation had taken place, and such were the problems of Spanish medical terminology that only one thing seemed clear: that in this case any operation would be a difficult one. Tony had formed the opinion – perhaps not unreasonably in a situation where this boy, had we not intervened, would have been left to die by the side of the road – that even now his chances of survival were slight, and he approached Anthony Walter with a suggestion. This was that the patient should be flown to England for the operation, and while Mr Morgan agreed that it would be a nice thing if it could be done, it was inevitable that the question should arise of who was to bear the cost, and I concluded that the idea was dropped.

Peru had not been an outstanding success, for we had seen little of the real country. A journalist may pass unperceived among the crowd and is sometimes rewarded by experiences from which the foreign traveller is carefully steered away. Tony's appearances in the headlines ruled out this possibility so that in the end what came to be written about Peru was hardly more startling than the information offered in the average travel brochure.

A few days later it was time for me to move on. Tony appeared in no hurry to return to London, deciding in the mean while to visit an uncle in the Caribbean, where he invited me to join him, but I had commitments elsewhere. Minutes before my plane took off from Lima Airport I was subjected to a baffling experience. A stewardess called me to the plane's open door where three Indians stiff in well-pressed suits, begloved and with highly polished shoes waited to see me. The man in the centre held a cushion on which rested three tiny white strips of bone. It was a moment of acutely mixed emotions in which embarrassment predominated. There was no way of knowing what these men wanted with me although it was clear that their presence was allied to the drama of the injured boy. It was evident, too, that an operation had taken place, but what had been the result? These obsidian Indian faces gave no clue to the answer. This was a ceremony in which I was invited to join, but was it in mourning a death or of thanksgiving for salvation? No-one in this plane, the stewardess at my back assured me, understood Quechua. This was a silence that could not be broken. Could it be that these slivers of bone had been brought as an offering in gratitude for my action, which I should accept? Since I would never know, all I could do, stiffening the muscles of my face in an attempt to match an Indian absence of expression, was to touch the bones with the tips of my fingers which the Indians watched unblinkingly. Then we all bowed and withdrew.

I suspected that the Indian boy's fate was the one episode of the Peruvian journey that would always remain in my mind. Had he survived the operation, or had he died? Despite all subsequent enquiries the enigmatic presence of the three Quechuas – still visible as tiny, motionless figures at the edge of the runway as the plane took off – was never solved.

Chapter Fourteen

WRITING IN THE influential *El Mundo* (Madrid) back at the end of the sixties, a well-known Spanish journalist expressed the opinion that Spain had gone through greater changes in the previous twenty years than in a whole preceding century, despite the disastrous civil war it contained. This he attributed to the influence of mass tourism upon all aspects of the national life. In 1950, with the war at an end, Spain was a country drained of resources of every kind. To some extent its culture had been preserved by poverty and isolation, but this, too, began to lose its uniqueness as the great flood of foreigners poured in exhibiting life-styles so different from those of the Spanish themselves. Most foreigners remained untouched by their brief contact with the Spanish way of life, but the delicate and subtle culture of the host country suffered increasing damage by its exposure to alien customs.

The social life of Farol, simple as it had seemed to me back in the fifties, proved on closer inspection to be like the mechanism of a fine watch in comparison with that of my own country. The people here were bound together by a network of blood relationships, age-old traditions, a religious philosophy which although strong was only in part Christian, and continuous emotional investment in each others' lives. Courtship and marriage customs were more intricate than ours. At betrothal, for example, a boy would be expected to set about building with his own hands the matrimonial home, and five to seven years would normally pass before this was completed, and the marriage could be celebrated.

This was the institution most undermined by sudden contact with the outside world. There was no divorce in Spain, and in so far as affairs existed outside marriage they were conducted with the utmost reticence. The thing that most amazed the Spanish when the foreigners from the north first came upon the scene was the openness and flexibility of their sexual relations. These freedoms they were bound in the end to envy and copy, often with disastrous effect.

Love in the new style provoked its disruptions, but once again, money was the root of all evils, for it was easy money that the foreigners brought with them. Hotels and bars to accommodate the newcomers opened in Farol, and in these the tourists spent what to the Spanish seemed inconceivable sums of money. One of my friends was a carpenter who carried out minor repairs to houses and boats. His wage, fixed by the fascist state at a time when the peseta was 30 to the pound, was 34 pesetas a day.

A young fisherman might average 20 pesetas, and a senior who managed a boat with a crew perhaps 40 pesetas. Due to the sudden tourist influx there was a demand in Farol for waiters. Although it was a form of employment at first considered demeaning, an evening's tips for a fisherman prepared to grit his teeth and take it on could amount to more than he earned in a week in his battles with the sea. Slowly but inevitably, proud men who like their ancestors had gained their living from the sea, learned the correct and inconspicuous way of holding out their hands for tips.

Next, the wholly new phenomenon of inflation made its appearance in Spain. The horde of affluent foreigners put up prices, producing a new kind of poverty squeezing out all those men left in useful occupations, and compelling them to surrender to easy money. Suddenly my friend of old, Dr Seduction, became impoverished when the fishermen (now waiters with the usual stomach trouble) could afford the taxi-fare to have themselves treated at Figueras, where medical science was known to be more up-to-date, even if enormously more expensive. In Farol of old, although there were no social classes, the best of the fishermen were much respected for their skills. Now they were fewer and poorer, but suddenly a class based upon wealth had been created. These were the families owning sea-front property, once considered of little worth but now saleable for development at astronomical figures. It was these families who suddenly came into prominence and learned to enjoy all the privileges and satisfactions of bourgeois society. In a decade Spain had at last caught up with the rest of Europe.

In the late seventies I slipped back to see what sort of a mess development had made of Farol. The first problem was to establish the position of the original village, of which I was to discover no trace had been left. A complicated one-way traffic system led eventually to a wide beach, once locally famous for its hundreds of thousands of translucent pebbles of various colours strewn through the sand, avidly collected by the children and stored in glass jars as 'precious stones'. Part of this was now the municipal car park, and if this happened to be full, as it was on the occasion of my visit, the only remedy was to follow the helpful arrows and park outside the town. Fish were no longer caught in Farol and all the handsome old fishing boats painted in purple and yellow were no more. Skiffs with glass bottoms carried visitors to view 'aquatic gardens' furnished with coral from the south seas fastened to the sea-bed, now cleared of its original rocks.

It was the same story wherever I went. In 1983 I visited Thailand for the *Sunday Times,* travelling through much of the country, including Chiengmai where thirty years earlier I had stayed at the headquarters of the Borneo Company. Again, the change was vast. At the time of my first visit the only tourists were a handful of foreigners who did the rounds of the pagodas in a maximum of two days before catching the train back to Bangkok. Now the local newspaper announced with some pride that 120 tourist agencies had opened in the town to cope with the huge influx of visitors, largely on trekking holidays into the once remote and 'wholly unspoiled' areas along the Burmese frontier to the north. An inevitable bottle-neck had developed, for there were far more foreign visitors than the total population of the twenty or so primitive villages to which they were to be taken. Cases arose where several parties bound for the same hamlet renowned for its isolation and the strangeness of its customs might find themselves in a queue while the villagers dealt with those ahead of them with all the speed they could muster. Business was stimulated by a variety of devices. There were up-market tours which included the smoking of a pipe of opium with a headman. The trouble here, I was told, was that only the poorest quality opium was provided, frequently producing alarming effects. There was a shortage of headmen, too, since most villages were too poor to support such ceremonial personalities. In case of emergency, some impressive-looking fraud would be quickly imported from Chiengmai to go through the motions of authority, or the tourist guide might make a point of carrying with him an old-fashioned mandarin-style gown hired from an antique dealer to dress up a poverty-stricken villager as a tribal authority.

Imposture, then, was the backbone of this business, and Chiengmai now both created and participated in a myth which sadly diminished the grace and style it had earlier possessed. The tours had now actually run out of genuine villages, which meant that by the coming season more imitations would have to be built. They were also on the point of running out of genuine mountain people to occupy them. In this case, I was informed, they might turn to Burmese refugees, or even to the most presentable beggars to be recruited from the city and rigged out in mountain-style garb.

A social and aesthetic climate in which fake peasants are paid to be photographed by foreigners in fake villages diminishes the attractions of any country, but the worldwide reputation of this once most charming of lands has been tarnished by the sex-tourism for which it has become notorious. The Thais have always exhibited realism in sexual matters and few brands of satisfaction are more easily obtained. It is probably this openness and liberality that has helped to protect them from the inversions and perversions self-inflicted by so many other peoples, in particular the Nordics arriving in droves in search of pleasures banned elsewhere by law.

The sex industry went into top gear at the spur of the Vietnam war, when 46,000 American troops rested here in the intervals of combat. Up to that point the art of healing as practised in Thailand was based upon an ancient conception that thirty-six bodily parts responded to massage. This had been practised since antiquity in numerous temples throughout the country, and prayers and invocations accompanied the physical ministrations. The Americans exposed to this novel treatment passed on their enthusiasm to their comrades who were quick to apply for sick leave. In consequence, even before the end of the war numerous massage parlours had opened up. Now 750,000 Thai women are said to be employed in this once basically religious exercise, in surroundings where the sounds of prayer are rarely heard.

From this blameless start, prostitution on a large scale rapidly developed and, in response to a Western taste for make-belief, often adopted bizarre forms. The Patpong and Petchiburi areas of Bangkok, for example, draw tourist crowds that outnumber the local populace and give the impression of being in revolt from normality.

It is hard to find a place of entertainment where strangeness does not pervade the atmosphere. Entering a bar one may be served by a bar-girl who wears absolutely nothing but a belt of silk round her waist, or instead a school uniform or perhaps a wedding dress complete with train. In one restaurant topless waitresses career from table to table on roller skates, and in another guests – whether they like it not – must actually expect to be fed.

The great stark buildings in which the multi-faceted edifice of sex is to be explored in modern style appear on their outside as copies of supermarkets, and only the stacked trolleys are missing. One enters to encounter the central feature of all such establishments in the shape of a well-lit room behind a glass screen and within it a row of dignified ladies seated on an example of what must be the largest sofas in the world. All wear pink evening gowns, are substantial without being fat and have expressions described by the *Bangkok Post* as of maternal indulgence. The illumination is as artful as the most up-to-date provided by Tesco to display to the best effect their vegetables and fruit – and these women, too, seem to glow. Each lady has a number pinned to her dress, and can be reached by dialling this on a telephone in the surrounding ambulatory. In this, potential clients prowl uncertainly, conversing in low voices in a cool twilight. The atmosphere is passionless and even institutional, and this shortfall of romantic inspiration is emphasised by the presence of an 'information and advice desk' staffed by female employees in airport-style uniforms. Nevertheless, the appetite for fantasy survives. Of this place the *Bangkok Post* reports that the most popular of the available pampering facilities involves dressing up and that any of the fifteen ladies seated on the long sofa and smiling a maternal invitation can convert herself in a matter of seconds into a stern headmistress, a nun of a strict order, or even an angel with wings.

Thirty odd years before, I had visited Pattaya in the company of somebody from our embassy who introduced me to a singular sport. In those days, like Torremolinos, Pattaya was a charming fishing village, with brightly painted boats strewn among nets drying on an immaculate beach. Inland from the village was a wide area of lagoons and creeks which attracted a great population of fish resembling the mud-skipper. They had developed the extraordinary ability to transfer themselves from one body of unconnected water to another by propelling themselves overland for fairly short distances on their fins. The sport was to lie in wait with a gun and shoot the fish as soon as they began these exertions. Many sportsmen travelled the fifty miles from Bangkok to amuse themselves by these unrewarding assassinations, although the flavour of the fish was irremediably affected by the mud in which they lived. The fishermen of old were infatuated with flying the high bellicose kites they made themselves, and for those who had finally escaped the boredom of shooting fish, there was no better way to relax than drinking a beer in the village's single fretwork-adorned bar and watching the regular evening battle between the kites.

As was to be expected, the Pattaya of the eighties retained no trace of the entrancing coastal settlement of the past. The town had come under heavy criticism by the *Bangkok Post* which said that foreign visitors had been alarmed to notice that quite often the smartly turned-out police patrolling the streets seemed to be drunk. More alarming still was the habit of the drivers of police cars, who were also assumed to be intoxicated. When passing each other, they took their hands off the steering wheel to press them together in the polite salutation that accompanied a slight bow.

Despite its 400 hotels, its fizzing nightlife and its almost hysterical pursuit of modernity, Pattaya had not quite recovered from the fascination with the American Far-West that had inspired the total rebuilding of Hat Yai as a replica of the old Dodge City, based on thousands of photographs taken in the last century. The town still had a few swing-door saloons, boarded side-walks and even hitching posts, although no horse had been seen in its streets for at least twenty years. When disputes arose, people still drew guns in a threatening manner, as I saw for myself, and occasionally shot each other. My experience of movie-style violence happened after I had taken a room for the night in a small hotel and settled for a nightcap in the bar. A man at a nearby table suddenly pulled out a huge revolver and pointed it at the man seated opposite. He was immediately overpowered and disarmed, a shouting match subsided in a matter of minutes, the dispute ended in embraces and smiles. When shepherded to my room, I pointed to several bullet holes in the floor. 'What happened?' I asked. 'Anybody hurt?' The boy smiled. 'Maybe two guys don't see each other for a long while. They shoot in the air like they say good to see you again. They don't fight. They happy.'

Escaping from Pattaya with its pampering and gun-slinging, I went to Phuket in Thailand's far south. It had been praised by friends who had been there only five years before, but by now I had learned that remote and reputedly unspoilt islands have become the most vulnerable to attack by the ugliness of our times. Phuket offered an extreme example of the strange impulses of the escapist who goes in search of the exotic yet cannot free himself from dependence upon a familiar background. South-east Asia is the scene of soft colours and gentle, blending shapes. What remains intact of the largest of Thailand's islands offers beauty of a subtle and intricate kind. There is a grey pallor in the blue of its lakes, and often a lavender mistiness across the sky. Its native houses are elegant structures of wood, built often in the shade spread by the dark, mossy foliage of a casuarina. Why should a Swiss enterprise in the village of Paton have added a breeze-block and cement suburb of mountain chalets designed to support loads of Alpine snow, and the Germans a Bavarian-style Bierkeller and Speisehaus, outside which an employee in lederhosen stands to hold up a menu. Inevitably the British are here, too, with a mock-Tudor pub in which the half-timbered structure is of concrete artfully painted to pass as wood.

The only obvious Thai undertaking was a tea-house in an old village building, which at least suited its background, although there was something in the atmosphere of the place and a familiarity in the manner of the woman who served me that left me perturbed. I finished the tea and got up and the woman came through the curtain dividing the tea-house proper from the family quarters at the rear. She beckoned to me and I followed her through to pay. The room at the rear held a wash-tub full of crockery, a thin cat, a parrot in a cage and an unmade bed. There was also a young girl in a grubby flowered frock with her head turned away, and the woman gestured at the girl and at myself in a way that was unmistakable. She then held up both hands for me to count the fingers, following this by two fingers held up of a single hand. I shook my head, paid her for the tea and went out. Down the road I stopped for a beer at Karon among the ironed-out dunes, the drained marshes, the streams corseted with cement, and the hills sliced away. It was here that I ran into my first British ex-pat, and I described my recent experience. He was both scornful and amused.

'They do it all the time,' he said. 'They tell you these girls are twelve to make the sale, but they're most likely to be fourteen or fifteen. She ought to be reported. It's something the police really crack down on here.'

A hundred yards out at sea, one of the new 125 hp Dragon Boats brought down from Bangkok 'to liven things up a bit', my friend said, went howling past. He jammed his fingers in his ears and I waited until he took them out. 'Reported for child prostitution, you mean?' I asked.

'No,' he said. 'For offering sexual services under false pretences. It really gets up their noses. It gives the place a bad name.'

Chapter Fifteen

I went to India four times in all, the first two of these journeys being at the beginning of the sixties when I wrote about India's takeover of the French colonial enclave of Pondicherry, and that of the Portuguese in Goa.

Pondicherry provided by far the more interesting of these experiences. I stayed in the Ashram of Sri Aurobindo, which following the Indian philosopher's death had passed into the firm control of his wife, known as the Mother. She was a little old French woman of extremely dominant personality who had come by a large number of Western disciples, most of them members of the English upper class, and of superior education. Their search for enlightenment in the ashram caused them almost to welcome physical discomfort and even to view the possession of wealth as a disadvantage. Many of them had placed all their worldly goods in the Mother's care, and were happy that she could be persuaded to dole out small sums in cases when some rare emergency might have arisen. One disciple had been a fashion photographer and, believing that his skills might be utilised by the ashram, asked for permission to buy a camera. The Mother assured him that a camera would be found for him without going to the expense of buying one, and sure enough, within days a new disciple arrived with a camera which he was assured would no longer be of use, and this was handed over to the photographer.

The ashram raised funds through vegetables grown in a garden surrounded by a high wall and guarded by armed ghurkas inherited from the British Army, and in these the disciples worked joyously and without pay for twelve hours a day. In the evening they squatted in a refectory to recite mantras before tackling vegetable curry with their hands. As a visitor who might possibly be persuaded to stay on, I received indulgent treatment, eating at table and sleeping not on a straw palliasse but a bed. As a supplement, perhaps, to sparse rations, there was an evening ceremony for which the disciples were assembled in a row to be fed by the Mother with nuts. When introduced to her on one of these occasions I was told by an attendant that I might take her sari between thumb and forefinger and count to five, in the course of which a discharge of power would pass from her into me. This, I was warned, was so strong that I might faint, and when the moment came an ex-British army regimental sergeant-major in charge of the ceremony placed himself behind me to catch me if I fell. There was no noticeable transfer of power in my case.

In a single instance in my life have I felt myself a subject of hypnotism. This was on leaving the ashram at the end of my stay, when I checked out through a kind of guardhouse, in which were offered for sale the whole gamut of Sri Aurobindo's philosophical works. Despite knowing full well I should never read a sentence of any one of them, I bought the whole collection, and lugged them with some difficulty and at substantial overweight cost back to England. I presented these books to Oliver Myers, whose eyes glistened with gratitude as he filled two suitcases with them.

After Pondicherry and the rapturous disciples, Goa was calm to the point, almost, of sluggishness. The predominant problem of the near-empty Central Hotel was the thievishness of invading crows with beautiful amber eyes that stole the guests' sun-glasses. The manager warned me that the town offered little in the way of entertainment. Night-clubs were banned, the cinema showed Western films only when a minimum audience of fifty could be rounded up. Otherwise there was snake-charming. Jose Custodio

Faria, who discovered the doctrine of hynotic suggestion, had been born here, and a club of Goanese hypnotists held regular meetings and practised his techniques on each other. The principal industry was the smuggling of gold carried in the bodily orifices into India, and caravans of young girls were daily marshalled to cross the frontier. Otherwise, a small army of the not-quite-destitute searched the beach for slivers of mother-of-pearl cast up by every tide, from which the handsome windows of Goa were made.

Coming back to the subject of entertainment, the hotel's manager said I should not fail to see the mummified body of St Francis Xavier in the church of the Bom Jesus. Until a few years before it had attracted pilgrims to Goa from all parts of the Catholic world. Lately there had been a falling-off as a result of the common trick by which persons pretending to kiss the saint gnawed off small portions of the remains and carried them away in their mouths, so that now not much was left.

By the time I returned to Goa in 1990 little remained that was recognisable of the old city. A laundromat replaced the Central Hotel with its jewel-eyed crows and the one-time white sheen of mother-of-pearl on the beach was no more. The iron statue of the most compelling of all hypnotists had gone for scrap, snake-charmers were banned as detrimental to the nation's image, and although smuggling flourished as before, it no longer involved gold but dope. Of the Saint's remains only an arm that had been severed and sent to Rome for application to the Pope's piles was still on view. In the old days all the lights of Goa had gone out at 10 pm on the dot. Now five cinemas blasted the night with the broadcast music and outcry of violent Indian films.

I was on holiday with my family and had chosen the north coast of Goa because I had been told it was relatively unspoiled. This might have been the case when my friends had visited it the year before, but it was no longer true because Indians are the fastest builders in the world, and holiday apartments were going up in a matter of weeks. What interested me about this upsurge of building activity was that most of it was carried out by young girls imported from Rajasthan. They worked a twelve-hour-day in the great heat, and were crammed at night into plastic shelters roughly four feet in height. These were bonded labourers who in theory did not exist because the Indian Act of Parliament known as the Bonded Labour System Abolition Act, 1976, had ensured their release. Nevertheless, in 1990, precisely at the time when we were in Goa, the Anti-Slavery Society published a statement that 'the majority of bonded child labourers, 20 million, are in India'. These cheerful, smiling little girls were some of them.

How many Europeans buying a cheap holiday home in Goa realise that it has been built by slave labour?

Converted to Voltaire's viewpoint by a personal experience of primitives, I had developed a near-obsession with the opportunity to study them in Central India. Here, although they had escaped the attention of the travel writers, I believed that I should discover remnants of those aboriginal peoples thrust into the background by the Aryan invasion and the invention of the caste system.

From preliminary enquiries I was to learn to my surprise that the Central Provinces still contained as many as 54 million tribal peoples, many of them at a bow-and-arrow level of development, and in possession of many of their ancient customs. The area of greatest interest was the unspoiled region of Madhya Pradesh, but on my arrival in India I was to learn that governmental problems with the tribals had led to Bastar being temporarily out of bounds. Orissa, I was told, would be the next best thing, sheltering in its mountains and forests tribes that had even remained nomadic and of which little was known.

In Bhubaneswar, the Orissa capital, I had the extraordinary good luck of meeting a young Brahmin, Ranjan, who had spent part of his childhood in tribal areas and spoke three of their languages. He was free to travel, he said, and mapped out an itinerary through 1,500 miles of territory seldom visited except by government officials, in the course of which we should see something of seventeen tribes. It turned out that an additional inducement in coming on this trip was a romantic involvement with a Paraja girl whom he was anxious to see once again before deciding whether or not to drop out of bourgeois Indian life by marrying her, renouncing his caste and settling in the Paraja village.

Ranjan found a car and a driver and we set out. 'Every experience of this journey,' I was to write, 'contradicted the image of India as presented on the films.' India has always been shown as overbrimming with people. Here it was lonely. Having left the main coastal road with its unceasing procession of lorries, there was no traffic at all except a single car in an occasional small town. There was in general nowhere to stay, nowhere to eat, and with Naxalite revolutionaries scattered through the hills it was not particularly safe.

The last car vanished and we saw the first of the Saora villages, cool places in a hot country, with the roof thatches sloping to within three feet of the ground, converting verandahs into deep havens of shade in which the Saoras, wearing sparkling white cottons, took their ease. These villages were dazzlingly clean. Some of the Saoras had decorated their walls with spirited naïve paintings on which magic symbols were scattered through scenes which might include a goddess, a plane piloted by an elephant, a man on a bicycle, a tiger, a village bus. There were no crops to be seen, instead a grove of pines dribbled their sap into bottles hung under incisions in the bark. This would become alcohol, and Ranjan said that the only form of crime in such tranquil villages was the theft of alcohol-making equipment or the alcohol itself. The equivalent of a policeman in a white toga leaned against the trunk of one of the palms, apparently asleep.

Such were the villages of the Saoras and after them the Kondhs, in the first of which a travelling medium was going from house to house offering to lay troublesome ghosts. In another house several jungle fowls sat on clutches of eggs in decorated baskets, soothed by a boy crouched nearby who played to them on a flute.

Ranjan, who was deeply attached to the Kondhs, described himself as particularly touched by their custom of building their villages so that the occupants of a house could stand at its entrance to greet their neighbours face to face across the street with the rising of the sun.

Indian tribal society is immediately observed as a tolerant and easy-going minority compared with the caste-dominated majority that encircles it. These primitive peoples have steadfastly rejected caste – the cruellest of burdens borne by the Hindu population. There are no crippling dowries to be provided for their daughters. As in all primitive societies, there is no drive to accumulate possessions, and therefore no rich and no poor. All students of the situation Ranjan and I were now observing at first hand have been impressed though often shocked by the relative freedom of tribal sex relationships, most strikingly exemplified in the areas where we now found ourselves. In 1947 Elwin Verrier wrote a book called *The Muria and their Ghotul* about the custom of a tribe in Bastar by which on reaching puberty the young of both sexes were expected to sleep together, praised for frequent changes of partners and criticised or even fined for over-exclusive relationships. Ranjan insisted that similar practices existed among the tribes in Orissa, in particular the Kondhs. 'But do not question them about it,' he warned me. 'They will be embarrassed.'

Celebrated in Orissa for the peculiarity of their sex and marriage customs are the Koyas, a flourishing, handsome and intelligent people we visited in their principal village, Bhejaguda, wedged into the Malakangiri hills. Among their many gods is a divine earthworm, and their unique sexual arrangements involve a union in which the wife must always be substantially older than her husband. One such couple was pointed out to us: a boy of about thirteen was trotting at the heels of an imposing wife of thirty-odd. The wife is supposed to wait for her husband to be full-grown before intercourse takes place, in the meanwhile guarding her virginity. Of this, after we had been in conversation with some Koyas who seemed highly amused by the topic, Ranjan translated. 'If a woman shows some impatience, her father-in-law may be called upon to do the necessary.'

The Koyas, like many tribal peoples living in circumstances in which civilised stresses are unknown, suffer from occasional attacks of boredom, and are delighted at the opportunity to fuss over strangers like us who drop in from time to time. They had grand manners, and were at pains to put their visitors at ease, and as soon as we came in sight a number of splendid matriarchs in crimson togas appeared at their doors and received us with expressions of excitement and enthusiasm. A large bed was carried into the street and covered with a clean mat and we were invited to make ourselves comfortable. More beds were then dragged out of neighbouring houses and upon these the women settled themselves to face us and unleash a barrage of smiling chatter, dealing, said Ranjan, with matters of general interest such as bovine sickness and the possession of a hen with four feet.

It was the women who mattered here. Someone had dashed off for the palm-toddy. We emptied the beakers pressed upon us, after which the women drank heartily, followed by a few patriarchs on the fringe of the gathering. What we took to be young husbands formed a meek background row, and were the last to be served. Ranjan pointed out that several had downy growths on their upper lips, achieved, he said, by the application of a kind of mud, to which were added the droppings of certain birds.

We happened to arrive when the Koyas were celebrating a ritual period of abstention from work, except for the making of alcoholic liquor. The principal activities at this time included the consumption of neat palm-toddy and the nightly staging of theatrical entertainments. To attempt to work – as a few sometimes did – was seen as anti-social and punished by severe public criticism.

A shortage of beds meant that a number of women were compelled to stand. To me they seemed to be swaying, and perhaps drunk. I mentioned this to Ranjan who put this to the headman who was also somewhat unsteady. He opened one eye with difficulty, and agreed that this was the case. 'It makes a good impression with your friends,' he told Ranjan, 'if you let your hair down at a time like this.'

In this situation it was a matter of politeness to ask what god the headman worshipped, and he said, between hiccups, 'the Divine Earthworm, creator of the world. There are many more, I am told twenty-three, although I cannot count myself. The Earthworm we borrowed from the Kondhs and are obliged to return it after this celebration. We have also two or three gods on loan from the Saoras, the most useful being a stone.' Ranjan showed surprise and, reaching for another toddy, the headman said, 'It is all a matter of belief. If you believe a stone is a god, then it is one.'

We had taken sweets for the children, and their mothers formed them into an orderly queue to receive them. They were a gaudily wrapped commercial product with a sharp synthetic flavour and the children sucked them reverently, frequently taking them out of their mouths to prolong the pleasure. Occasionally I noticed a child who appeared to stagger. I asked Ranjan if the boy could possibly be tipsy. The headman, blinking with difficulty, thought this over. He pointed out to us that the lined-up jugs of liquor were kept carefully out of their way, but explained that the Koya women breast-fed their children up to five years of age. 'There is palm-toddy in these women's milk,' he said.

The theme encouraged the headman to philosophise. 'There's no sickness here,' he told Ranjan. 'The white people who come here offer us medicines, but we don't take them. We listen to the Earthworm's advice in these matters. He tells us to enjoy life, and that we do. Some of us expect to live for ever.'

Ranjan, toying with the romantic possibility of turning his back on the strain and stress of life in Bhubaneswar, marrying a Paraja girl and adopting the genial life-style of a Paraja village, had collected facts and figures that supported the divine advice. The average life-expectation of the non-tribal Indian of the capital of Orissa was fifty-seven years; that of a village tribesman was sixty-three years. The Koyas did even better than this, he had discovered, by another five years. Sometime during the next two weeks we should reach the Parajas; by then, Ranjan assured me, his decision would be made. How would he cope with the problem of ritual idleness, he wondered. It had been published in a government report that the Koyas only worked 1½ hours a day, and he suspected that the situation among the Parajas would be roughly the same.

Leisure, envied in the bustling cities of India, was in unlimited supply in these country places. Few people could have made better use of it than such tribals as the Saoras and the Kondhs who were enabled by it to fill their lives with the satisfactions of art. Almost all these primitives had developed some absorbing skill. The Saoras and Kondhs were by any standards great painters and wood-carvers. The Parajas and Godbas (who unaccountably occupy the same villages, although they are racially and temperamentally quite different) spent much of the time rebuilding and improving their houses – in one case rectangular and the other round. The Mirigans, living in extreme isolation on the frontiers of unexplored jungle, took young parakeets from their nests, so outrageously spoiling them that they could hardly be separated from their foster-parents who were to be seen with the birds fluttering round their heads wherever they went. The Mirigans carved, too, but in their case only tigers and elephants, explaining that this was no more than an act of homage, which they believed helped to protect themselves from attack. The elephants remained a problem, for they sniffed the Mirigans' alcohol supplies at a great distance, continually raided the stores kept under the roofs, and were enraged and incited by the liquor into acts of vandalism such as tearing off thatches and butting down walls.

The Lanjia Saora village of Potasing was the undisputed capital of the naïve art of tribal India, producing *anitals* of the most complex kind, painted after locally famous artists sit alone in a dark place waiting for an image to form. There are special societies of women who are entrusted with the painting of certain patterns, and, as in many parts of tribal India, the women of Potasing cover the interior walls of their houses, and sometimes even the surface of the street, with exuberant and complicated designs. Until the recent past, it was the men who carved the doors, door-posts and lintels.

The Indian government is to be praised for its exclusion of American genocidal missionary sects from any part of its territories, but it is said that it has tolerated the assault by Lutherans and Catholics upon tribal customs and religious beliefs. We were a year too late in arriving in Potasing, the Athens of the Indian primitive world, for the Lutherans were already at work, with depressing effect. We were told that they had descended on the village in an epidemic of malaria and an absence of medicine. The missionaries had plenty of Nivaquine but the magic tablets were on offer only in exchange for conversion. Our informant complained of unfairness. 'We have twenty-three gods. Most of them have been kind and useful to us. The missionary is asking us to exchange twenty-three for one, plus a month's supply of Nivaquine. It is unreasonable.'

Inexplicably, as in this case, evangelists in the Third World see godliness as incompatible with the pursuit of art, so the art has to go, and the Lutherans in Potasing worked with zeal to destroy all the pictures that could be found, and defaced or ripped out innumerable carvings. The effect was all the more grim because areas of woodwork where the carving had been stripped away were often patched in with metal or concrete.

People had also been compelled or persuaded to part with their beloved *anitals*. A government-appointed postmaster – who also managed to be the Lutheran representative on the spot – took us to see the one remaining example of Sudha Saora art, now kept in a locked house. It was very large, painted in white upon a red background, recalling the paintings of palaeolithic hunters on the walls of caves. Soara manikins pranced and capered in ceremonial hats under ceremonial umbrellas, rode elephants and horses, pedalled bikes and were carried by fan-waving attendants in procession. They played musical instruments of the past but shouldered the guns of the present. Gourdfuls of wine awaited their pleasure, displayed like Christmas gifts on the branches of palms. The postmaster shook his head in disbelief at this relic of the wanton past. Before Potasing's desecration there had been no locks on doors throughout tribal India, but the destroyers of art had insisted on locks, and four out of five houses in this strangely deserted village were locked up. I asked why this should be.

'They are working in the fields,' the postmaster said. 'They are very active in employment.'

'But this is an in-between season, with nothing to do.'

'If there is willingness to work it is always to be found. In the old times people were lazy. They were drinking much alcohol. That was bad. We have cut down those palm trees that were giving that wine. For those who were carving wood, we are making enquiries. Soon they may be making toys for shops.'

This, then, was the struggle faced by the tribals in India. The world of art for art's sake, of amateur dramatics, self-entertainment and the long, lazy summer was slipping away, and the world of regular work in the employment of others, of money and buying and selling, was about to reach them by the roads to be built and the airfields to be opened. It was a bleaker prospect than they realised, for India was hard on the poor and those of lowly birth, and all the more if they were women. The year of my visit, 1990, was the Indian Year of the Young Girl, and the newspapers, including the respected *Times of India,* unhesitatingly reminded their readers how atrocious their fate could be. Young Indian wives, they informed us, whose families had failed to produce promised dowries, died by the hundred, even the thousand, by 'kitchen accidents', i.e. by incineration on kitchen stoves. Shocking things, too, happened to under-privileged males. The newspaper that day recorded the case of an untouchable who had married a high-caste woman and was beheaded by her brothers – the girl herself being locked up in an asylum for fallen women. The same page recorded the fate of a bonded labourer who made a dash for freedom: he was punished by the amputation of a limb – a penalty commonly inflicted in such cases, said the paper.

The postmaster would have been the last person to question in such matters. He radiated optimism. 'Everything is different in Potasing now,' he said. 'We cannot say it is all work. On Sunday we are attending church. Practising to sing hymns. They are telling us that soon a bus will be coming on Fridays for the cinema at Gunupur, for which we are all very glad. But if we do not sell, how can we have money to buy?'

Down the road at Rayagada a kiosk had opened to sell such country medicines as dried bats, curative snakeskin, and above all hornbill beaks, administered in a ground-up form for every known illness. There was a trickle of cash here in circulation, but most of the customers, unable to cope with it, still arrived with vegetables and bags of rice with which to negotiate a deal.

We were at the very end of scenes of this kind. Until now, what I had seen of the tribal heartland was the India of Calcutta as it had been 2,000 years ago, and there was no affinity, no point of contact between the people who had remained unchanged in these mountains, and the brand of human society that was slowly closing in on them, and into which they would shortly be absorbed.

*

Ranjan was clearly a romantic whose romanticism was the product of the stresses of mundane life in Bhubaneswar and the vision of an attainable Eden over the horizon. He was a Brahmin wearing the sacred thread, and in theory firmly sustained by his religion, but he was doomed to work in an office among colleagues of lower caste although often with more money in their pockets. His common-enough tragedy was that of so many Indians: the cost of finding dowries to marry off his three sisters had ruined his family. He longed to have been born in the free air of the tribal land in which he had spent part of his childhood.

The next leg of our journey together would reach Kangrapada, which he would be revisiting after a year's absence. There – although nothing had so far been decided – he might take the plunge, marry the Paraja girl and exchange the heavy responsibilities of civilisation for the calm satisfaction of tribal life.

The encounter with the Parajas which had led to Ranjan's inner confusion had happened almost exactly a year before. Quite by chance, the travel agency he worked for had employed him to explore this remote corner of south Orissa bordering with Andhra Pradeṣh, where a few villages tucked away in the jungle were marked only on the largest-scale map. The majority of such villages were to be reached with difficulty, and on foot, but a minor road took him by car to Koraput. Here he learned of Kangrapada, a village at the end of an unfinished jungle track. It had only been visited by a government official and the occasional itinerant trader.

He went there and found it extraordinary. The village had been splendidly built in a jungle clearance in such a way that every house was shaded by the trees. Stranger though he was, he was received everywhere with smiles. Kangrapada was saturated with a kind of drowsy calm. People gave in to pleasant impulses. A man would pick up a musical instrument, strum on its strings, and those within hearing often started to dance. All the Paraja girls were pretty and returned an admiring glance with an encouraging smile. An old man who spoke enough Oriya to be understood explained the workings of the community to him. Except for the money-lenders, everyone was welcomed in Kangrapada with open arms, the old man said. The jungle was full of edible berries and fruits so no-one went hungry. There were no disputes or quarrels, little sickness and people lived to a reasonable old age. He ascribed this pleasant state of affairs to the full-time presence in the village of the goddess Hundi, represented as a pile of stones round which benches had been built where the elders sat to discuss local affairs in loud, clear voices the goddess could easily overhear. Any problems arising from their discussions could be instantly settled by Hundi on the spot. Nothing could be easier in Kangrapada than to strike up a warm and instant friendship, as he did, with a member of the opposite sex. This, Ranjan decided, was Eden.

He slept that night in the village and was about to leave next morning when he found himself encircled by elders who gently restrained him. Once again an Oriya speaker was found who warned him that he had succeeded in offending Hundi by not formally presenting himself to her and requesting her permission to be in the village. It would be necessary to sacrifice a buffalo to her before removing his car. His admiration for the people of Kangrapada grew when he was assured by them that the goddess was very easily moved by a hard-luck tale, and that the villagers would set to work to persuade her to change her mind. This they were able to do and the demand for the sacrificial buffalo was reduced to one for a white cock costing ten rupees.

Ranjan spent another pleasant night in the village and at leave-taking in the morning the Paraja girl brought her father to say goodbye. He had obviously made a good impression on the family, for the father said that if Ranjan wished to marry his daughter he could do so without payment of the usual bride-price. He also assured Ranjan that the villagers would build a house for them in a matter of days. Taken by surprise, Ranjan asked to be given time to consider the proposition, and the Parajas, reasonable as ever, smilingly agreed. Back in Bhubaneswar, he discussed the situation with his friends, most of whom seemed alarmed. The marriage of a Brahmin to a tribal was unheard of and there was some uncertainty as to whether or not there was a law against it. There followed several months full of setbacks to his suit of one kind or another, but now he was on his way to resolve his future.

The nearest place to Kangrapada in which we could stay the night was Koraput, and the made-up road passing through it had tipped all the refuse of any small provincial town into its narrow streets, and urban noise filtered from it far into the silence and peace of the tribal backlands. An Indian television crew filled the meagre spaces of the hotel: they were friendly men with loud, confident voices and a command of American slang. Ranjan found it hard to explain what they could be doing in a town full of buffaloes going through the rubbish, and unemployed rick-shaw-pullers, and in the end he plucked up courage to ask them. They replied that they were down from Hyderabad to make a film about a village where round houses were made. 'Kangrapa-da?' Ranjan said.

'Yes, I guess that's the name. Kangrapada,' the man said. 'You guys know the place?' he asked, and Ranjan told him he did. It was an encounter that filled him with gloom.

'They can put one of their houses up in five days,' the man said, 'and we already filmed the different stages. Tomorrow we'll be filming a fiesta. Let's say we hope we will. You never know with the tribals. Anyway, we've paid for it. Why don't you guys come along?'

There was some trouble with the car in the morning and we made a late start. It was two hours to Kangrapada, most of it through lush, bird-filled jungle. There, just as Ranjan had described it, was the abandoned road-making machinery on the unfinished track, and within minutes we drove into Ranjan's Eden. At this moment he had become silent, and I understood that something was wrong. What I saw here was so wholly different from the picture of this place he had so repeatedly painted, I began to suspect that he had been the victim of self-delusion brought on by pressures suffered prior to his visit, and that his Kangrapada was part of the delirium of hope. None of those elegant Parajas I had heard so much of were to be seen making silk on their balconies, and the men who should have been relaxed in the tribal manner appeared to be hurrying on urgent errands. Only an itinerant trader with a tray of cheap watches was to be seen. Ranjan asked him sternly, 'With what will they buy these things?' and the man returned an impudent smile. 'They will buy them with money,' he said.

Where were the women parading in their tribal finery, the spontaneous outbursts of music that set them dancing while the mild, white cows looked on? The shrine, coming into sight, was hardly more than a pile of stones tipped from a lorry, but what had become of the village elders gathered here on the surrounding benches to discuss village politics within earshot of their reasonable goddess? Instead, a makeshift fence had been put up round it, decorated with coloured ribbons. There were wide gaps in the row of circular Godba houses which overlooked the shrine, and which had featured in Ranjan's repeated accounts of this place.

Leaving the car to go off and make enquiries, Ranjan returned with a depressing story. He had already mentioned that the Godbas had been persuaded to send a copy of one of their unique houses to a Bhubaneswar exhibition, where much excitement and admiration had been aroused among visitors who until then had believed that most tribals lived in conditions of primitive savagery. Now he had been assured that Godba houses were in demand and were being snapped up. Paraja 'square' houses that were easier to build were to fill the gaps.

'The beginning', Ranjan said, 'of the end.'

We walked on, turned a corner and came immediately on the TV group from the Koraput hotel busy with their filming. A line of Godba girls were performing a dance in which a girl at the end of the line who carried a long-handled broom suddenly broke off to sweep vigorously at the ground. In the usual way, the action stopped for frequent repeats and the cameraman dashed about, climbed a step-ladder to film from above, then squatted to get a low-angle shot as close as possible to the ground. In the course of these repeated manoeuvres the Godbas maintained the habitual stolidity of expression imposed by their culture, which ruled out smiling except in private.

The director held up the action and strutted across to us. 'Could I shift you guys a few yards out of the picture?' he asked. He was friendly and polite. We backed away and he followed us. The dancers had fallen into listless postures, except the one with the broom who had continued to scrape at the earth. 'Excuse,' Ranjan said, 'but what is this dance? No-one in this village will dance in this way.'

'Or anywhere else, I guess,' the director said. 'This is a standard routine. You can change it around like you want, like we did with the broom. It's easy for them to dance and easy for us to film.'

'Do they take money for this?' Ranjan asked him.

'Not really money. Maybe a little inducement. I guess we put them to some trouble. This is supposed to be a fiesta and the dresses had to be made up specially.'

'What happens next?'

'We'll film them dancing round the shrine,' the director said. 'After that it's back to Koraput. Maybe we'll see you there?'

So far as I was concerned, there was no point in prolonging our stay, but I waited for Ranjan to make some reference to his quest. Inconclusive minutes drifted by and I asked him what he was doing about the girl.

He seemed embarrassed. 'She will be told that I am here. She will take friends to wait outside the village. That is custom.'

'In that case, let's go.'

We set off, driving slowly, and hardly had we passed the last village house when we saw the Paraja girls in a group on a slope by the road. There were eight of them of the same height, in identical scarlet dresses, and otherwise remarkably similar in appearance. The one Ranjan had come to see detached herself from the rest and came down to the car. She bent down to talk to Ranjan through the window. None of the tribals, Ranjan had told me, knew their ages, but I would have put her as seventeen. Her eyes were extremely wide, and she was smiling, as were all her friends, and there was something about her face that reminded me of the goddesses that had stared out at us from the many wall-paintings we had seen on this trip. Ranjan showed no signs of emotion and looked straight ahead. Five minutes passed, the low-voiced conversation tailed off. 'Now we may go,' Ranjan said.

They nodded to each other and we moved away. 'A disappointment?' I asked him, and he said, 'I am relieved.'

Nothing more was said of the episode until we reached Srikakulam, where the meagre trickle of traffic was snatched up in the roaring cataract of lorries on the National Highway NH5. Night was suddenly upon us, with open exhausts, a fog of dust and blazing headlights that identified the many wrecks by the side of the road. We were back in the old world we knew so well, but the full realisation of this only struck us when we ran into a police check. A smiling policeman told us we could expect a long wait while the cars ahead were being searched. He then held out his hand for a fifty-rupee bribe, and we were sent on our way.

The Film-Star hotel in this town had no rooms, but Ranjan, nodding at the reception clerk, said, 'You may give him one hundred rupees and he will find one.' Instead we went to the General Lodgings, and settled over drinks to discuss the events of the day.

'I don't understand why you should feel relieved,' I said.

'Because I am one year trying to make a decision. Now that decision is made for me. I am happy because if that place is staying as it was I will never get away from it. Now it is ugly and I am free.'

'So it's to be one of those arranged marriages for you after all?'

'There is no alternative. To marry a tribal person is easy. The father says, I give you my daughter. You go to get drunk together and it is finished. For me an arranged marriage is difficult. My father must find me a wife but he is poor. It must be a Brahmin lady but only an elderly one will marry a poor man. Or maybe some marriage-broker will be telling my father frankly we can offer a young girl but she is a little short, or suffering from one slight limp that can easily be put right, or there is small discoloration of the face not to be seen beneath the hair.'

'The Parajas were very pretty,' I said.

'Please don't tell me that. They are all looking the same. When I first went to that place I did not see this, but now I am realising it is so.'

'It's to be expected with inbreeding, I imagine.'

'Yes, it's to be expected. I was wishing to conceal this from myself, but now I must admit. I am happy that you also are telling me this is the case.'

There was an influx of affluent-looking guests who had clearly been unlucky at the Film-Star. The tribal environment was a land of lean men, but in returning to Srikakulam we seemed to have crossed an invisible frontier. Here, where success counted, it was advertised – as in this case – by bodily fat. Three of the newcomers wore blazers with brass buttons and all spoke in loud, confident English enlivened by slang from the days of the Beatles. All these men ordered whisky and Ranjan, whose caste obligations ruled out spiritous liquors, decided that for once it was in order to break the rule. Our neighbours exchanged slightly off-colour jokes, laughed loudly and slapped each others' backs. The strains of a quavering Indianised version of Mendelssohn's 'Wedding March' squeezed through the cracks in the partition separating us from the next room. Down in the street the lights changed and the outer wall palpitated like a trapped bird's heart as the lorries roared into action. A single whisky had restored the normal composure of Ranjan's patrician features. 'So we are arriving at the conclusion of our adventure,' he said. 'I have settled my problem, and for your purpose may we be calling it a success?'

'Immeasurably so,' I assured him. 'It confirmed opinions already held, and that is generally satisfying.'

Ranjan had become more talkative than usual, to the point of letting fall odd facts relating to an unsatisfactory childhood. This, I understood, was to be put down to the whisky. I risked a question which, in his present mood, I felt he would be happy to answer. 'Tell me,' I said. 'What are you looking for in life?'

'Freedom I am looking for,' he said. 'Of that there is no doubt.'

'I guessed that would be the case. And where and how do you find it?'

'From what my father is telling me, life is game to be played by the rules. Namely I must worship the gods, give alms, and if they are taking a prisoner away for his crimes I must bring food for that man. Things not to do are kill or rob, also sleeping in my neighbour's absence with his wife. Meat not for consumption at any time. Pity this was not spoken of before drinking the whisky.'

I agreed that it was a pity. 'But does it affect your freedom?'

'Accomplish all these things, my father is telling me, and freedom is there.'

'It's a simpler business with our tribal friends,' I said. 'Naturally you were tempted to take the short cut.'

'You have explained the fact of this matter.'

'Although we're both agreed now, it would never have worked.'

'That, too, is the case. At the back of my mind there was always this feeling.'

'Still, it was good while it lasted. Is there any chance you might be available for another trip of the kind we've done? I mean in a different area?'

'The wishing to do this would be very strong for me. Now I am wanting to ask a question. Why are you travelling so much? Is someone telling you you must do this?'

'No,' I said. 'It's just a compulsion I've always felt. It's the pull of the world. I spent most of my childhood on my own, and some of it was in the mountains of Wales. I would go exploring with the idea in my head that the farther I was from home the better it would be. The next valley would always be wilder. The lake would be bottomless, and I would find a mysterious ruin, and there would be ravens instead of crows in all the trees. Now it's not just the Black Mountains of Dyfed, but the world.'

He seemed in part to have understood what I had been struggling to explain. 'Could you call this freedom for you?'

'No, not quite. It's never quite that.'

'And you are not looking to find people in your mountains?'

'Nowadays, yes. I'm looking for the people who have always been there, and belong to the places where they live. The others I do not wish to see.'